Endors

When in the presence of the truth, the ~~....~~ rejoice. With each page, my breath got deeper and my heart opened. Dunion is able to, in easy and accessible language, examine the path home to ourselves. He offers us a way of being in and with life that is skillful, dignified and allows us to access the grace that is everywhere. From descent to a humble and meaningful liberation.

Jen Cohen, Co-Author – *The Seven Laws of Enough*
Seven Stones Leadership Group, Mobius Executive Leadership

Dr. Paul Dunion's *Wisdom* is a must read for anyone on a path of personal development or spiritual seeking. It is a handbook for a modern seeker who wishes their life to be infused with meaning, joy, closeness and devotion. It's precision, practicality and beauty are the fruits of Paul's lifetime exploring the human psyche, intimacy and attachment, and the embodied path of meeting the Mystery. This is a rare and sweeping look at where modern life places us away from immanent experience and inside a series of costly bypasses in habit, mindset and practices.

At the same time, it is a beautifully articulated call to descend into life, encounter the nature of the forces that move and shape us, and enjoy the fruition of a life elevated by wisdom, compassion and love. I recommend this book for anyone wanting to address an addiction, repair a relationship, or apprentice themselves to a life-long journey of awakening.

Amy Elizabeth Fox
Transformational Coach and CEO, Mobius Executive Leadership

Fate makes only one promise: endless opportunities to heal and learn. (p.172)
I have used Paul Dunion's books for years in my university teaching and in my consulting practice; and *Wisdom* proves his finest offering yet. Through the use of ancient myths, Bible stories, and Jungian psychology, he challenges all of humanity to see and heed an ever-persistent call to grow in Wisdom. This is not a book about how to live, but a book about living. It is not a book to merely be read, but a call to enter a relationship with yourself and with fate. With his trademark style of weaving piercingly reflective questions throughout each chapter, Dunion gives us yet another book that is best received in small doses with a pen and journal nearby. May you experience the blessings of responding to the call.

Peggy Andrews, PhD, SPHR
Senior Lecturer and Leadership Curriculum Coordinator
Hamline University School of Business

Wisdom: Apprenticing to the Unknown & Befriending Fate is a lucid invitation to let go of trying to get life right and allow life to get you right. In his usual profound and mystical style, Paul Dunion offers mythological counsel as well as numerous stories supporting what it means to remain an apprentice to life's teachings. The apprentice learns to live life on life's terms rather than his or her own. At a time when truth is literally under siege, this clear path to wisdom is a most welcome offering.

Jennifer Read Hawthorne, Co-Author - *Chicken Soup for the Woman's Soul* (#1 *New York Times* bestseller), Author – *Life as a Prayer: Poems*

As Humanity Faces Extinction…

To be alive and in tune with our body and soul's longing means spiritually engaged to grow beauty. To give more than take.

This book brings forth life saving truths… tools made new from our ancestral journeys, polished brightly by the authors long experience in the animal belly and study of human healing.

We are re-imagining how our powers of choice to create compassion or destruction work through our uninitiated actions or the disconnection from a knowing heart.

Immensely important at this time. I will be chewing on its inspiration a long time.

Jeffrey Duvall, Author - *Men, Meaning and Prayer: The Reconciliation of Heart and Soul in Modern Manhood*

WISDOM

WISDOM

*Apprenticing to the Unknown
and Befriending Fate*

Paul Dunion EdD

Columbus, Ohio

Paul Dunion's Other Works

Seekers: Finding Our Way Home (2016)
Path of the Novice Mystic: Maintaining a Beginner's Heart and Mind (2014)
Dare to Grow Up: Learn to Become Who You Are Meant to Be (2012)
Shadow Marriage: A Descent into Intimacy (2006)
Temptation in the House of the Lord (2004)

Wisdom: Apprenticing to the Unknown and Befriending Fate
Published by Gatekeeper Press
2167 Stringtown Rd, Suite 109
Columbus, OH 43123-2989
www.GatekeeperPress.com

The editorial work for this book is entirely the product of the author. Gatekeeper Press did not participate in and is not responsible for any aspect of this element.

The conversations with clients offered here are all true. Names and identifying characteristics have been changed or omitted to protect their privacy.

Library of Congress Control Number: 2020950380

ISBN (hardcover): 9781662907340
ISBN (paperback): 9781662907357
eISBN: 9781662907364

Contents

This book is dedicated to our granddaughter, Erika "Beanie" Dunion, who possesses heart-eyes. She knows, at 16, how to see with her heart. It will be very difficult to derail her from the wisdom path. Her heart, her intuition and her values comprise a revelatory network allowing her to remain a devoted apprentice to the unknown.

Foreword

Thomas Moore

I love the word apprentice, probably because when I was a child my father taught plumbing in a trade school where all the young would-be plumbers were apprentices. My father's job was not only to teach them how to fit pipes in buildings but also to become masters in this work. Some of them aimed to get a master's license, and often an apprentice would come to our house regularly. My father would meet with him in our finished basement and help him prepare for his master's license exam.

An apprentice is someone who works along with a master to learn skills and concepts firsthand, more by osmosis that by instruction. You could say that apprenticeship is one of the more soulful forms of learning. So I am happy to see my friend and colleague Paul Dunion writing about apprenticing to the unknown and mysterious. What a rich idea! We don't have to learn all the many explanations for the unknown that fill theology books. That is a contradiction in terms anyway. If you explain the mysterious, it is not longer a mystery, and that is a mistake if you appreciate the place of mystery in human life.

But how do you apprentice yourself to the unknown. If you follow my father's example, you find a master who knows how to do this and spend time with him or her. If your apprenticeship is to the unknown, you notice how a master not-knower may be comfortable not knowing something, even something important. He may not know where his life is headed. He may sense a change taking place and wonders what he will be invited to do next. I have been in that position many times. The skill required in that circumstance is an ability to remain in the domain of mystery— patient, trusting, and willing to consider a new direction.

I realize that in reading Paul's carefully structured book, I am an apprentice to Paul's mastery. I felt in reading his stories especially that here is a man who has faced his own sometimes harsh challenges and has worked with people who were dealing with unusually raw and difficult life circumstances. From his often extreme existential encounters he has found a clarity about the ingredients of a trusting, self-aware kind of existence. His book is the gift of that clarity that could help anyone sort out the stuff of their lives so it will not be overwhelming.

Emerging from the hazy mist of the unknown is fate, what life has in store for us. I have never liked the idea that we create our own existence. I see a human life as a response to invitations and opportunities. I imagine that each life is a long series of turning points, rites of passage. If you say yes to life, you move along toward wisdom. If you say no—and sometimes in every life one says "not now, please"—you are that much removed from wisdom and a sense of fulfillment. Paul says, "Befriend fate," and he offers many elements involved in such awesome befriending. Don't see life as an enemy to conquer but as vitalizing power to befriend.

I suggest you take this thoughtful book, obviously based on an intelligent, open-hearted willingness to live fully and courageously, and read it slowly. Write in the margins and empty spaces. Make it your own. See how each particle of the big picture applies to you. Don't over-intellectualize your life. Read the book the way it was written, distilling a livable philosophy of life out of a willingness to cooperate with what life wants from you.

Follow your deep desires. The soul is motivated by love and attraction, not by principles or rules. Meander creatively and see your life as an odyssey, a twisting voyage full of challenges that demand resourcefulness and imagination. Keep moving. Don't be embarrassed by blockages and detours. They are part of the journey. They make the trip your own, not one that someone else has charted for you. Be bold. Have courage.

Acknowledgements

I have been deeply privileged to have been surrounded by students, colleagues and friends committed to pursuing the best version of the truth accompanied by compassion. I initially felt layers of presumption as I began to write about wisdom. It was the curiosity and wonder expressed by those with whom I travel that helped me to remember that I too remain a student of the human condition.

I want to acknowledge my protegees who have become colleagues. Peter Drake who models what it means to remain an apprentice to the unknown. Margaret Harris who brings an open heart to her work, allowing her to be deeply touched by human suffering. Mary Kenny who lives the ancient meaning of the word *curiosity,* which is "to care deeply." And to Jennifer Jondreau Thompson who knows how to summon an unbridled attention and regard for family, friends and clients. Much appreciation also to Jody Grose who holds a passionate devotion to support the maturing hearts of men.

Many thanks to Norcott Pemberton for her unequivocal faith in my gifts and my capacity to serve, while modeling a soulful path to elderhood. Much appreciation to my friend and colleague Wendy Shami who understands and walks the path of the Wounded Healer. Appreciation to Walter Van Sambeck for the offering of vibrant collegiality that evokes passion for the art of healing. I am deeply grateful for the collegiality and friendship of Jen Cohen and Ester Martinez for their commitment to serve human potential, bringing more ground and meaning to those we serve.

I am enormously appreciative to Amy Fox for calling me out of the basement, into the world, where I continue to refine my gifts and their offerings. Amy's summons both deepened and broadened my understanding of serving. I continue to be thankful to the entire Mobius community for their faith in the possibility of Transformational Work resulting in leaders stewarding what is truly sustainable.

I want to acknowledge Amy Mercury for moving my articles and blogs into the world and Heather Fessenden for gathering my teachings such that they easily translate into the written word.

Much appreciation to Thomas Moore who endorses what I write, which is especially helpful when I'm wondering why I do it.

I am only able to continue to ask what life is requesting of me because of the care of my friends: Ray Di Capua and Marie Pace who continue to offer me a welcome for my joy and my weariness. Special thanks to Ray for living life on life's terms and calling me to the question: What courage is life asking of me? Gratitude to my friend Thom Allena who remains fervently introspective reminding me of where my attention belongs. Appreciation to Gary Blaser who knows how to hold his experience with sweetness, teaching me about the power of softness. Jeffrey Duval whose devotion to the wellness of the planet reminds me where home is. And appreciation to Deirdre O'Connor for accompanying me while facing medical challenges and reminding me of the beauty and wonder surrounding me. Many thanks to Michael Paprocki for an enduring friendship that continues to feed both men in the winter of our lives.

Immense gratitude to my wife, Connie Jones Dunion, for walking with me in my triumph and in my defeat. Typically, Connie's eyes are the first to review what I write and the first to bring attention to excessive abstraction in much need of grounding. When I fall prone to either catastrophizing or protesting my life experience, she pauses and curiously remains engaged with what is happening. It is an honor to grow old with her and I do so, in the hope that I might offer as much support for her creativity as she does for me.

1

Meandering

Improvement makes straight roads;
but the crooked roads without improvement are roads of genius.

–William Blake

I t was late October, with the first frost heralding winter. I pulled into George's driveway, glad to be arriving for our regular 8:00 AM meeting in his basement office. The rural surroundings invited me to let go of what seemed time-consuming and trivial. I entered his home through the front door, took off my shoes, and stepped upon a dark blue-and-gold Persian rug. There was something uplifting and regal about walking slowly across such a plush floor covering. The sight of George emerging from his office with a robust greeting only amplified this feeling.

"Good morning, good morning, my friend! I watched you walk from your vehicle to the house, looking very much like Alexander the Great crossing into Mesopotamia," cried George, once again offering unsolicited feedback regarding my persona.

"Well, I don't feel much like Alexander," I responded.

"Okay then, come in, and let's talk about this less-than-Alexander feeling of yours," George offered.

I took my regular seat: a beige leather chair with oak-grained armrests. George sat across from me in a large rocker that swayed in tune with his excitement. He was dressed in a blue denim shirt with a brown leather vest and a pair of baggy khakis. He leaned forward, ready to hear my truth.

"I've been committed to living a self-examined life, and I don't feel closer to attaining any measure of wisdom or enlightenment. After all, I just turned fifty!" I proclaimed, attempting to convey my frustration and disillusionment, as if something might be wrong with the self-examined life itself as opposed to my deficient efforts in seeking it.

"It sounds like you've been on some kind of quest for wisdom and you're not thrilled about the outcome," George reflected.

"No, I'm not thrilled. I continue to make choices I regret. I hold some adolescent beliefs, and what's really unfortunate is that I don't ever seem to make any profound statements," I continued, building a case for why I should be seeing more impressive results due to my investment in being wise.

"So, you want to make more profound declarations," teased George, making no attempt to withhold his amusement.

"Come on, George, you know what I mean. What's the use of attaining wisdom if you're not able to demonstrate it and allow it to benefit others?" I suggested, attempting to bring a measure of altruism to a statement laden with a desire to impress.

"I really appreciate your willingness to gift humanity with your wisdom, and I'm sure there'll be an outpouring of gratitude from the multitudes," responded George, his soft tone failing to buffer the jocularity and sarcasm revealed by the sparkle in his eyes.

"Okay, so maybe I don't get why I haven't acquired some level of wisdom. I don't know how to make it happen," I confessed.

"You don't make it happen. It happens to you. You make yourself available to be touched, moved, and mindful of your experience. You'll need to learn to let go of trying to get life right, and let it get you right instead. The gods willing, you may stumble more in the direction of enlightenment. However, you'll first need to get accustomed to fumbling along a more circuitous route," instructed George, bringing a more sober resonance to the conversation.

"Can you tell me more about being available and the purpose of fumbling along a circuitous route?"

"The key is to honor the meandering and not the arrival. There'll be no arrival. Attachment to your arrival at some place of wisdom is simply another attempt to impress. Such an attachment will take you a long way from your truth and an even longer way from life as a sacred odyssey. Meandering loses its ability to teach anytime you judge a moment as falling short of your expectation. You'll get lost because you turn your back on where you are now.

Do that many times and you are many times lost. The journey becomes sacred when you live the questions of meandering rather than pretend you're not lost or that the moment is somehow an unfortunate belch of life, signifying nothing because it doesn't meet your expectations."

George continued by suggesting that I live the questions that allow *fate*— defined here and throughout as the "will of the gods"—to teach me. "Questions of meandering include: What is here? How did I get here? What else is here? Who is here? How am I responding to this situation? What is this situation asking of me? Do I know how to be defeated by things larger than myself? Can I respond to these questions more honestly? And when you ask them, see if your responses carry adequate heart, measured by compassion, generosity, and gratitude. And then, ask these questions again and again. The path is circuitous, with ample opportunities to be distracted, get lost, and act foolishly. And you will get distracted, again and again. You're only asked to be honest about your distraction while paying attention to the messages carried by the redundancy of your experience.

"Your ego will insist on being above such impediments. However, you're asked to remain an apprentice of distractions, getting lost and acting foolishly along the way. Do that well, and you'll be welcomed into an apprenticeship with the unknown," offered George with no hint of condescension, leaving me touched by his encouragement.

"Well, George, you certainly left me with a bundle today. I'm going to get on the road, arrive home, and do some journal writing," I said, thankful for his insight.

"One more thing before you leave. Remember to remain an apprentice to defeat. It's the best way to become acquainted with the contours and edges of your soul. You might learn where you begin and end. You might open to whatever invitations the gods are extending to you. Oh yes, make sure you greet the fool when you encounter him," George added with a drop of his chin, his gaze sustaining a downward slant and his lips separating into a smile that baffled me.

"Why the fool?" I asked, hoping for a more uplifting suggestion.

"The fool because only he is willing to be seduced by fate and continue to meander, holding a kind of naïve faith that more will be revealed, even when feeling deeply lost. And you will get lost, again and again. **Fate is all that you encounter; it is the people, places, and events that constitute your outward experience. This is what you can call your life: your dance with fate and the destiny you create by such a dance**," explained George.

"George, I've never heard of someone singing the credits of the fool," I pointed out.

"Right, it's not a very popular topic. Remember, you can't get life right," he added, moving to a standing position.

"What the hell?! Am I supposed to get life wrong?" I shouted.

"That's it! Now you've got it! Make sure you get life wrong!" George exclaimed, giving me one of his typical bear hugs and laughing uncontrollably.

As I drove away from that conversation some twenty years ago, I could not help but wonder if George had serious doubts about his own ability to get life right. Much time would pass before I began to understand the relationship between getting life wrong and living wisely.

That was the last time I saw George. He died shortly after that meeting. Like all good mentors, he enhanced my vision with his strengths and weaknesses alike. He was a bold man who sometimes stepped away from his limits, confident he could wrestle with life victoriously. George taught me that, in the quest to be rightsized, one must err in the direction of going too big and allow life to make the appropriate modifications. Slowly I learned that fate was not shy about modifying me. But first, I needed to befriend fate as its apprentice.

Life guarantees that we meander. It also guarantees that we get lost. If we can tolerate and be honest about being lost, then we may come to see being "lost" as the transition from old to new eyes. We are touched by genius.

Fate makes its strongest alterations by defeating us. Just as defeat can devastate us, so can it steer us away from where we do not belong, moving us in the right direction. The risks are inevitable. Yet fate favors those who show up in a big way, vulnerably placing our self-inflation in the hands of life's immensity. And from that place, life might get us right. We shall see that our fall from self-inflation may be what apprentices us to the unknown, making wisdom possible. Until this occurs, we must acknowledge how we get distracted from understanding ourselves and the journey on which we have embarked.

The ego knows how to build a case in favor of meandering. Efforts toward some success or achievement, as well as exhortations of being correct, will bring some credibility to the circuitous path, even if it is the only one initially available to us. What we encounter in our meandering informs us about the relationship we have with ourselves and with life. Each situation offers an opportunity to deepen our mindfulness of how we become distracted, lost, and ready to learn.

White-Bear-King-Valemon

This Norwegian myth portrays the necessity of meandering and the distractions and opportunities for learning that ensue in the pursuit of wholeness. We are told of a king who has three daughters. The youngest is beautiful and gentle, while the others lack her appeal and sweetness. In her nocturnal meandering, the youngest daughter dreams of a golden wreath, which the king's blacksmiths are unable to reproduce. I am inclined to see the golden wreath as symbolic of wholism or becoming more mindful and accepting of oneself.

While meandering through the forest for no apparent reason, the youngest princess comes across a bear in possession of the wreath. Yet the bear, who manifests the power of spirit she will need to support her wholism, will not give her the wreath unless she agrees to go away with him. He gives her three days to prepare for departure.

The king, wishing to support his daughter's ardent desire for the wreath without losing her to the bear, instructs his soldiers to acquire the wreath by force. The bear easily defeats them. In response, the king sends out his oldest daughter to join the bear. She mounts the bear and he rushes off with her on his back, asking her if she has ever "sat softer or seen clearer." The oldest daughter avers, "Yes, on my mother's lap I sat softer, in my father's court I saw clearer." The bear returns her to the castle. Next, the king offers his second daughter to the bear. When the bear asks the same question of her, she responds similarly to her older sister. The bear returns her to the castle. Finally, the king offers his third daughter, who tells the bear that she has never "sat softer and seen clearer." The bear takes her to his own castle.

The two oldest daughters are not ready to meander. Attached to the softness and clarity of home, they are content in honoring the strong connection they share with their parents. The youngest, however, is ready and willing to risk losing known comfort and clarity for a new adventure. But why is she ready to meander while the older sisters are not?

We are told that they do not possess her beauty and gentleness. Beauty here may be more than skin-deep. It may reflect the beauty of her youth, innocence, naïveté, curiosity, and spirit of adventure. The story may be suggesting that a woman will need to rely on these qualities if she is to remain loyal to herself and continue to meander away from the hearth of the home.

At his castle, the bear turns into a man at nightfall and enters her bedchamber. She bears him a child, but he rushes away with it. This takes place three years in a row. Thus, the princess and the man-bear cannot psychologically guide the development of their own children in the context of a loving family. Their unity is limited to penetration and insemination.

At the end of those three years, the princess requests of the bear that she be able to visit her parents. During that visit, her mother gives her a candle so that she might see the man-bear who comes to her during the night, when his beastly energy transforms in the dark. By that point, she has already received his primal power as he mutates into a human man and unites with her in the shadows of her unconsciousness. All she and the man-bear have to show for their nightly congress are their three children, but even these are lost to her. Yet her prolific creativity and seemingly harmonious life with the bear are not enough. Following her mother's suggestion, she lights the candle to gaze upon the slumbering face of the man with whom she has been cocreating. But when molten wax drips onto his forehead and wakes him, he tells her that just one more month of waiting would have freed him from an evil witch's spell, and that now he must go and betroth himself to that very witch.

Not all meandering, as we can see, leads to positive results. In meandering back home and falling under the spell of her mother's bad advice, the princess has prioritized her daughterhood over her womanhood and adulthood. Due to maternal influence, she has prematurely attempted to become conscious of her nightly male visitor, who is an incarnate symbol of her inner masculinity.

In this part of the myth, a woman has gained premature clarity with regard to her own masculinity. Alongside the many gifts of feminism, there is a hasty encouragement to clarify and take on masculine traits that enable a woman to compete in the marketplace and in politics. This may be a premature grasping of traits commonly perceived as masculine, such as aggression, willfulness, rational thought, and independence. These are, in fact, traits available to all genders. Could it be that a woman's wholism is obstructed if she loses an appreciation for the value of passivity, compassion, feeling, and dependence?

The princess expresses her desperation to connect to the masculine within by insisting she go with him. Despite his refusal, our heroine "seized hold of the fur all the same, flung herself up on his back, and held on fast. Then they were off over the mountain and hill, through grove and thicket, until her clothes were torn off, and she was so dead tired that she let go her hold, and knew no more." Might the suggestion not be that attempts to feverishly own what is masculine can lead a woman to physical and emotional exhaustion, or depression?

Because our heroine falls off the bear, she can resume her meandering, only now in a forest where she encounters four separate cottages, each housing an old crone and a little girl. Each cottage offers much in the way of learning, as an old woman and a little girl reflect an entire life span. In other words, the apprentice must be willing to serve wholism for an entire lifetime. Thus, we are reminded of the depth and breadth of learning.

At the first cottage the heroine is given scissors, and when she cuts the air, silk and velvet appear. Given my association of air with thinking, I see her as learning to cut away excess thoughts, beliefs, and opinions that do not serve her. Silk and velvet are made directly from nature. Moreover, silk possesses a protective quality, as it is difficult to cut through. She may be learning to protect herself on a deeper plane.

Another interpretation is that she is cutting away what does not pertain to her inner nature. She may be learning to cut the psychological umbilical cord connecting her to her mother, allowing her to approach the essence of her unique character. This is why she gives the silk and velvet to the woman in the cottage instead of keeping it for herself. She is learning about the importance of giving over grasping.

The old crone and little girl in the second cottage give her a never-emptying flask that pours out whatever her heart desires. What transpires at this second cottage also has important implications for the apprentice to the unknown. She is encouraged to trust her wishing. Wishing is a powerful way to connect us to whatever fate presents. It keeps a woman grounded in her own story rather than living in someone else's. Of course, it is critical to acknowledge that whatever is wished for will have unforeseen consequences. There will be pleasures as well as trials and ordeals meant for deepening a woman's capacity to create a well-lived life.

Our heroine meanders to a third cottage, where yet another little girl offers a cloth that can conjure up food. This gift from a child suggests that genuine nourishment is born of curiosity, wonder, and awe. Food is whatever sustains us not only physically, but also intellectually, emotionally, and spiritually. To conjure is to awaken. Thus, she is learning to awaken her capacity to identify what truly sustains.

The princess meanders to a fourth cottage, where an old woman and many children are wanting for food and clothing. Our heroine feeds and clothes them. In so doing, she learns how to manifest her gifts and serve. In gratitude, the old woman's husband crafts her a set of iron claws. These will enable her to climb the mountainside to reach the witch's castle, where the man-bear is being held captive. This fourth encounter reveals her capacity to be generous with her gifts. The claws she receives are resonant with the instinctive acts of climbing, killing, digging, and grasping.

In order to make her ascent, she must combine the humanity she has deepened in each of the four cottages with something primitive and corporeal. This interface of what is human and creaturely allows her to climb that mountain and unite with her core masculinity in a meaningful way. She possesses enough feminine essence to go higher in pursuit of her quest.

Our heroine reaches the witch's castle where the man-bear, who we learn is a king in his own right, is being held captive by the witch in question. The witch serves as a symbol of the dark feminine principle within the king, prone to malevolence, trickery, and deceit. He is unable to claim his ability to be approachable, to nurture, to be merciful and tender. The king can only be seen in daylight for his animal nature: brutish, aggressive, and coarse. The fullness of his humanity remains obscured by the darkness of night, and if his humanity is witnessed, he must marry the witch and spend the rest of his days as her spouse.

The princess bribes the witch twice—first with the cloth, then with the flask—in exchange for one night with her sweetheart. But the witch drugs the spellbound king to prevent him from waking up whenever the young princess approaches.

An artisan overhearing the witch's plan tells the king of the drugging that has taken place the past two nights. It is worth noting that an artisan is one who remains devoted to his craft. It may be that his devotion to creative spirit in the presence of the young princess awakens his senses, allowing him to see that his connection to the deep feminine is being sabotaged. The king does not drink the witch's offering on the third night and remains lucid, plotting the death of the witch once and for all with his true love.

They decide to have the king's carpenters install a trapdoor in the bridge extending over the deep chasm leading to the castle. When the witch arrives to marry the king, the trapdoor is opened; the witch and her entourage tumble through it to their demise. The bridge, symbolizing the connection that will unite the witch with the king, is disrupted by another, purer unity.

Our heroine has learned to protect herself, honoring her desire by serving others. Her movement toward wholism is enhanced by a masculine devotion to her craft, honoring her gifts. Likewise, we move toward wholism, not arriving but ever-deepening, remaining intimate with fate.

The king and the princess gather the treasures of the witch's castle and flee to his homeland. Along the way, they reclaim the young cottage girls, who happen to be their daughters. The king had housed them in those cottages to aid the princess in her quest to find him, but for our purposes they embody the assistance of youth. Their lack of inhibition, guile, and contrivance, as well as their spontaneity, aid in our meandering. Meandering begins when we are open to experience, as we will see when we visit the story of Parsifal in Chapter 6.

Our heroine is mostly distracted by allegiance to her mother. Such distractions show us where we do not belong. This lesson is one of the apprentice's most critical.

Distractions

All distractions possess some measure of allure. We cannot enter the house of wisdom until we come to terms with the distractions that have their talons in us. The more we are distracted, the more our meandering lengthens. Wisdom, like anything worth cherishing, calls for a deep understanding of what does not really matter. Our ability to discern what matters depends on our ability to identify what lacks credibility. Ironically, we must meander enough and get distracted enough to know what we walk away from in our distractions. The following are some popular distractions of which we never completely divest ourselves.

Seduction – An old definition of the word *seduction* is "to lead astray." It is natural to be led astray while meandering. Seduction will likely remain a powerful teacher throughout life. But while it may appear that the seduction has all the power, in reality our ego decides where our attention and intention will go.

The ego abhors the heavy lifting involved in generating an honest self-acceptance of strengths and weaknesses alike. The ego is poised and ready to welcome any flattery that eases the task of maintaining a compassionate relationship with ourselves. Meandering is a time for giving away power as we bask in others' admiration. As we shall see later, however, giving away power is one of the most effective ways to deepen our understanding of it. The cognizant apprentice will learn time and time again the price paid for such relinquishment.

Seduction offers feelings of safety, self-worth, belonging, and empowerment. The ego finds the arduous work required to sustain these four states somewhat distasteful. It takes considerable meandering, defeat, and mindfulness to reclaim responsibility for these four human essentials. The ego remains vulnerable to producing stories about others and our own accomplishments to feel worthy, safe, and empowered. Such responsibility points the apprentice toward the path of wisdom. We begin to understand the immensity of life as we get seduced and defeated in our meandering.

I often think of myself as a slow learner. At 13, I left the parochial school I attended for nine years and ventured into one of the largest high schools in the state of Connecticut. Looking considerably older and tall for my age, I discovered that girls found me attractive. I easily found my place with members of the opposite sex, as well as on several sports teams. Being elected class president two years in a row only added to my feelings of security and belonging.

My hunch is that I was supposed to start learning about seduction early, which I doubt I did. The path of the golden boy came to an abrupt halt when I entered college. I lost my girlfriend, flunked off the basketball team, and began allowing the debauchery of fraternity life to define me. It was not until my junior year in college, when I fell in love with philosophy, that something deeply soulful replaced the array of sirens who had their hold on me. Only years later would I come to understand that what had been given to me as a teenager had to be taken away if I was ever going to find my way back to myself.

But then, at age 30, my meandering found me seduced beyond measure once again. My mentor at the time established a human relations training program that met one weekend per month for nine months. The training began with a five-day retreat aimed at building the community needed to support our imminent learning.

During the first day of the retreat, my mentor explained that he wanted to read a graduation address he had recently heard. He suggested that the major tenets of the talk would serve as guiding principles for our training. After hearing the first line, I immediately recognized it as a talk I had delivered three months earlier. Upon completion of the reading, my classmates eagerly expressed their curiosity about the author. He paused and said, "It's Paul, one of your classmates."

For the next five days, my need for safety, self-worth, and belonging was held in the hands of the other fourteen participants. I was the recipient of admiration, respect, and ongoing invitations for affiliation. Whenever I spoke, heads would nod in the affirmative long before I finished a sentence. Whenever I entered a room, I would be met with multiple gestures of greeting and updates regarding what had taken place before my arrival. The eye contact I received seemed to transcend normal limits, stretching beyond the spoken word. Getting my attention appeared to be a prized commodity. Without reservation, I allowed my fellow trainees to take responsibility for my safety, self-worth, and belonging.

Once those five days came to an end, I drove home convinced the gods had finally brought me to where I needed to be. As the days passed, I noticed a palpable melancholy, sadness, and a deep feeling of loss. My initial response was to see it as nothing more than a reaction to the loss of a fulfilling experience. Yet my struggle to regain myself continued. I needed help to process what was going on with me.

My mounting curiosity began to reveal deeper happenings rather than the end of a lovely event. I had given the other participants power and responsibility for my safety, self-worth, and belonging. I wandered anxiously, vulnerably, and without certainty of being okay. I was scattered about the Northeast, a long way off from my center.

I was being asked to learn again about seduction and the challenge of being thrust into the light of acceptance, respect, admiration, and love. I needed to learn how to accept a genuine compliment and to appreciate my gifts while drawing enough boundaries to remain the author of my essential worth.

Seduction is problematic when it leads us astray from responsibility for our safety, self-worth, belonging, and personal empowerment. Sources of seduction may have little or no need to call us away from our responsibility. Even if the sirens do intend to call us astray, we are ultimately responsible for cooperating. I once heard a man say, "I'm so easily seduced by such and such." I immediately respected his acknowledgement of where he was vulnerable to seduction. It may be the fool in us who gets seduced again and again, and who ultimately supports the apprentice's relationship to the unknown, evolving in the direction of wisdom.

Letting the Banners Fly – "Human events become trapped at the soul-starved surface of life where brief flashes of fame become a substitute for struggling to live the dreams inherent in one's soul. Narrow forms of egotism pass for accomplishment, and cleverness takes the place of genuine learning and the search for real knowledge" (Michael Meade). We can be distracted, marching while waving our banners in declaration of our achievements, knowledge, acquisitions, or pedigree.

This distraction can deepen as we grow obsessed with our own performance. Often, the desire to impress drives performance. When driven to impress, I do not really know who I am in your presence and I certainly do not know who you are in mine. In fact, I am not here to actually be with you in any meaningful way. I am here simply to wow you and give myself a temporary respite from self-contempt.

Recently, over coffee, my friend looked at his watch and said, "I'll need to get going soon. I want to catch up with my brother before he begins four months of silence." I lost my breath and felt a bit numb. I moved toward my vehicle in a robotic fashion and drove two miles down the road before I realized how shallow my breath had become. My friend's words echoed within me, as if yelling into a steep canyon. Why was his brother's intention to remain silent for four months having such an impact on me?

Twenty-four hours later, I got it. I had scheduled the autumn months such that I would be dancing as fast as I could, my banners flapping wildly in the breeze. Could it be that my father's son was continuing to seek his father's blessing? When I thought of my father on the other side, separated from this earthly plane, I imagined his satisfaction and joy regarding who I was, with no need for me to win his favor. Was I waiting for the world to confirm my worth? The lifelong task of remaining responsible for my essential goodness was again knocking at the door.

Life was asking me to slow down and let go of an attachment to be chosen by someone or some organization outside of myself. I was being asked to remember that no one can hold our value the way we can, just as no one can really know us the way we can. It was helpful to hear a colleague say to me: "You've downloaded quite a bit of learning. If you don't slow down, your rapid pace will be an impediment to wisdom."

We must become mindful of an attachment to impression. We can begin by noticing how impressive we were in retrospect, without harsh judgment. The more we are able to notice an urgency in the moment to impress, the more choices we have. Having the choice to impress or not impress is empowering. Knowing the need to impress is personally disempowering, I was convinced it would be no problem to simply interrupt my desire to arouse some favorable reaction. Time and time again, however, I felt a wave of heat gathering in my chest as an opportunity arose to stir an admiring gaze in my listener. I finally admitted that I was truly a novice when it came to laying down my banners.

I knew I did not want to grow old striving to move others toward perceiving me in some glowing fashion. It was simply too much work. I had repeatedly experienced the emptiness of walking away with flattering words drifting out of reach. Still, I occasionally allow myself to be seduced by a quick fix. The good news is that I seduce myself less often; and when I do succumb to a vigorous wave of my banners, I hear a voice within asking to be remembered and cared for.

Some questions can help to identify when we meander into being impressive: Where in my body do I feel the urgency to impress? What do I have to gain once someone is actually impressed? What is lost in my most impressive moments? What must take the place of my desire to impress? Lowering our banners becomes easier as we allow ourselves to feel the emptiness of striving to look good.

The emptiness that often follows banner waving is a good place to begin understanding the price of being impressive. The resounding hollowness of an impressive moment can be highly instructive. We step away not really seen, heard, or understood, and certainly not chosen in any meaningful way. Only in choosing to be authentic can we know the richness of genuine connection and, possibly, deep belonging. We must be in the presence of another to be appreciated and loved. Our banners merely generate a moment of attention and possible fascination.

There is an immense gift in an apprentice's banner waving. In our efforts to impress, we are unable to fully take in our life experience. A profound settling accompanies the acceptance of our essential goodness. Such acceptance can give rise to a celebration of our gifts and accomplishments. We are not attempting to impress, but rather inviting the other to join us in our celebration. I recently experienced such a celebration with my friend Ray.

"Ray, I'm experiencing a sense of expansion as I'm invited to teach internationally. It's very exciting and touches me deeply," I related to him in the hope that he might be able to join me in my excitement.

"I'm so glad for you. You've been developing your craft for many years and it's certainly time to share it with the world," Ray responded, his eyes glowing as he leaned forward.

"I can feel you're glad for me," I added.

"Oh yes, I know you're on the path that you belong," he said with confidence.

"It does feel right. And here you are celebrating it with me. I guess I respond to a man hearing of my good news either by deciding I'm excessively boastful or deciding there's something wrong with me," I admitted.

"Shit, as long as there's nothing wrong with me, I'm fine," screeched Ray, laughing with tears rolling down his cheeks.

I cherished this moment of a friend sharing a celebration of my path. I could feel the desire for celebration in my throat with no attachment to Ray being impressed. It was reassuring that celebration could be an option to either waving a banner or simply remaining mute with no sign of rejoicing.

Striving – Striving is the first cousin of performance. It can be extremely seductive and distracting since it is often camouflaged as either moral or spiritual laboring. Meandering in the embrace of striving may therefore go on for some time. No wonder that a root meaning of the word *strive* is "to quarrel."

Striving has a double edge. On the one hand, it may be quite helpful in allowing us to "quarrel" with contrived or artificial limits. We live within constricted margins, driven by fear and lethargy under the influence of striving. We become more of who we are meant to be by striving. Another perspective is that in our striving we are "quarreling" with our essential worth, determined to better ourselves. In the words of Sheldon Kopp: "I am no longer interested in character development, as long as that implies in any way that my Buddhahood is not already at hand." Kopp apparently understood the price of striving. He refused to toil in the mere interest of developing his character, as long as that suggested his goodness was not already present. Were he not presently accepting his goodness, his essential worth would continue to elude him. How many pure thoughts and noble deeds will it take?

Quarreling with our essential worth does not allow us to fully apprentice ourselves to the unknown as we meander freely in the grip of striving. Such feuding keeps us busy trying to get life right or get ourselves right. Living in pursuit of alleged betterment does not allow us to be informed by our wandering. Striving points us toward possibility and not what is. The striver often feels the exhaustion and inadequacy of unfulfilled arrival, resulting in a posture of moral superiority. It sounds something like: "I must be better than most folks. Look at how much I do!" Striving can be a compensation for shame.

Each excessive act of fortitude, or so we tell ourselves, keeps us just one step ahead of the shame running us down.

We can interrupt the meandering of striving by becoming curious about our striving: How might I labor in a way that fosters growth, without discrediting who I already am? It may be helpful to acknowledge that our soul's task is not to become better but to remove whatever obstructs the life of our uniqueness. Carl Jung suggested that individuation is "the psychological process that makes a human being an 'individual'—a unique indivisible unit or 'whole man.'"

In the Jungian sense, we might conceive of four steps in the individuation process:

1) **We can substitute individuating for striving.** We can cast off or give back to the culture what is incompatible with our values and our hearts' desire. Not all cultural influences will impede our individuality. An educational or religious institution might very well serve the individuation process. Getting clear about what to keep and what to give back is a lifelong process. For example, as an introvert living in an extroverted culture, I have become sensitive to how culture can call me away from introversion and who I am. I know the feeling of being summoned away from my shyness, solitude, and quietude. I work with this process by honoring these qualities. I also translate extroverted dynamics such as love, trust, loyalty, and welcoming into my experiences of introversion. I especially like the notion of a welcome offered to the self.

2) **We can deepen personal acceptance of our wounds and our gifts.** We come to this planet, where we receive wounds and gifts. Our wounded caregivers pass on legacies of both psychological injury and strength. Wounds and gifts call us to the business of being fully human. The apprentice is asked to respond to fate with a renewed willingness to heal and learn every time. We remain open to the wound's request for healing and the gift's request for learning. We are asked to identify and develop our gifts, then allow them to serve others.

3) **We can remain curious about what fate is asking of us.** Fate must be treated like any person we care for. We are in constant relationships with the people, things, and events of fate. If we fail to be curious and caring about our experience with these materials of fate, we impede

fate's ability to teach. Our apprenticeship with the unknown can be sabotaged indefinitely.

4) We can encourage the individuation of others. I was in a psychology training recently when I noticed that the other trainees only asked the instructor questions for the sake of embellishing or clarifying the position she was offering. There were no questions suggesting a different view. Regretful that my students tended to do the same, I began encouraging them to find their own diverse voices.

Caught in Hierarchy – Nothing thwarts learning more while meandering than getting caught in hierarchy. Most folks will struggle to liberate themselves from the shackles of hierarchy. The eyes of hierarchy see others as either above or beneath us. Meandering in the grip of this distraction can be a lifelong process.

The ego abhors being ordinary. It is, however, quite comfortable with being exceptionally superior or uncommonly inferior. Time and energy are spent swelling the ego with either self-aggrandizement or evidence in support of our deficient character.

Giving up this distraction, or at least diminishing its potency, calls for adequate support. We need an ally who is familiar with the seductive lore of hierarchal terrain, both the high road and the low. We need assistance to clarify how we allegedly benefit from where we take up residency and what is at risk when moving from one territory to another. Our goal should be to make peace, going home to the sacred ordinary guided by unity consciousness.

Given that other people are vital facets in our relationship with fate, it behooves the apprentice to devotionally deconstruct hierarchal perceptions. Through a commitment to unity consciousness we can see ourselves and others sharing a common humanity. We see their need to love and be loved, to be acknowledged, suffering loss, losing their way, afraid of being forgotten, getting sick or injured, feeling insecure and lonely.

Attached to Being Victorious – The distinguishing feature of this distraction is a motivation to conquer, itself driven by a primal competitive spirit. The ego easily becomes enamored with this distraction, its purpose to gain victory over life. An advantageous job promotion, some lucrative financial investments, and the acquisition of a desired spouse are all it takes for the ego to be convinced of its superior destiny. It is now ready to escape the perils of rejection, addiction, loss, physical and emotional suffering, and, with a little luck, death itself. Such was the shadow that haunted Odysseus after his victory at Troy.

Being an apprentice to the unknown quickly fades into the background as we immerse ourselves in the revelry of our victories. Hungering for further conquests, we no longer see the nuances of our experience. We become strategically obsessed, convinced that making the right moves is all that matters. Arrogance renders our vision myopic. We can no longer respond to fate meaningfully, dulled as we are to what it wants to give us, what it asks of us, and what it will inevitably take away. Thus limited, we are no longer in a dynamically creative relationship with fate. If anything, we are enveloped by the illusion that we are in charge of defining our lived experience. Old thinking sometimes suggests that an alienated and adversarial relationship with fate guarantees serious defeat, as fate shows itself to be far superior to the ego's alleged sovereignty.

I am reminded of the sizable defeat I experienced when our daughter Sarah was born with a rare neurological disorder. I had placed myself on a lofty pedestal when it came to fathering and marriage. But the pillars supporting my elevated station began cracking and tumbling over in the face of Sarah's diagnosis and prognosis. My heroic self-image was taking a serious hit. I drank more alcohol, pretended I knew what I was doing, resisted asking for help, and denied the impact that keeping Sarah at home would have on her siblings. It took a number of years before I could admit the absence of victory. My tenacious pursuit of victory was dying, with no idea of what would take its place.

I will never find that pristine, non-heroic place. I am humbly called back to being more of an ordinary man as I face the vastness of the unknown when it comes to caring for Sarah, for myself, and for other family members. I have only brief moments of comfort and reassurance. They usually happen when Sarah and I are engaged in play, laughing all the while.

I continue to mindfully meander with Sarah: Who is Sarah and what does she need? Who is Sarah's father and what does he need? Who might be a resource to help us both? What does my apprenticeship as Sarah's father teach me? A major Sarah lesson has been to realize that what replaces the death of the heroic and the hunger for victory is an apprenticeship with the unknown. My ego's fascination with itself periodically has me believing I am in the know. I am asked by fate at those times to pause, notice how aggrandized my thoughts are, and remind myself not to believe everything I think.

Victimhood – Most of us at some point will find ourselves meandering into the land of victimhood. The most obvious experience of victimization happens when our physical, sexual, or emotional boundaries have been violated. This level of victimization is not about meandering. It is simply reflective of the inherent hazards of being alive and results in some form of trauma in need of healing. Let's see what might draw someone to their meandering as a victim:

1) An insidious form of empowerment - Curiously enough, attachment to being a victim can be an insidious attempt at gaining power—insidious because it is so indirect and subtle. As victims, we may believe we are more entitled to compassion and consideration. We may also believe our victimhood can control the expectations others have of us. Why would others have large expectations of someone already struggling so much, especially with regard to self-accountability? Another expression of empowerment is the belief that some sensitive souls will attempt to take care of us and, with a little luck, may even be willing to neglect their own needs to address ours.

2) Legitimizing our emotions - If we have either shamed or ridiculed our emotional lives, then the ordeals that left us feeling victimized can bring legitimacy to our emotions. We gain permission to feel hurt, angry, sad, fearful, and desperate. How could anyone question the rightfulness of our emotions in the wake of such hardship?

3) Entitled to attention - The suffering and trauma of being victimized can be a ticket to getting the attention we always wanted but did not quite know how to ask for.

4) A protest - Meandering as a victim is often echoed in protest of life's inequities. The protest suggests we deserve better. It becomes an opportunity to pity oneself in lieu of genuine self-care. The protest implies we are exempt from living life on life's terms. We deserve a more pleasant life; one divorced from trauma and pain. Such a position is often driven by a longing to return to the magical thinking of childhood.

5) A dispensation from the hard work of healing - Hanging on to victimhood allegedly offers a dispensation from the responsibility to heal. Meandering into victimhood is often the result of either having our hearts broken or experiencing a serious defeat. Instead of taking on the task of healing, we lament our misfortune, embracing self-pity with its cry: "My situation is beyond any hope of healing!"

6) **An illusion of safety** - The "stimulus generalization" suggested by John Watson, father of behaviorism, lures us into an illusion of safety. Stimulus generalization takes place when we respond to current situations as we have to a past situation. For example, a boy responded to the trauma of his father's brutality by isolating in the hope of avoiding that wrath. Now, as a man, he avoids almost anything reminding him of that formative experience. He continues to isolate and remain anonymous with little or no discretion regarding who might be a safe ally and who might be an enemy. He is ever in survival mode, a potential victim of all relationships.

Like any distraction, victimhood presents a massive opportunity to explore authentic empowerment, self-love, healing, and the legitimacy of our emotional lives. The perennial danger lurking in the land of victimhood is the possibility of taking up permanent residency there, irreversibly derailed from the path of wisdom and our apprenticeship.

Meandering cannot serve us until we realize we are somewhere we probably should not be. We experience the loss of having wandered off course, away from what we truly desire. There may be a period of mourning that loss, accompanied by sorrow and regret. By experiencing the defeat inherent in our obsession, we begin to open to what it means to get back on course. Before that can happen, we must be honest about how we have either oversized or undersized ourselves to cope with the unpleasantness of life. The ego would sooner create some alleged effective strategy than admit powerlessness.

Oversizing and Undersizing

Confusion over our actual size is common while meandering. The ego is preoccupied with strategically demonstrating its worthiness. The ego cannot imagine that being authentic is the most rewarding way to hold value and be loved by others. It becomes obsessed with employing strategies to demonstrate its credibility.

Undersizing and oversizing are two of the ego's fallback strategies. Oversizing appears to be more obvious, as it overtly energizes itself through arrogance. The oversizing voice cries out, "If I'm big enough, you'll see me, admire me, and never accuse me of not being enough." The illusory promise of oversizing is that we can actually control how others perceive and respond to us.

Sadly, I have watched oversizing do just the opposite. The more oversizing gives testimony to its extensive knowledge and achievements, the more others back away. The oversized individual may then decide that the adverse reaction calls for strategic reinforcements, which only distances others more. Occasionally, a few undersized folks are seduced by the oversized exhibition, misinterpreting it as confidence. In which case the oversized is reinforced by the enamored reaction. Both remain confused about the rightful role of authenticity.

We cannot step from an oversized position into an apprenticeship with the unknown because we spend too much time pretending to know. The unknown remains an enemy to be avoided, as does the vulnerability of feeling lost and bewildered. The risk of growing too attached to oversizing is meandering indefinitely in the depths of isolation. The only way out is to face the terror and powerlessness of stepping away from the strategy. The path of wisdom is not available until authenticity is fully embraced, at least with respect to ourselves.

I think back to one of my first wake-up calls around my own oversizing. A student of mine wanted me to meet her mentor. We scheduled a meeting, during which several hours of stimulating conversation took place. As the evening came to a close, with pleasantries exchanged regarding how glad we were to have met, my colleague turned to me and said, "It certainly was a full evening. Meeting you was like having three hot fudge sundaes."

As I left her driveway, I kept wondering about my company being described in these terms. Were three hot fudge sundaes too many or not enough? By the time I finished the thirty-minute drive home, I decided that being likened to a dessert fell somewhat short of complimentary.

Because I believed the person describing my impact on her was relatively perceptive, I struggled to write off her feedback. One hot fudge sundae was a treat. But three? I decided she was describing me as a bit much.

I never ordered another hot fudge sundae. I was 33 years old at the time and not quite ready to admit she had caught me showcasing my best wares, so to speak, although I did become gradually interested in the man attached to showcasing his best wares. I discovered how convinced I was that being genuine would never be enough. The work of my rightsizing had begun.

Undersizing is not quite as popular with men as oversizing. The undersizing voice says, "I'm no threat" or "You'll find me to be amiable and easy to get along with." The undersizing strategy has two purposes. The first is the entitlement to be risk-avoidant due to the absence of inner resources and skills. Translation: "I don't have what it takes to fully participate in life." The second purpose is to engender the acceptance of others by posing no threat to their desires and beliefs.

The undersizing strategy guarantees isolation by prohibiting us from engaging life to the fullest. The undersized remains poised, ready to be told what to believe and what to do. Because this strategy interrupts a turning inward, allowing for a deeply personal encounter with ambiguity, it also obstructs an apprenticeship with the unknown. We saw the young princess in our Norwegian folk tale undersize herself as she returned home for maternal guidance rather than trusting herself.

It can be difficult to interrupt the undersizing strategy when others only seem to reinforce it. The oversized can feel better about their alleged dominance over the undersized, prey to the seductive belief that being likened to three hot fudge sundaes is pretty nifty. Such false modesty is the life blood of undersizing. How often do you hear someone being accused of false modesty?

If we think of false modesty as a minimization, and dishonest assessment, of our actual gifts, then its duplicity is no less misleading than that of arrogance. The insidious nature of false modesty is disrupted only when we stop feeling good about ourselves because we are relating to those who undersize themselves. It can also be helpful for those who undersize to be honest about their false modesty.

Undersizing can also be a compensation for oversizing. Recently, while I was responding to questions about my life's work, a colleague overheard my responses. He quickly suggested, "Paul knows how to greatly understate the extent of his work." I became more aware of rightsizing as deserving lifelong attention. Such a focus inspired me to be more honest about my arrogance and false modesty. The result was an ensuing invitation to authenticity held with compassion. Such soul work has the capacity to frame an apprenticeship with the unknown.

It is no small accomplishment to get through some meandering alive. With the ego holding authority, our ability for fine-tuned discernment is typically skewed, leading us into distortions. We are not sure who we are, nor do we have any clue about the journey. The hope is that we have gained some familiarity with our favorite distractions and where we are most susceptible to being seduced. When our meandering yields self-revelation, we gain understanding of how we either inflate or deflate ourselves as we cope with life's challenges.

Sometimes meandering calls for more meandering. Fear, feelings of unworthiness, or some early childhood injury may prevent us from seeing and accepting ourselves for who we are. Life feels like too much. We cannot imagine what it would mean to be ready to live it fully, so we retreat into feeling lost, confused, vulnerable, and, at times, deeply worthless. The ego recoils in the face of challenges, prepared to strategize, finding some way around life's demands. Such a reaction is the breeding ground for generating a Bypass, a detour around life's impositions on our will.

A Blessing for Meandering

I always believe I'm ready, ready for something larger than I am now. Ready for more insight, more responsibility, and more offerings of leadership, ready to impact the world in a favorable fashion. Oh, so ready am I, for that larger stage.

I am so willing to be distracted by rationalization: some skewed thinking comforting the appetites, turning me away from myself. These distractions will come in the form of denial and its first cousin, rationalization, convincing me that nothing of any importance is at the door—just some annoying clamor.

Performing and striving always feel holy. I'm just trying to get you to see how good I'm doing. Have you noticed yet? If not, I'll strive to get it right. Certainly, my moral and spiritual laboring deserve your attention. I'm really trying hard to get it right. Why does the final destination seem so out of sight?

Could there be no better demonstration of my earthly prowess than to set out to conquer life? Surely, my will is ready to be victorious. And then defeat comes. Shame and helplessness weigh heavily at the back of my head now, not knowing if I'll ever stand erect. I hear the call of victimhood, to one unjustly treated by life. My defeat will know redemption. My suffering is no longer ignoble. Certainly, such pain deserves your kind attention, no need of expecting so much from someone so mistreated by the gods. I'm sure that this victimhood can be some new kind of victory.

I'm so alive, seduced, and obsessed. I can feel the blood pumping from an eager heart. I am so completely where I should be. You bring me all that I wish for, desired, loved, and adored. You are the well of my redemption, finally liberated from the shackles of self-contempt.

Could it be that the great lesson of meandering is not being ready, accompanied by the fool who thinks I am? Must I allow rationalization and denial to indulge me in eating more, drinking more, isolating more, and working more? Can there be great teaching held by the emptiness of these mores?

The fool believes that performance accompanied by you being impressed will feed my soul with your delight. And when it comes, it passes through me like a warm Spring breeze followed by a cold chill caused by the absence of your favor.

What of this fool who introduces me time and time again to where I don't belong? Is he the younger sibling of wisdom? And does he know my unknowing and take on the mission of introducing it to me?

And what of these encounters with my unknowing? As each distraction loosens its grip, am I emptied a bit of some distortion? Now, understanding that I do not make this wisdom happen, I meander, guided by a fool. I empty, waiting to be touched and moved by a new light patiently waiting to offer me its illumination.

2

The Bypasses

To nurture a resilient human being, or a resilient city, is to build in an expectation of adversity, a capacity for inevitable vulnerability.... Resilience is at once proactive, pragmatic, and humble. It knows it needs others. It doesn't overcome failure so much as transmute it, integrating it into the reality that evolves.

–David Sloan Wilson

Bypasses are attempts to avoid life's intensity, mystery, insecurity, adversity, and inevitable vulnerability. Our inability to accept life's perilous journey compels us to take every possible detour as a way of circumventing life's undomesticated power. The ego flatters itself in the belief that it can outwit life without having to succumb to life's whim. The ego either is adequately defeated, willing to surrender to all that is out of its control, or maintains an attachment to the illusion that some Bypass will win out. Where the former opens us to being informed by life's limitless lessons, the latter deludes us into thinking the perils of fate can be avoided.

The Spiritual Bypass

Spirituality, like all human endeavors, can be reshaped to avoid the tough stuff of life, which includes what fate presents and how we respond to it. Nothing is more demanding than deepening and broadening our psychological maturity and choosing to live fate on fate's terms. The word *psyche* originally meant "soul." And so, we might say there is soul work to do. At the very least, the soul alerts us to any aspects of fate within our grasp. We must then decide if, and how, we want to take action with regard to what is in our control. We must also discern what we cannot control by letting go of it. As Albert Einstein put it: "It's not that I'm so smart, it's just that I stay with problems longer." Einstein's remark captures the steadfastness needed to craft a reliable level of discernment.

Tolerance for confusion and ambiguity can yield more information about what is and is not in our control while also determining how we respond. The decision is ours to make: **Either we are bigger than fate, protesting what we find unfavorable, or there's something wrong with us.** Staying with a problem longer may reveal something about us we are not ready to see or accept, such as our limits.

Typically, this staying power calls for a ruthless inventory of the soul. We become more honest about our positive and negative traits alike. It also calls for enough humility to accept how small we are in comparison to the vastness of what fate hands us.

"The ego wants to eliminate all bothersome, humbling, or negative information in order to 'look good' at all costs" (Richard Rohr). A Spiritual Bypass offers the ego an alleged path to human development, adorned with icons, hallelujahs, and protocols aimed at reassuring one's ability to "look good."

The Indicators

A number of indicators suggest the possibility of an active Spiritual Bypass:

- **We deny unresolved wounds.** The fact that we are constantly invited to deny abuse or neglect means that healing is unnecessary. We decide that affiliating with the God of our choosing automatically redeems whatever trauma was conveyed in childhood.

- **We exaggerate our sense of compassion.** Pseudo-compassion is the alleged declaration of one's holiness, allowing for the denial of hatred, jealousy, competition, and feelings of revenge. Pseudo-compassion's closest companion is self-righteousness. Inevitably, darker elements find their way to the surface by way of projections and passive aggression, both of which are unconscious. Whatever we deny in ourselves skews our vision of others, in whom we see what we reject about ourselves. Our compassion translates into a pity that denounces others as unfortunate. Passive aggression commonly manifests as seemingly positive assessments that also demean: "It's not your fault you lack intelligence." "You acted inconsiderately, but maybe they deserved it." "Sorry, I just forgot to pick you up." "You seem very kind, but then you let people walk all over you." "When will they get their act together?! They could surely use the support."

- **We hold tightly to "delusions of having arrived at a higher level of being" (Robert Augustus Masters).** Our tendency is to vault ourselves into "awareness" without taking on the arduous work of mindful living. How seductive it is to bask in the light of having arrived!

- **We reduce our primary spiritual task to ideological compliance.** Taking on the task of serious personal reflection is suspended. Neither do we live a rigorous, self-examined life. We tell ourselves that all we must do is familiarize ourselves with holy books, as if that alone will make us holy.

- **We deny darker elements of the psyche, such as arrogance, greed, vanity, and false modesty, as well as any positive traits we deem unacceptable in the eyes of others.** In lieu of significant psychological work, we promote an attractive persona, all the while pretending we have dealt meaningfully with the darker elements of our character.

- **We engage in pseudo-self-love.** Genuine self-love is significantly inhibited when darker elements of the psyche are denied, thus disallowing acceptance of our whole selves. Pseudo-self-love leaves the ego capriciously in charge of our perceived worth.

- **We treat being born again as our attainment of some refined spiritual status.** The ongoing seduction of the Spiritual Bypass is its suggestion that we have "arrived," as if the work is already over. The ego rejoices in the illusion that it has found immunity from the slings and arrows of the journey.

- **We deny a destructive dynamic.** Rather than confront some destructive dynamic in our lives, be it a betrayal, addiction, or loss, we focus on uplifting exhortations pointing us away from destruction: "My marriage works perfectly now." "I no longer resent my alcoholic spouse." "My children have all found the Lord." "I'm sure my son's overdose was part of God's plan." "My husband's rage doesn't really effect the children."

The New Age Spiritual Bypass

New Age spirituality has become increasingly popular because it avoids religious dogmatism as well as exhortations of fire and brimstone. It also restores sovereignty to the ego, securing its dominion by validating the powers of desire and intention. This thinking is epitomized in Rhonda Byrne's bestselling book, *The Secret*.

The Secret assures us there is no reason to consider fate as anything greater than the sum of your desires and intentions. As long as those desires and intentions are sound, fate will be attracted to supporting your every wish. Nothing could be more seductive to an ego eager to maintain its supremacy and reduce life's mystery to a well-organized intention. Some of *The Secret*'s urgings include: "You will attract everything you require—money, people, connections." "Go for the sense of inner joy and peace then all outside things appear." "The Universe will rearrange itself accordingly."

Thinkers like Joseph Campbell, however, believed that *fate* ("will of the gods") would prevail beyond the hero's best intentions: "The fates lead him who will; him who won't they drag." Responding to adversity presented by fate often exceeds the ego's skill level. Celebration and a measure of gratitude are the best that can happen when the universe provides.

When fate refuses to cooperate with our intention, we are presented with an opportunity to learn about the power of surrender, becoming humbler, more forgiving, and more compassionate. We create ourselves again and again. Even Campbell is suspicious of living with alleged clarity: "If the path before you is clear, you're probably on someone else's." In other words, following our unique passion and vision will inevitably lead us across unknown terrain. Learning how to be lost is central to the development of true character. An honest spirituality cares nothing for aspirations of prosperity.

Another appeal of New Age spirituality is that it lines up well with our culture's love affair with expedience. We want our spiritual task to be accomplished as quickly as we can download it. A weekend workshop or retreat in Sedona, we tell ourselves, is enough to bring us to enlightenment. But, as theologian Pierre Teilhard de Chardin reminds us, "Above all, trust in the slow work of God."

It was around my sixtieth birthday that I began to realize the most important learnings take a lifetime. My ego was repelled by this awareness. How could it be that learning about compassion, freedom, love, simplicity, grace, gratitude, and generosity would take me many decades to yield some inkling about what truly matters? Only in the wake of this epiphany did my illusion of prodigy subside, leaving me stumbling toward enlightenment as the flawed human being that I am.

The Psychological Processing Bypass

The Psychological Processing Bypass, an outgrowth of the New Age Spirituality Bypass, is perhaps the most insidious Bypass of all. It is accompanied by a sturdy denial. Even those witnessing it are hard-pressed to identify that a Bypass is actually taking place. But Bypasses are like that. They conceal the truth of what is happening while making us look good doing it. The following are some basic characteristics of this ByPass:

- Psychological processing is a verbal exploration of emotional life. It often includes an examination of how early wounding impacted future decisions and relationships, with considerable emphasis on organization of self-concept. It is often done in the presence of a psychotherapist and/or support group.

- This Bypass defines personal growth as creating and participating in opportunities for verbal processing. Transformation and change are not identified as valued outcomes of psychological work.

- The person engaged in the processing may be willing to express deep emotions, including sorrow, fear, anger, and despair. Such expressions tend to elicit very favorable responses from therapists and support group members, who will view the individual as courageously attending to needed healing.

- When a man exercises this Bypass, he is received with admiration and respect. He appears to be interrupting the cultural mandate that "real" men avoid deep emotional work.

- The ultimate goal here is to bypass living life on life's terms while looking good doing it. This Bypass entails the elimination of courage to face life's challenges in support of genuine personal transformation.

The Price Paid

When personal growth is reduced to expressing emotions, fate is stripped of its ability to teach. We sacrifice our ability to live life to its fullest potential. The apprentice is inoculated against taking the kinds of risks that would allow fate's penetration. One's coping skills are likewise arrested. The emotional resources gained through direct experience are forfeited in favor of mere talk about such resources. False modesty haunts the psychological processor, who denies innate skills and talents as ways of reducing life to something emotionally discussed but never lived. A need prevails to present oneself as too small to live life on life's inherently risky terms.

Genuine emotional maturity is disabled. Maturity is dependent on a willingness to learn from life, while learning itself is dependent on a willingness to fully participate in life. When the apprentice does not fully participate, he or she cannot grow into personal truth. Relationships become severely limited. The psychological processor enters into them with the following directive: "I'm willing to talk about our relationship but not fully be in it." Relationships become yet another way of declaring that life is too big to warrant total commitment.

Impact on Others

I became more aware of the impact this Bypass has on others when a client of mine, Patrick, a human relations consultant, wanted to discuss a personal challenge:

"I'm in a men's support group with my friend Mac. We've been in the group for almost five years. I have a great deal of respect for Mac's ability to process his emotions and support the emotions of other men," explained Patrick, shifting his gaze downward.

"Sounds like Mac knows how to show up and allow his emotional life to be visible," I replied, aware there was more to Patrick's story.

"Absolutely, he fully partakes of the support group. In fact, he belongs to four different support groups. Sometimes, I think he sees life as a support group. What's been bugging me lately is how alone I feel when I'm relating to him in the group," Patrick pointed out, his head dropping toward his right shoulder and both hands turning palms up.

"Something is missing for you," I suggested.

"Yes, if I'm grieving some loss in my life, he's right there with me. But the minute I start talking about a new professional undertaking, I can't find him. He fades whenever I'm breaking new ground in my life," asserted Patrick, with a sense of satisfaction over having deepened his understanding of this challenge.

"It sounds like you now have a better understanding of what's going on between the two of you," I noticed.

"Yes, I think it's something about change and taking risks. He's sixty and rents a yurt on his uncle's farm. He professes a devotion to ecology and clean living, and yet what I pick up on is an excessive austerity. It's as if he's trying to strip life of its immensity. Does he actually believe he can decide how big life is?" said Patrick with a note of skepticism.

We spent several weeks focusing on Patrick's friendship with Mac. He came to understand that Mac did not want his support regarding personal empowerment and that Mac did not know what to do with Patrick's willingness to look inward. Patrick also came to understand that he and the other men were colluding with Mac's attachment to the Psychological Processing Bypass. They were all willing to make sense of Mac's inertia by deciding he was excessively wounded. Patrick expressed great remorse concerning this appraisal of Mac. He refused to see him as damaged goods. He decided to leave the group, finally accepting that Mac did not want his support and that Mac would not support Patrick's commitment to living life on life's terms.

The Psychological Processing Bypass is especially attractive to those wishing to benefit from being perceived as committed to personal growth while avoiding the risks of transformative work. Can it be they simply will not forgive themselves if some risk yields unfavorable results? Forgiving ourselves for meandering, getting lost, and accepting defeat is crucial when befriending fate.

The Violence Bypass

It seems unthinkable. Could thoughtful, compassionate folks actually prefer violence to living life on life's terms? It may be that remaining an apprentice to the unknown calls for a devotion to pacifism. Because fate's terms will always be greater than what lies in our control, the apprentice is destined to feel helpless over that which cannot be controlled. We will now explore violence's subtle mechanisms, whether directed at others or toward the self, as compensations for powerlessness.

How Violence Becomes an Attractive Option

At its heart, the word violence refers to a force by which we inflict harm or fear upon others. Because our ability to harm or frighten may reflect an arousal of sadistic tendencies, it is vital to explore our attraction to use of strong force. Guru Nanak, for one, points out that the ego struggles to accept its impotence or passivity. Nanak goes on to define compensatory violence as "a substitute for productive activity," adding that "a man cannot tolerate absolute passivity."

We can understand "absolute passivity" as the inevitability of our impotence against life's challenges. Obviously, one way to compensate for feeling powerless is to exercise brute force. Violence need not be limited to acts of sadism. Harm may result regardless of our intentions. Whether violence is committed consciously or unconsciously, however, accountability should prevail.

Violence Against Others

Enacting force to harm or frighten others is often obvious and less insidious than self-violence. Everything from murder, schoolyard bullying, raging at family members, and objectifying the female body reflects a measure of violence against others. It is natural to visit these darker expressions of the human condition. But to take up residency in them is poisonous to our collective spirit and emotionally sedative to the heart. A heart sedated is limited to necrophilia (love of death). Compassion, expression and acceptance of love, authentic self-appreciation, generosity, gratitude, and cocreation all begin to atrophy. As the capacity for these life forces withers, so does the hope of maintaining any intimate kinship with life.

Violence may be physical, emotional, or intellectual. The most ostensible expressions of violence, such as assault, rape, and murder, are physical. Emotional violence includes bullying, sarcasm, ridicule, shaming, and name-calling. Ignorance and disregard, despite being more passive, are also forms of emotional violence. Whatever form it takes, emotional violence renders its recipient "undeserving" of attention.

Intellectual or mental violence is perhaps the most complex of all, and takes at least one of the following four expressions.

1) Preaching, lecturing, and moralizing - These are the most obvious expressions of mental violence. Its message to the recipient is that he or she is somehow depraved, lacking in virtue. Intellectual violence can also be inflicted by insisting we know what is best for others. In the words of Ron Kurtz, "When someone simply assumes they know what is best for others, you have violence." But what could be violent about assuming we know what is best for others? Kurtz is highlighting a narcissistic component to violence. When sadism drives violence, it is difficult to look good while pulling it off. When narcissism propels violence, however, it is often cloaked in veils of teaching, healing, help, and rescue, making it appear noble. And yet, to suggest we are somehow a more reliable source of truth than others are for themselves is harmful. Our recommendations, teachings, and guidance compensate for our own lack of self-worth. We get a temporary boost when others take up our hallowed prescriptions. How could we not have value when others appreciate our counsel?

I have often witnessed people feeling significantly diminished by being told what is best for them. The message is clear: "I know something you don't know." The force of the advice, however well-intentioned, may even be expressed with condescension, pity, self-righteousness, or a sense of admonishment. Recipients of advice often feel inadequate, as if they could never know what might be best for them. The more the advice is related to significant life issues and not simply something perfunctory like offering directions to the post office, the more harm can be done.

It is important to distinguish offering choices from asserting our knowledge of what is "best." An offering is not a declaration of infallible truth. It is an expression of our experience of another's behavior or of life in general. For instance, saying to someone wrestling with alcohol, "I notice you've decided to keep drinking alcohol," is a way of stepping into a collaboration with the drinker. It takes practice to hold a view as nothing more than that: a view and not an ultimate truth.

Even in response to a request for guidance in relationships, education, and job selection, one must see those making the request as having the ability to decide what is best for themselves. Nonviolent responses to those struggling with such significant life endeavors include telling stories about similar situations, generating questions aimed at focusing and enlarging the inquiry, and inviting emotions surrounding the issue in question.

We can interrupt an attachment to narcissistic violence by pausing before we speak. A pause is especially important when feeling urged to open our mouths without thinking. In such cases, violence occurs not because of what is said, but how it is said. As we habituate ourselves in effective pausing, we exercise more suppleness toward others, loosening our attachment their value and acceptance of what we offer. Our offering is made by acquiescing to recipients' best judgment as to whether they feel served by what we say.

2) Unbridled attempts at influence - We can also support pacifism by deepening our understanding of attachment to influence. An old definition of the word *influence* is "the power to act on others." We come to understand acting on others as our intention to push them in some direction only we deem favorable. The violence inherent in this message is clear: "You need to clean up your act and be what I want you to be."

It would be naïve to suggest that all attempts at influence are violent. We might just as easily "act on others" in a way that calls them to hold more compassion for themselves. We also might wish to influence them into collaborating with us in service of a mutually desirable goal. In doing so, we become more mindful of our desires to influence, reducing rather than enhancing violence. We might even openly declare our desire to influence, asking if the other is open to being influenced. We may also ask: What drives me to influence others in this particular situation? Am I attempting to change them in a way contrary to their wishes? How do I feel about myself when I suspend attempts at influence? How might I more effortlessly interrupt my attachment to influence?

3) Social dissociation - We can think of dissociation as translation of emotions and bodily sensations into ideas. Dissociation happens when children realize they are only susceptible to harm because they exist in a body. Consequently, they learn to step outside of their bodies as a way of protecting themselves in unsafe environments. A prototypical example of dissociation would be turning hurt into an insistence on humanity's insensitivity. Thus, sorrow becomes an abstract consideration of the inevitability of loss. Social dissociation takes place when we respond to the despair and pain of others by advancing a theoretical perspective. In such instances, we send a clear message: "I will not join you in either empathy or sympathy. I'm okay with you being alone in your suffering." Even dissociation may be an attempt to avoid our helplessness with regard to remedying someone else's pain.

4) Projections - Four forms of projection constitute a more insidious way of enacting mental violence against others. The first form of projection happens when we unconsciously identify someone in our present lives with someone from our past who was unkind to us. We erase the present individual's uniqueness, replacing it with the unacceptable traits of another. If the historical individual was tyrannical, abusive, or inconsiderate, then the person to whom we now relate can be nothing else. This often happens when we did not get what we needed in childhood. Such was the case with Joan, a 35-year-old primary school teacher, who came to our first appointment visibly upset with herself.

"I thought I was simply doing a good job as a parent," she confessed, her voice trailing off and eyes cast downward.

"How did you come to decide that your parenting wasn't meeting your expectations?" I said.

"Well, my husband kept pointing out that I give my five-year-old daughter more attention than my other children, especially the baby," she admitted, her tone suggestive of the struggle she likely experienced with regard to her husband's feedback.

"It must've been difficult to hear your husband," I suggested.

"Yes, initially, I was convinced that my seven-year-old son and the baby had nothing to do with his issue. I figured he was complaining about not getting enough of my attention for himself," she said by way of suggesting a reasonable interpretation of her husband's complaint.

"Sounds like something changed your mind along the way."

"I'm not sure. But I started to wonder if my mother dying when I was five might have something to do with the attention I give to my own five-year-old daughter," she pointed out, looking to me for agreement or disagreement.

We spent time exploring Joan's maternal loss at five years old. Eventually, it was easy for her to see she was projecting that loss onto her own daughter. The projection was accompanied by an inordinate amount of care and attention that was, in her words, "enough for three children." She learned to pull her projection away from the past and begin to care equally for her children, who needed to be mothered in the here and now.

Joan's form of projection is often accompanied by expectation of compensation. Consequently, we go from expecting those we project upon to treat us unkindly in the manner of someone from our past to expecting the present individual to make up for what we believe "should have been." Joan expected to compensate by giving more to her five-year-old daughter, on whom she projected her own five-year-old self. Thus, projection, coupled with the expectation for compensation, leads to emotional violence.

Once our hearts are committed to someone, we create an opportunity to redeem the past. When that happens, the expectation for compensation increases exponentially. The current relationship is burdened with the onus of making up for what came before. This dynamic can be as destructive to relationships as addiction and domestic abuse. The prospect of redeeming someone's past begins to collapse under the weight of an impossible expectation.

I am especially sensitive to this form of violence, since I engaged in it during my first marriage. Although not the only factor, it contributed greatly to the marriage's fall. I constantly projected my mother onto my spouse, expecting her to compensate for an entire childhood of emotional deprivation. It took years of self-directed work to reclaim responsibility, thus providing myself with the emotional support I needed.

A second form of projection happens when we reject some aspect of ourselves by relegating it to our unconscious, where we deny it or pretend it no longer exists. When family or society deem the trait taboo, we feign its lack to safeguard the acceptance of others. When a daughter or son figures out that a parent feels threatened by some positive characteristic like leadership or decisiveness, then that trait runs some risk of being denied, to secure acceptance.

These denied traits seem to have a life of their own. If we do not claim them, then they get projected onto others. We see our denied self-righteousness in others, leading us to treat them as if they actually possess what we project. The projection may be directed at an individual or an entire group, either way setting the stage for violence. We treat others as if they are inferior, because we see the darker elements of ourselves in them. This can lead to violence on a large scale, such as genocide or war.

The third expression of projection is something I term "masochistic projection." In this case, when being cruel is our default method of treating ourselves, we decide that others will be unkind to us in turn. Once this kind of projection lodges itself in the bedrock of the psyche, we live as if being hurt by others is inevitable. We create defenses through withdrawal or aggression in the name of protection. Ironically, the presence of such defenses practically guarantees callous responses from others, thereby confirming the narratives we spin around the inevitability of harm.

I describe the fourth expression of projection as a "beatification projection." This projection involves ascribing our essential goodness to another. In other words, attributing our divine spark to another, as happens when we fall in love.

To Project or Not to Project

Unfortunately, the choice of whether to project or not to project is not really a choice at all. In order to eliminate all possibility of projection, we would need to have experienced a perfect childhood and learned to accept the full spectrum of our characteristics as acceptable to others. Moreover, we would need to be perfectly at peace with the unknown. We project onto others as a way of coping with the tension we feel when encountering the unknown. Our projection tricks us into thinking we actually know the other person.

Why bother paying attention to the violence of projections when we can't extinguish them? Asked another way: Why love when we can't ever become perfectly loving? Working with projections holds us accountable for our perceptions and actions. It helps us eliminate violence in small, incremental ways. We can start by becoming more mindful of what kinds of projections have taken hold of us:

1) **Historical projection** - We project somebody from our past onto someone we are currently related to.

2) **Shadow projection** - We project some aspect of our personality we find unacceptable, deny we have it, and relegate it to the unconscious.

3) **Masochistic projection** - We project that others will treat us as cruelly as we treat ourselves.

4) **Beatification projection** - We project our own essential goodness or divine spark to the other.

In acknowledging our deification or demonization of others, we are proving ourselves to be in the throes of a projection. Another likely indication of projection is an intense need to fight against or flee from the presence of a particular person. An exaggerated attachment to be critical may also indicate the activation of a projection.

The following are some ways of dealing with projections:

- Acknowledge that we easily slide into projections and be willing to work on undoing them.

- Ask ourselves: Does the person we are reacting so strongly against remind us of someone from our past? If so, address our unfinished business with the historical person in question.

- Ask ourselves: Are we reacting to some specific trait of the other person, and can we own up to our possession of that very characteristic?

- Learn to let go of sanitizing our personalities by welcoming anger, arrogance, vanity, impatience, and insensitivity.

- Cultivate a broader welcome for what we deem positive and negative about ourselves.

Benefits of these strategies include:

- We are less likely to alienate others by idealizing or belittling them.

- We interrupt living in the past by seeing who we are actually relating to now.

- We gain internal serenity by accepting both what is laudable and less admirable about ourselves, thus honoring the wholeness of our humanity.

- We gain the ability to live with a depth of unity as we learn to see ourselves in others.

- We are less likely to go to war, in both the physical and metaphorical senses.

There will always be some level of projection in our views of others. The key is whether we allow a projection to prevent us from seeing their goodness and uniqueness.

Avoiding Feeling Helpless

Our use of harmful force is driven by an attempt to mitigate helplessness:

- **Helplessness suggests a diminished sense of self.** We experience it as the impotency of our wills and therefore an assault on our humanity. Helplessness is the antipathy of strength. It compromises our maturity. We feel like pseudo-adults or children.

- **When our adulthood is discredited, we lose self-worth.** How can we imagine that everything is okay when we feel like a child? As our personal value dissipates, so does our expectation that anyone might genuinely love us.

- **Once we decide we are unlovable, the natural consequence is to believe we will be alone.** Somewhere in the recesses of our DNA lies the fear of our ancient ancestors, who surely equated solitude with death. Thus, our hopelessness becomes intensely taboo.

The ego's need to compensate for helplessness activates destructive forces within us. This is especially true when feelings of inadequacy have been building over time. Under such circumstances, the force of aggression is by no means easy to resist.

On the surface, it is difficult to see the self-harm experienced by perpetrators who impose violence on others. In the words of Hesiod: "He's only harming himself who's bent upon harming another." We injure ourselves in precisely this way whenever we give in to revenge, rage, hatred, ruthlessness, cruelty, sadism, or narcissism.

The aggression behind infliction of harm is felt throughout the body, and its resulting violence often obscures a vulnerability that might otherwise cause the perpetrator to tremble. Anxiety gnaws just below the surface. Nightmares remind us of the harm we have incurred by enacting violence. The perpetrator's soul is straddled with toxic feelings.

This feeling of power, in tandem with the cultural injunction that renders helplessness "inappropriate," compels us to treat ourselves violently. The ego is impartial to where it directs its force.

Self-Violence

Self-violence is typically expressed through euphemisms: "I've always had low self-esteem." "I should've known better." "I can't believe how stupid I am." "I don't know what's wrong with me." "I wish I had more confidence." "I don't have what it takes to create real friendships."

I often find that folks who treat others kindly can be quite cruel to themselves. Although self-violence may reflect one's need to compensate for feelings of helplessness, it also has other precipitating factors. Below are several ways we commit violence against ourselves:

1) Collusion with a parent - A father possessed of sexist qualities sends a message to his children that intelligence is inherently male. A daughter in such a situation could easily support her paternal connection by deciding she possesses subpar intelligence due to her gender.

2) Filial loyalty - It is common to treat ourselves the way we were treated by parents or other authority figures. Filial loyalty protects against fears of abandonment, which the child comes to see as worse than abuse. When such loyalty extends into adulthood, one loses the ability to connect to others on an even keel.

3) Supporting an aversion to taking risks - Treating ourselves violently results in a diminished sense of self and confirms the inadequacy of our best efforts. Defining ourselves through multiple deficiencies exempts us from taking risks, since there is no reasonable hope of favorable outcomes.

4) A call to be taken care of - Beating ourselves up is often a call to be taken care of by others. Enacting violence toward ourselves presents caregivers with a clear opportunity to offer a type of support we ourselves are incapable of giving. This form of self-violence can actually be leveraged as a means of connecting to others.

5) Protesting against life's immensity - Self-violence leaves us feeling too diminished to live life on life's terms. This protest keeps us wallowing in victimhood, risk-averse and quick to offer a reason why someone should save us.

6) Maintaining an identity as negatively special - Since the ego abhors the idea of being ordinary, it eagerly identifies itself as either positively or negatively special. The ego's imperative is to secure its uniqueness, at either extreme, no matter what it takes.

7) Convinced that, by shaming and ridiculing ourselves, we avoid making the same mistake twice - This is bad self-parenting. Not a shred of research supports shame as a viable device for correcting behavior.

Developing curiosity about the purposes driving our decisions to be violent with ourselves can be a major spiritual undertaking. Kabir reminds us where our pacifism must begin: "[W]hen deep inside you there is a loaded gun, how can you have God?" If we are truly going to learn from fate, then we will need to treat our apprenticeship nonviolently. The key is committing ourselves to pacifism, interrupting violent thoughts and actions against the self.

The Violence Bypass takes the apprentice away from the self and from life itself. Violence breeds immunity against helplessness and inoculates our hearts from feeling the depths of our lived experience. Feeling helpless is therefore not so much a reflection of who we are as it is a testimony to the immensity and mystery of life. The more we relax into that knowing, the more capable we are of remaining apprentices to the unknown.

The Trivia Bypass

Nineteenth-century Danish philosopher Søren Kierkegaard coined the phrase "tranquilized by trivia." Although this sentiment was a reaction to his times, he was likely unaware of how prophetic it was. As acquainted as we are with the popularity of sedatives like alcohol, street drugs, and pharmaceuticals, we might not normally include trivia among them. And so, we do well to ask ourselves: How does trivia sedate and serve as a way of bypassing real life?

The Sedation

Preoccupation with trivia is one way of anesthetizing the tension and shame that often accompany uncertainty and ambiguity. Sedation sets in as we think and talk about nonessentials such as the weather, our possessions, the condition of our property, the status of our mobile devices, the final scores of athletic contests, and anything else that might be in vogue. It is as if knowledge of popular minutiae adds to the credibility of our knowing.

We live in a culture that prizes certainty and denounces uncertainty. So many of us experience the weight of our culture's condemnation of doubt to the point where it becomes extremely difficult to be shamelessly uncertain. Our wonderment loses its power to explore and create under a siege of cultural balefulness. And so, we attach our intellect to trivia or, as James Hollis points out, generate a "contrived certainty"—which is to say, we make believe we are certain. Either way, we seriously sabotage our capacity to remain apprentices to the unknown.

The Compost

We have moved far beyond the Socratic invitation to remain close to our uncertainty and our questions as the compost for wisdom. In Plato's *Apology*, Chaerephon (a friend of Socrates) has returned from visiting the Oracle at Delphi, who told him that Socrates was the wisest man in Athens. Chaerephon is excited to convey the Oracle's praise to Socrates. Initially skeptical about the report, Socrates wonders why he and not, say, an Athenian politician should hold rank as the wisest. After exchanging words with one such politician, he leaves the conversation thinking, "Well, although I do not suppose that either of us knows anything really worth knowing, I am at least wiser than this fellow— for he knows nothing, and thinks that he knows; I neither know nor think that I know. In this one little point, then, I seem to have the advantage of him."

Not on Fate's Terms

Our Bypasses are attempts to avoid the tension of living fate on fate's terms. Leaning into trivia as an attempt to avoid the unpredictability of fate to decide what can be controlled and what to do with it. It may be that on some level we decide we are never going to feel okay about ourselves facing the immensity of life. We believe we will never have what it takes to live fate on fate's terms. We cannot imagine ever being good enough, so why not change fate? Do we remain in the stranglehold of early abuse, where the only explanation for being violated was that we were never good enough to be loved?

We attempt to live fate on our terms by reducing it to a laundry list of petty details: Does the lawn need cutting? Do the windows need to be cleaned? Which player should be traded from my favorite baseball team? Who was the best-dressed actress at the Oscars? These are not inhuman considerations. Yet they become dehumanizing when allowed to prey on our conversations and sabotage our deepest considerations of what it means to remain apprentices of the unknown.

The Price Paid

There is an immense price to pay for trivializing fate. The problem is that fate refuses to be put into a small box. It relentlessly presents us with loss, new challenges, and trials for which we are never ready. There are several distinct consequences for attempting to reduce fate to manageable trifles.

First, we are ill-equipped to have significant relationships. We are unable to effectively address diverse views, resolve conflict, identify and ask for what we want, collaborate, or take emotional risks that build trust and rapport. Our relationships become superficial encounters signifying little or nothing. We draw people to us who are likewise interested in sequestering amid minutiae in lieu of extensive learning.

Meaningful relationships are a major source of the unknown. When two people are genuinely committed to one another, they each bring an attachment to support the development of their own uniqueness as well as their connection to the other. As these four energies constellate, there is an enormous opportunity to explore what support each person's autonomy will add to their connection. Such was the case when Martha and George came in to see me complaining of unworkable breakdowns in their marriage.

"We don't seem to be able to talk anymore without someone feeling rejected or afraid of hurting the other person," Martha shared as she made eye contact with me and quickly glanced at her husband, apparently scoping for some reaction.

"I think she's right. The tension created by either anticipating being hurt or hurting the other is immense. As a result, our conversations are typically about nothing important," George quickly chimed in.

"Is one of you more concerned about being hurt versus hurting the other?" I asked, wondering if they had in some way divided up their fear.

"Well, not that I'm insensitive, but I think I'm the one mostly afraid of being hurt," George added.

"That sounds like a tough way to be in a relationship," I offered.

"It's miserable. I end up avoiding the very person I want to be closer to," George explained, sounding both sad and defeated.

"And you, Martha, are you carrying the fear of hurting George?" I asked.

"Without a doubt. Don't get me wrong, I don't want to be hurt, either, but I mostly worry about hurting George," Martha added, appearing to feel relieved by her disclosure.

Over the next dozen sessions, it became obvious that Martha and George loved each other dearly and wanted to stop taking sanctuary in trivial conversations, instead learning how to work creatively with their fears. George began to understand how he was bringing an early abandonment wound into his relationship with Martha, since his mother had surrendered her parental rights to a relative and stepped out of George's life when he was nine. Martha, for her part, had significantly sacrificed herself in her first marriage by catering to her husband's every need.

While George was learning how to expand his support network so that Martha would not be his only source of emotional support, Martha was learning to delineate clearer boundaries around her need for solitude and time with female friends. As they began discussing what really mattered to them, each conversation contributed in some small way to rebuilding their emotional intimacy.

Second, we are unable to generate a meaningful life. Inasmuch as we strive to reduce life to a favorite TV show, we know the emptiness of minutiae. We cannot escape the question: What makes life worth living? When survival overrides our yearning for meaning, we return to the comfort of incidentals. Early trauma is characterized by feeling out of control and alone. Control, we tell ourselves, is restored by our preoccupation with minutiae.

Third, we are straddled with ineffective problem-solving skills, leaving our ability to cope impaired and our anxiety free to run wild. Large questions are either discarded as unnecessary or they end up overwhelming us. The soul wants to live in larger questions: What's my purpose? Who actually knows me? What risk awaits me? How effective is the support I currently live with? What do I truly love? Do I live my love? What do I long for? Who do I want to get closer to? What important task is asking for my attention?

Fourth, we advance a life of ignorance, relying on clichés, innocuous comments, and platitudes, blinding ourselves to wisdom's light. The unknown is deemed unacceptable. When ignorance prevails, fate must be reduced to whatever can be easily explained. Otherwise, it is relegated to the realm of the irrelevant. When experiences germane to love, freedom, compassion, accountability, generosity, and courage are deemed impertinent, soulful maturation is stifled. It becomes very difficult to see beyond the neatly stacked soup cans in the cupboard.

The Intellectual Bypass

The Intellectual Bypass paves a detour around the necessity of living life on life's terms and prevents us from being apprentices to lived experience. As first cousin to the Psychological Processing Bypass, the Intellectual Bypass favors thinking to being. The only difference is that the Intellectual Bypass is not limited to perseverating on psychological issues, but will obsess over anything it deems interesting. The classic example of a character attached to this Bypass is Shakespeare's Hamlet.

In his famous soliloquy, which begins "To be or not to be," Hamlet is not simply questioning whether to live or die. Rather, he is philosophically debating the value of existence versus nonexistence. He remains trapped in a web of rumination. He does not like suffering the "slings and arrows of outrageous fortune" and the implied passivity of such a condition.

Hamlet is troubled by the quandary of desiring to avenge his father's murder while not wanting to act immorally. When he questions suicide as an active way to confront life's suffering, he is reminded that the afterlife remains a significant mystery which may end up being even less rewarding than life. His ongoing cogitation contributes to his eventual demise as he duals with Laertes, motivated by a readiness to die.

The Origin and Construction of the Intellectual Bypass

Several elements support the origin, construction, and perpetuation of this Bypass:

- **Discovering we get hurt because we have bodies** - We are all raised in environments harboring at least some level of aggression and hostility. Children intuitively learn they can get hurt because they have bodies. Both physical and emotional suffering are corporeal experiences. Removing our bodies by spending more time outside the home is one option. The other alternative is to lift our energetic fields out of the body toward the mind.

- **At home in the mind** - One abstract concept can exponentially lead to an unlimited number of ideas.

- **Cognitively anesthetized** - Ideas do not feel. Due to the numbing effect of mental life, it is easy to think about important matters rather than be in them. Why not think about experiences such as risk, rejection, fear, hurt, and failure instead of getting involved with the messiness of these bodily experiences?

- **The power of dissociation** - We all have the power to translate emotions and internal bodily sensations into thoughts. Indulging in this ability minimizes having to deal with the autonomous nature of emotions, which come and go of their own accord. One's hope is that dissociation restricts the involuntary nature of an emotional life.

- **Can be impressive** - The Intellectual Bypass is often experienced as impressive. Our culture endorses the ability to express multiple abstract concepts. Those who are engaged in dissociation will be quite taken with others who dissociate. It is quite possible that we relegate the capacity to be emotionally moved to children, leaving those insulated by a sheathe of heavy abstraction basking in a supposedly evolved state of maturity.

The Price Paid

As with any Bypass, there are sizable prices to be paid when we decide to replace being with thinking. **The body is no longer viewed as a valuable conduit of information.** If the new neurology is correct, then ignoring data being relayed by the vagus nerve constitutes a significant loss of direct communication with regard to instinct, emotion, intuition, and imagination. When it comes to identifying what constitutes safety, nothing is more effective than instinct.

I was recently prepared to write off a strong bodily message of my own. I was watching the end of a TV movie in which a character named Jenny had secluded herself in her office after feeling betrayed by the man in her life. Suddenly, the boyfriend and two dozen others arrived, calling out her name: "Hey, Jenny. Hey, Jenny." I gently sobbed as she turned toward those assembled, and each of them described how their lives had benefited from some choice she had made.

My first reaction was to ridicule my sloppy emotional reaction to a scene lacking in meaning and depth. I finally paused and asked, "What does this scene call me to?" I let the question sit with me overnight. By morning I was flooded with childhood images of my friends standing outside our family home. They would call my name in a singsong fashion: "Hey, Paulie. Hey, Paulie, are you coming out?" Each time I heard those melodic voices, anticipation and excitement filled my chest. I was being called to some adventure by my gang. I never doubted that some novel expedition into the woods was to take place. Maybe we would discover a new cave or a game, promising some desired victory.

My tears carried a gratitude for those boys and the adventures we shared. They also held the sadness of no longer hearing that call. I wondered whether I might be able to recreate it. I was reminded that my initial criticism of oversentimentality simply reflected my fear of wandering too far away from my intellect. Yet the wandering allowed a genuine longing of my soul to surface. Below are some further consequences suffered by an apprentice caught in an Intellectual Bypass:

- **Untouched and immovable** - Life teaches us by touching and moving our hearts. But when we are smothered in abstraction, our capacity for empathy suffocates. Empathic injuries make it difficult to be touched and moved by others' experiences. Learning from another's engagement with life can become seriously restricted.

- **Blurred vision** - When our focus is on the relationship of ideas, we often miss what is right in front of us. Recently, at a dinner party, a woman and I were engaged in a conversation about inclusion, exclusion, and marginalization. The conversation became laced with an increasing number of abstract concepts. As the evening was drawing to a close, I asked a woman sitting near us if she had felt at all included in our conversation. She quickly responded, "Not at all!" I shared regret over getting caught up in my own cerebral activity. It prevented me from seeing what was right in front of me.

- **Confusion over what truly matters** - Psychologically navigating from one concept to another interrupts our ability to be informed about what we love, what we desire, and what deserves our devotion and passion. We struggle to identify the risks we are willing to take. Perseveration of thought leads to another idea worthy of our consideration, restricting actions that would support the apprentice's connection with fate.

- **Impairment of our ability to be seen, appreciated, and chosen by others** - Mired in abstraction, others cannot see where we live. They cannot see our losses, our triumphs, our failures, our heart's longing, and our love. Those who cannot see us cannot choose us.

None of the above is meant to give clear thinking a bad rap. I am reminded of another quote attributed to Albert Einstein: "I don't know why I get so many job offers. I'm only curious." The issue is not whether we reject our propensity to be curious, to initiate and sustain a thorough inquiry. The apprentice confronts attachment to an Intellectual Bypass by tracking her or his own tendency to dissociate.

We are likely dissociating, translating emotions and internal bodily sensations into abstract concepts, when we speak without pause. Excessive use of language lifts us out of our bodies and focuses our energy toward the face and throat. We do well to pause and ask: What does the application of this idea look like? Do I have any investment in identifying how my ideas can live?

A Blessing for the Bypasser

You always knew you were traveling a mysterious and unpredictable journey. You were not properly initiated into such a pilgrimage. You were not given the resources needed for such a trek. So, you did the next best thing by denying the immensity of the unknown. You decided that, with the right stuff, it would be quite manageable. You tightened your grip on the belief that the right education, the right job, the right financial investments, and the right spouse would ensure that you, the one traveling on this odyssey, would also be right.

But you discovered that being right would be but a temporary massage for the ego. The life you call your own would eclipse your best efforts at getting it right at every turn. Now, trapped as you are, you either turn against fate as a ruthless perpetrator or against yourself as essentially flawed.

When the chains of being fate's victim break through the skin and the noose of self-contempt tightens, you may be ready to negotiate a deal. You decide there's only one way to get it all right. Find some detour, some way to bypass fate's treachery and the slow death issued by self-loathing. Now, you're convinced you've found some formula, some circuitous route around life's inevitable insecurities.

You may be drawn to a spiritual detour, offering repose from hard soul work. Magic and delusion are rendered by the words "I believe." There's no longer a need to authentically forgive yourself and others. A self-examined life melts away, replaced by a "Hallelujah" and the sovereignty of dogma. Or maybe you succumb to the yearning of the sacred ego whose intention overrides the will of the gods. Of course, the result is more self-deprecation as the gods have their way.

You may seek refuge in your thoughts. No need to suffer the worry and angst of taking risks. A good idea beats quaking in the face of some action offering no guarantee of a favorable outcome. You know how to recline upon a bed of abstraction, where you are destined to endure an unlived life.

Oh Blessed Bypasser! You were not given honest directions about how to live. So, you searched for an inoculation against feeling helpless and insecure. You did what you needed to do, even searching for power by turning against yourself. Be gentle now. The soul does not feed on dogma, abstraction, or violence. It longs for warmth, tenderness, and sweetness.

3

Beyond Bypass

It is not necessarily those lands which are the most fertile or most
favored in climate that seem to me the happiest, but those in which
a long struggle of adaptation between man and his environment
has brought out the best qualities of both.

–T. S. Eliot

How long is the struggle that might lead you to living passionately and resiliently, until you are willing to let go of your attachment to some Bypass? The goal of a Bypass is to detour around and away from life's challenges, the unforgiving nature of fate. Because the ego wishes to live on its own terms and look good doing so, vanity accompanies each Bypass. Our culture colludes with the ego, suggesting that, with enough knowledge, skill, money, and the right friends, we can find a way to live fate on our own terms.

So much of wisdom is about letting go of your insistence on living fate on your own terms. And yet, while the life you create is yours to some degree, your creation will always be the outcome of both will and surrender. Your participation is reflected in active engagement and in receptivity to what fate brings you. Let us now examine a life that entails fate, your will, and your eventual destiny.

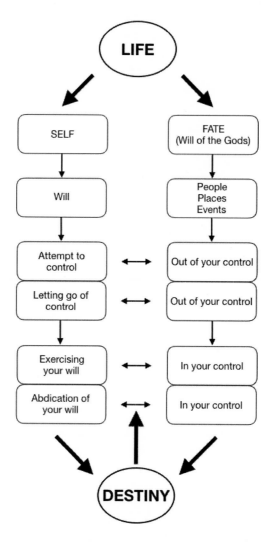

The above chart is but a small road map of life. Everything we experience, via our senses and intuitions, constitutes fate. An ancient definition of the word *fate* ("will of the gods") suggests just how much of our experience of people, places, and events is beyond our control. Because the consequences of our will have yet to take form, the apprentice works a great deal with the unknown.

We have two choices when fate comes to us with people, places, or events out of our control: attempt to control the uncontrollable or let go of that control. Either choice leads to internal reactions while also setting external consequences in motion. One example would be an attempt to dictate a child's academic success, which is fundamentally out of your control. Possible internal reactions include frustration, anger, resentment of the child or the school, feelings of inadequacy, and failure. Possible external consequences include the child growing hateful of learning, acting out at school, family dysfunction, and marital issues.

But what if the parent remains involved in a child's academic success as a consultant, collaborating with teachers and the child in support of educational success, accepting how little can be controlled? In this case, the parent holds no illusions about dictating the process. Possible internal consequences for the parent include acceptance of the child's progress and learning style, support of the child's interests, clarity around what actions might actually be helpful, and deeper satisfaction. Possible external outcomes for the student include treating studying and learning more favorably, discovering genuine academic interests, freedom to explore, and rapport between teachers and the parent.

What happens when fate presents us with people, places, and events we can control? It is very important to note that control over others only happens when they give us that control to begin with. Another thing to consider is how we exercise control, be it with curiosity, compassion, courage, and generosity of heart or with ruthlessness, ignorance, and self-indulgence. Our method of control determines the outcome. Everything from cooperation to sabotage, satisfaction to discontent, destruction to sustainability, and growth to inertia is possible.

Letting go of what is in our control also has varied consequences. The more innocuous outcomes happen because we have low interest in what fate is advancing. An example might be having control over cutting the lawn, which you decide not to do, instead allowing a landscaper to take on the responsibility of lawn care. Or letting go of control because you perceive someone else as more qualified to complete a task, as when you hire an electrical worker to fix some wiring in your home.

Of graver concern is when your control overlaps with responsibility. Examples include self-care, dreams, job and vocation, children, finances, government, and the planet you inhabit. As soon as you let go of your control over things for which you hold responsibility, you deliver a powerful message to fate: "I don't want to befriend you." The natural consequence is that you create an adversarial relationship to fate and feel victimized by it.

Whether or not you choose to befriend fate, fate will always define you. Living in your own story is easily replaced by living in someone else's. Such a situation places you in a position of excessive dependence and resentment.

Depression and anxiety ensue; personal meaning wanes. Underlying our choice to let go of control over responsibility is the need to avoid making mistakes. The price of this risk avoidance is a malaise of emptiness and the suspension of our ability to apprentice the unknown. Authentic engagement is replaced by passivity.

The apprentice must be willing to fail over and over again in her or his attempts to discern what should be controlled or set free. Failure engenders wisdom, the clarity of letting go and how to do it. Letting go means suspending attempts to influence or shape what fate presents. It also means redirecting our attention and intention toward something over which we have some level of control.

We can say that our destiny is a co-creative act of our own ability to exercise our own wills and our own capacity to surrender to what fate presents. We can also say that destiny can sweep over fate as a destination calling to us. Of course, we still have the choice to reject the call or respond favorably. However, there does appear to be a link between the call of destiny and an individual's purpose.

I refer to destiny's call as an irrefutable summons when the call obviously disrupts what should be an ordinary experience. Some years ago, while having lunch at a ski lodge, I received an irrefutable summons. Having finally found a seat in a very crowded area, I looked up to see a middle-aged man in a green and red plaid shirt, sitting with a monkey on a leash. The gentleman was obviously not dressed for skiing. He proceeded to explain how he would soon turn the monkey over to Boston University where it would be trained to become the companion for a quadriplegic person. As I ate my lunch, I continued to listen to the gentleman's description of a variety of tasks in which the monkey would eventually be competent.

I proceeded to finish lunch, stood, and wished the man well in regard to preparing the monkey for her education. I took two steps away when the man yelled, "Hey, do you know that if the monkey's mother died soon after giving birth, the other female monkeys would automatically mother the chimp? Do you think that level of community was transferred to us humans?"

"I don't know," I responded, surprised to be asked such a question, as I took several more steps toward the door.

"Hey, I have another question. When this monkey is assigned to a quadriplegic, she will remain with this person until one of them dies. Do you believe that level of loyalty was transferred to us in evolution?" he asked with an entitlement suggesting he was sent to the lodge to specifically ask me these questions.

I once again told him that I didn't know, now feeling annoyed as well as surprised, as if I had not signed up for such a quiz while resting before heading back to the slopes.

Two weeks later I was petitioning the local high school principal regarding the creation of a mentoring community for 14-year-old boys, which continued to serve boys for the next 12 years. I had been irrefutably summoned by destiny and glad I responded favorably to the call.

Deciding Not to Live Fate on Fate's Terms

It takes little to understand that fate is not only very large but can also be quite hazardous. We must take care of ourselves in light of failures, losses, defeats, injuries, illnesses, and betrayals. Once we are duly acquainted with the dangers of fate, three attitudes generally give rise to one of the Bypasses:

1) **Protesting the perilous nature of fate** - Protest is a common reaction to fate's dangers, especially when we come to terms with mortality. Protest is driven by the illusion of not having to play by life's rules. Protest keeps us in an adversarial relationship with fate, driven by anger and rage. We delude ourselves into thinking that rather than needing to surrender to all that is out of our control, we have the power to protest. Such power is illusory. Our protest keeps us at war with fate, insulated from the possibilities of beauty, love, and fulfillment. Yet protest does not emancipate us from the slings and arrows of fate. Suicide may be the only possible way to revoke our membership.

2) **Deciding that our desire and intention hold sovereignty** - This is a heroic gesture whereby we pretend to hold domain over people and events beyond our control. Arrogance and rage lock step to avoid helplessness, fear, and feelings of inadequacy. Fate works on such inflation by offering myriad opportunities to experience defeat and failure. If the defeat does not open us to living fate on fate's terms, then we fall prey to addiction, anger, and cynicism.

3) Deciding that fate is just too big to deal with - I call this the "I'm taking my ball and going home" syndrome. Lured by the attraction of keeping ourselves tranquilized, we shy away from risk under the delusion that failure and its attendant feelings of remorse, guilt, and inadequacy can be avoided through passivity. The reality is that when we forsake our desire and intention, we betray ourselves by living in accordance with someone else's desire. The outcome is a lack of self-respect, diminished confidence, and resentment, all feeding a passive aggression directed toward the person choreographing our life.

Our attempts to protest or conquer fate interrupt the learning of the apprentice, diminishing her or his capacity to become wise. We neither are informed by our experience nor do we understand ourselves as the ones responding to it.

The above three reactions prime our lapse into one of the Bypasses. Instead of seeking a relationship with the challenges fate presents, we flounder to maneuver around its insecurity and unpredictability. When things fail to work out the way we planned, we blame ourselves for not having what it takes. We remain stranded in the paradigm of being able to eclipse fate's severity, wrapped in the comfort of our delusion. If we are to move beyond an attachment to any Bypass, we must be willing to live fate on fate's terms. This is never easy. But there is no other viable way to learn from experience. The key is being willing to acknowledge an attachment to a Bypass, the courage to interrupt it, and the boldness to explore how we want to relate to fate.

Your Life, Your Destiny

Your life is determined by your relationship with fate. As in all relationships, you adopt an attitude with regard to fate, some way of thinking, feeling, and acting toward it. We lose much when we do not pause to examine the relationship we are constructing. And so, let us explore what it means to befriend fate in a viable relationship.

The Promise

So far, we have been dealing with four specific Bypasses. There are numerous other Bypasses, such as the Addiction Bypass and the Work Bypass. The alleged promise of any Bypass is to be saved. An old definition of the word *save* is "to keep safe." Are we searching for some form of safety that will protect us from the slings and arrows of life's journey? Either way, safety is a precarious way station. In order to move beyond a Bypass, we will need to understand safety as being more than shelter from harm. The following are several principles that will help to expand our understanding of what it means to be "saved."

Acceptance

Is that which flows in the name of acceptance ever pure? Acceptance is a welcoming of someone or something into our neighborhoods, homes, bodies, minds, and hearts. Uncle Fred arrives for Thanksgiving dinner, but our welcome is mitigated by the expectation that he will be obnoxious, drink too much, and offer a lengthy account of his recent achievements. Fate is constantly presenting us with the opportunity to decide whether we should deepen our capacity to accept what is coming or exercise our wills, enacting some form of change.

The will is either like a warm spring breeze, calming everything it touches, or a cold arctic blast. The challenge is to discern how much will to put forward. When some aspect of fate is clearly within our control, discerning questions can guide us in our handling: Is my will being influenced by some agenda rather than what fate is currently presenting? Are there any unfavorable consequences to enacting a strong will? Am I attempting to avoid something by being excessively willful? Am I attempting to prove something? Will I fracture a rapport with my willfulness?

When fate acts against our desires, our wills recoil at some unwanted piece of life. The ego, convinced it knows better, tries its best to summon tolerance. This is especially true when we feel misunderstood or misrepresented. In my own experience of such situations, my ego cries out, "That's not who I am!" This happened to me after a psycho-dramatic intervention with a participant during a workshop. He asked for my attention and said, "I didn't appreciate the way you were yelling at me." In my mind, I had employed a soft, modulated tone. On the inside, I said, "Are you kidding me?" On the outside, I responded, "I regret that you had such an experience."

Later, workshop participants approached me to confirm that I had indeed spoken in a gentle, subdued voice. They wondered why I withheld my account of what happened. I replied, "Who would've benefited by my insisting that I'd employed a tender tone?"

They were baffled when I added, "My ego would simply have enjoyed a temporary massage." I walked away both satisfied and sad as I recalled the numerous times my ego demanded to be heard at all costs.

Pride is quick to join forces with the will. Each strokes the other. Pride then proceeds to offer arguments for why and how life went astray. The will stands strong, indignant about fate forgetting its mandate to serve our revered lives. How could life forget its purpose?

Wave upon wave of defeat crashes over our wills, eroding the illusion that fate is in our employ. We may gradually come to notice, then accept, that fate does not appear to be in the business of serving us. There might still be a place for our wills to participate, living out some desire. It may take a while for the dizziness to subside as we gain some understanding of how small that place may be. Fate does appear to crave our participation, content in pulling us into depression and cynicism when we become disillusioned about the level of our participation. Fate welcomes us as friends. We can notice small expressions of life's invitation when we are acknowledged, seen, and appreciated by others.

Seeing, Overlooking, and Serenity

"God, grant me the serenity to accept the things I cannot change, the courage to change the things that I can, and the wisdom to know the difference" (Niebuhr). These words from the Serenity Prayer, coupled with a quote from Pope John XXIII, grant us perspective: "See everything, overlook a great deal, correct a little." It takes a while to domesticate the ego's tyranny accordingly. I still hear the voice of my own: "Are you crazy? Given how hard I've worked to see what lies in my interior landscape as well as what surrounds me, why would I want to overlook anything?"

The response is: "Because a great deal will be out of your control." **It is important to note how deeply personal "seeing" is. It is not meant to equip us with a formidable virtuosity aimed at strengthening our authority** over others. **Rather, it is an honoring of the apprenticeship we have been invited into and the humility needed to maintain our apprenticeship to the unknown.** When urged to see everything yet overlook so much, the lessons slowly begin to reveal themselves. If control is not an option, then relinquishment, acceptance, love, tolerance, forgiveness, and compassion are the only alternatives by which we have to learn.

Simple prayers remind us to renew our relationship with life. Our request for "serenity" is a supple expression of hope for life's cooperation. **We gradually shift away from the view that fate is either helping or hindering us. Such a shift suggests that the ego is willing to reconcile with fate's inevitable dominance. In that reconciliation, tolerance morphs into welcome.**

The apprentice understands that serenity best prepares us for learning. It diminishes reactionary response, heightens mindfulness, expands curiosity, and deepens our capacity for awe and wonder. Yet the apprentice is also restless, eager to draw nearer to what the gods have willed by fate. Thomas Merton wrote, "Paradoxically, I have found peace because I have always been dissatisfied. My moments of depression and despair turn out to be renewals, new beginnings." **The apprentice is a seeker, living in the paradox of serenity and restlessness.** Such a paradox may be what Jack Kornfield is working with when he describes an old teacher, Dipa Ma, as "empty and radiantly present."

This does not mean we always like how fate impacts us. The ego may need time to lick its wounds, gradually restoring enough courage to tend to what remains within its purview. The wisdom needed to distinguish what is in and out of our control deepens as we quiet our protest over life's challenges and losses. Curiosity becomes our default mode and yields more clarity about what we can actually control. Still, the appropriateness of acting courageously may not yield the immediate satisfaction of complaint.

Wisdom with regard to what is in and out of our control has a double edge. On the one hand, it allows us to let go of fruitless efforts directed at people and situations in which we are powerless. On the other hand, we are left with the task of tending to our own lives and finding the courage to pose questions that matter: What am I being asked to learn? What do I need to let go of? What is difficult for me to admit? Where do I come from? Where am I going? Who is coming with me? What do I love? To whom or what am I devoted? What are my gifts? What are my wounds? What healing is my life asking for? How effective am I at allowing love in?

Ultimately, whether or not we allow ourselves to be guided by the Serenity Prayer depends on knowing we are here to serve fate, not the other

way around. A centuries-old definition of the word *serve* is "to meet the needs of." In so doing, we move our lives to a new level by asking, "What does fate need from me?" This question helps the ego find its rightful place and surrender claims to supremacy, as well as support our friendship with fate.

There are endless ways to respond to the question, "What does fate need from me?" I typically do not need to ponder the question for very long. Like any good friend, fate has a way of getting my attention whenever it has a need. Over thirty years ago, my spouse at the time and I were in a couples counseling session in which I found a measure of comfort complaining about my wife's behavior. The counselor quickly mitigated the potency of my courage and said, "I think the real problem is not your relationship with your wife, but rather your relationship with alcohol."

One month later, wrestling vehemently with my pride, I acknowledged my drinking problem and committed to sobriety one day at a time. I then accompanied my 12-year-old son, Jason, to his postseason basketball banquet. The event was held at a local VFW, where the other fathers were making sure every pitcher of beer on their tables was filled at all times. So began my battle with the aroma of brew filling the room. I ingested one ginger ale after another, determined to take in enough liquids to meet my oral needs and in the hopes of bloating me beyond any desire for a beer.

Throughout the meal, a table with numerous trophies caught my attention, as I assumed Jason was hopeful of acquiring one. The meal came to a close, and the presentation of trophies began. I watched as one kid after another stepped forward to claim his award. My anxiety mounted for worry that Jason would receive nothing. Gulping down my twelfth ginger ale, I felt the need for any alcoholic beverage that might anesthetize the pain of witnessing my son go unacknowledged. Only one trophy remained. It also happened to be the biggest. I prepared myself for the worst as the presenter announced that the last award would be given to the best player in the league, and who also displayed the greatest amount of sportsmanship.

"This year's recipient is Jason Dunion!"

There I sat, overwhelmed with a joy that could not be numbed by any number of ginger ales. I decided then and there that life needed my sobriety and my recovery. It felt bigger than my life, because it was also about Jason's life, about the life of his own son, and of his son's son. And even the lives of my ancestors.

Deciding to live fate on fate's terms is an endearing task that reflects our acceptance of who we are while honoring the immensity of fate. When grace guides our acceptance, we no longer see what is out of our control as unfortunate, but as an opportunity to be further informed by fate. When schooled by loss, suffering, and violation, we may find it extremely challenging to live the question: What is fate asking of me? The following can help us maintain focus:

- **Accepting how little is in our control.** This calls for an evolving humility. Our natural tendency is to turn away from life, as if retreating from an enemy. A return to fate heals our experience of having felt betrayed by it.

- **Becoming risk amenable.** It is not the risk we fear, but how we will treat ourselves if the risk bears unfavorable fruit. In order to accept life's terms of living our desire, we must forgive ourselves when our actions do not generate the results we crave.

Benefits of Living Fate on Fate's Terms

There are a number of advantages to living fate on fate's terms.

Learning how to live from our desire – We experience the fulfillment and meaning of living our own stories. A life of desire entails learning to identify desire in the first place, how to act in support of that desire, how to be grateful for the opportunity to manifest it, how to make clear and concrete requests of others, and how to effectively cope with delayed gratification.

Acceptance of the extremely small role we play in the grand scheme of things – This leads to a deepened capacity for humility and honesty. We also learn to accept the likelihood that our finest achievements will go unnoticed.

More serenity – As we call off our attempts to change or control what is out of our control, our lives are touched by an abiding equanimity.

Reverence for the immensity of fate – From our acceptance of fate's terms often sprouts a reverence for its mystery and vastness. The word *reverence* means "deep respect." If we are to serve as an apprentice to the unknown, then reverence is essential. It has the strength to disrupt a cavalier attitude toward fate's teachings. It keeps us from slipping into the haze of mediocrity.

Opportunity to learn – We begin to appreciate how much we can learn from living on fate's terms. When fate is an impediment to our desire, we have ample opportunities to learn about love, forgiveness, patience, surrender, acceptance, compassion, asking for support, and self-awareness. Living fate on fate's terms is the motto of the apprentice, as leaning into the unknown with curiosity and wonder becomes a way of life.

Living fate on fate's terms means learning how to live over and over again. The bad news is that such learning never comes automatically. We can spend time defining ourselves as too small to live life or convincing ourselves of being able to master and conquer it. It can take a while before we give up being wrongsized. Fate grants us the fire of desire and a restlessness to illuminate the path on which we belong. When our desire is accompanied by acceptance for everything beyond us, we agree to fate's terms and live life well. Before we can deepen our capacity for acceptance, we must let go of the alleged promises of whatever Bypass has led us astray.

You Can't Get Life Right

One way we turn against the mystery of life is by reducing our experience of it to whatever is practical. The concreteness of life lends itself to some sense of correctness. We learn about personal hygiene, bringing beauty and order to an environment, procuring and preparing healthy food, getting formally educated, acquiring a job, managing money, and acquiring social skills. Once we reduce life to these measurable items, we comfort ourselves by getting them done right. Unfortunately, life does not appear to be content with being reduced to what brings us comfort. Natural disasters, loss, illness, oppression, and other unsolvable predicaments remind us of life's immensity. It is all we can do to dare to bring more depth and meaning to our lives by not closing down.

"If your everyday practice is to open to your emotions, to all the people you meet, to all the situations you encounter, without closing down, trusting that you can do that—then that will take you as far as you can go. And then you'll understand all the teachings that anyone has ever taught" (Pema Chödrön). Chödrön's suggestion has us shifting from the paradigm of getting life right or wrong to a choice between emotional responsiveness or apathy. And so, when it comes to expressions of life's greatest mysteries—love, freedom, generosity, gratitude, humility, creativity, courage, compassion, etc.—we must be ready to let go of getting life right. If not, we turn against ourselves with accusations of stupidity, insensitivity, and lack of vision. These indictments suggest that the core of life's mysteries is penetrable and that we can shame ourselves into getting it right. If we are willing to let go of turning against life or ourselves, then we may allow life to get us right. **Allowing life to get you right may be the only true form of being saved.**

Life Can Get You Right

Allowing life to get us right is a powerful spiritual axiom. It refers to everything fate brings to us as well as the myriad feelings, thoughts, and actions with which we respond. It speaks to a willingness to allow fate to touch us, move us, and teach us while refusing to shut down. It calls for a serious downsizing of the ego. Because most of life's experiences are out of our control, it makes sense to allow life to be mostly in control.

By allowing fate to be in control, we create an opportunity for it to get us right. We return to who we were meant to be rather than pursue who we thought we should be. Chödrön's admonition against closing down echoes Thomas Moore when he writes: "Real strength of character shows itself in a willingness to let life sweep over us and burrow its way into us." Life sweeps over us from the outside (fate) and from the inside, the latter being the thoughts, feelings, and actions we harbor in response to fate. As we allow life to "burrow its way into us," fate and our responses to it to become integral to who we are. We take on lessons that endure throughout our lives rather than be merely satisfied with, say, knowing how to operate the latest technology. Let us examine how we can allow life to teach us with both ferocity and gentleness.

Letting go – Learning to let go of what is out of our control returns us to who we are, so that we might shun illusion and pretense. Less distracted by what is out of our control, we are more receptive to life's teachings.

Remaining a student – In order for life to get us right, we must remain a student of it. This happens by being aware of our attachments to contrived certainties whose purpose is to massage the ego. Remain curious. Hold your unknowing without shame. Have faith that more will be revealed, especially when you feel lost and are convinced you have attained some significant truth. Always listen more than you speak. Stay close to the questions: Where in my life are my actions yielding unsatisfactory results? Has complacency numbed my curiosity? What is my heart's longing? Is there a particular life pattern repeating itself in want of my attention?

Getting support – One should never weather life's unknowns alone. We need viable support. The process is too big and there is always the seduction of giving up and returning to something more parochial. Eventually, we feel overwhelmed to the point of needing others to carry us for a while. We can ask: Who in my life is a seeker? Am I willing to ask for their help? How might our collaboration be mutually beneficial?

Self-referenced but not personal – Remaining self-referenced means staying focused on what we desire, what we love, what we feel, and what we value. Not allowing ourselves to take life too personally means noticing that most of our experiences and choices are much more reflective of the human condition than a personal one. Making mistakes in relationships, crafting a vocation, and living with more generosity and gratitude are all bigger than who we are. We may acknowledge one of our shortcomings while also holding the immensity of the undertaking and the inevitability of oversight.

Self-forgiveness – We remain flawed, imperfect human beings stumbling toward enlightenment. We must dare and risk, stepping into the unknown, while learning to forgive the stumbling. Without forgiveness, we grow increasingly preoccupied with self-abuse. We ignore the teacher and the lessons, shrouded by a perseveration of criticism.

The fact that any effort to get life right is destined for failure may just be its greatest gift. Failure interrupts our fascination with getting life right. Life continually introduces its impenetrable mysteries until failure brings us to our knees for want of another option. Only then do we have enough humility to become and remain devoted students of life. Learning to die may be a prerequisite to allowing life to get us right.

Death Class

Given that we are being asked by fate to accept impermanence and the unknown, we cannot serve life well without learning how to die. Death is the largest unknown we face. Because we live in a death-denying culture, the first lesson in our Death Class is to interrupt denial.

Interrupt denial. Interrupting denial means building an honest and mindful relationship with endings. The word *change* is a euphemism for birth and death. We can practice honoring the smaller deaths toward strengthening our ability to honor the ultimate one. Days come to an end, meetings end, seasons end, jobs end, relationships end, formal schooling ends, beliefs and dreams end. By acknowledging our experiences of endings, we honor what took place in the life of that which has ended. I recently participated in a four-day professional training. Upon leaving, I was aware of a friendship emerging with one of my colleagues. I emailed him a week later, acknowledging the joy of having come away from the experience with a new friend. He responded, "Your message meant a lot to me." An ongoing assignment in Death Class is to practice refining your experience of endings. This includes acknowledging what ends with those who participated while expressing regret, gratitude, and joy along with a hope for the future.

Ritualize endings. Ritualizing an ending brings more refinement and reverence to the life and ending of an experience. A ritual activates a story. When a story's action allows us to open our hearts and give witness to what lives and dies, it embodies the meaning of what was lived. Participants step across barriers of time through an interface of "then" and "now," feeling the depth of their ancestors doing their best to offer reverence and meaning to death. One example is a ritual we enacted in our Mystery School, in which students gather in parallel lines facing one another. At one end of the line, with eyes closed, a student steps into the space between two classmates, who each take a hand of the student. The two communicate verbally and nonverbally by gentle touch what it meant to share this learning experience with the student who stands between them. They then pass the person to the next two folks, who will do the same. A soft chant usually plays in the background while all this is going on. Once everyone has made their way through the gauntlet, we stand in a large circle. Every gaze palpably honors the life and death of what has transpired. The ritual allows us to touch the learning and healing that took place in our community. I often step away from the circle well-fed, wishing for more yet willing to let go.

Give yourself permission to grieve. The emotional body lives much closer to death than the mind. The mind often reacts to deep mystery by denying and/or moving away from it. Practicing endings means allowing our emotional bodies to feel anger, sadness, regret, relief, and gratitude in kind. Unfinished grief knows how to breach the surface with its periscope, gazing on vice through the cleansing waters of tears, as happened in the case of a client named Maryann. She and I had been working for some time when her friend's daughter died of an overdose:

"I've been crying for days since June's daughter died. I didn't even know her. I don't know where all this grief is coming from," she explained, wiping the tears from her face.

"Sometimes, a current loss opens the way for grief related to some prior loss," I suggested.

"I didn't really mourn my father's death. His alcoholism and abuse mostly left me feeling relieved," she pointed out, appearing more composed.

"And before your father's death, does any loss get your attention?"

"My grandparents, but I hardly knew..." Her voice trailed off, drowning in sobs.

I continued to hold the silence, believing she had come into an important awareness.

"It was my abortion!" she bellowed out, her tears now flowing profusely.

We later created a ritual, which included one letter to the fetus and then, in her non-dominant hand, another in response from the fetus to herself. She read her letters to me, then took them to a wooded area behind her home and buried them. After praying at the burial site, she felt forgiveness emanating from the aborted fetus. Maryann was learning a great deal about death in her permission to grieve. Grief keeps us attuned to the rhythms of life. As John O'Donohue once wrote, "Life is a growth in the art of loss."

Remain an apprentice to sorrow. Only when we allow our sorrow to inform us are we able to learn from life. Sorrow can teach us about where we belong and do not belong, what we value and cherish, what makes life worth living, and what we might be willing to die for. Sorrow is an honorable way we allow ourselves to be crafted by life. As Francis Weller puts it: "In truth, without some familiarity with sorrow, we do not mature as men and women. It is the broken heart, that part that knows sorrow that is capable of genuine love."

Let go of catastrophizing a broken heart. Apprenticing sorrow is like apprenticing the unknown. As Weller points out, "it is the broken heart... that knows sorrow " and "is capable of genuine love." When we are willing to restrain our inclinations of bringing unbridled romanticism to our loving, the idyllic is replaced by an acceptance of the inevitable risks involved. The more risk-friendly we become, the more we allow sorrow to teach us we can love again and again. To love is to know loss, because sorrow prevents us from closing our hearts. Sorrow tells the story of a heart fully lived. Rather than catastrophizing a broken heart, we should be grateful for the courage to live with an open heart, keeping us on its path. Such an opening strengthens our ability to remain an apprentice to the unknown.

From Survival to Devotion

An old understanding of the word *devotion* is "vow or solemn pledge." By its very nature, a solemn pledge will be motivated by some measure of self-interest even as it transcends the ego's borders. Such devotion is not an attempt to accrue praise or recognition. Nor is it an investment in becoming more virtuous. We will now examine how we save ourselves through some chosen devotion and how safety takes on a distinctively different quality.

Something larger than ourselves – Once we become devoted to something larger than ourselves, the ego's obsession with safety is eclipsed. The soul's task now is to be protected. As Atul Gawande writes: "The only way death is not meaningless is to see yourself as part of something greater: a family, a community, a society." We have learned to accept the perilous nature of life and the inevitability of death. We can vividly see the shift from ego-orientated safety to something larger in the lives of Mahatma Gandhi, Nelson Mandela, and Martin Luther King, Jr. Devotion to something larger may not garner the notoriety of these esteemed figures. As we shift to supporting our soul's task of safety, we accept that our work might very well remain anonymous. Our attachment to recognition, along with the gravity we attach to embarrassment, diminishes. It is not that we become cavalier about how we present ourselves to the world. Rather, our soul's task simply calls for more of our abiding attention. A sacrifice will accompany our devotion to something larger than ourselves.

Willing to sacrifice – An old definition of the word *sacrifice* is "to make sacred." We can say that our lives are sanctified as we sacrifice time and energy in support of that which is larger than ourselves. Yet the act of sacrificing is not necessarily about martyrdom. The time and energy we bring to our devotion are energized by a great deal of heart, thus yielding fulfillment.

Accepting that we can't get life right – It can take a long time before we understand and accept that we cannot get life right. Our culture insists we can acquire everything we need to get it all right. This entails an allegiance to two illusions: first, that life is essentially understandable, and second, that we are all capable of such understanding. In the face of failure, we either turn against life for having done us wrong or condemn ourselves for being so inadequate.

"There is a cumulative and exponential growth in peoples' perception, for those who do their inner work" (Richard Rohr). Rohr's statement attests to the simple truth that we are the closest thing we have to understanding life and what it asks of us. The more we are willing to look at ourselves with curiosity and compassion, the more we are willing to be instructed. Self-revelation reflects the nature of life as we experience it.

We should never see curiosity as a demand for clarity but rather as the connective tissue between fate and ourselves. This bond strengthens with compassion. Curiosity speaks to us in an intimate voice: "I want to see more of you. I will wait for you in the faith that more will be revealed, and I will allow my restlessness to continue to turn me toward you." It may be that saving ourselves devotionally depends on cultivating an abiding friendship with fate.

In the next chapter, we will turn to what it means to triumph over defeat and victory as the most endearing way to remain befriended to fate.

A Blessing for Going Beyond Bypasses

You did the natural thing, you attached to a Bypass, an alleged detour around the grievous dictates of fate. You simply wanted to be saved and live on your own terms. But that wish would be frustrated over and over again, baffled by the prospect of living well.

As your favored Bypass failed to offer you a much-desired salvation and needed protection, you began to lose faith in your chosen detour. Fate cries out, "Don't turn against yourself. Neither turn you against me!" Let your lamentation be short-lived. There will be some grieving as you get honest about the shortcomings of your beloved Bypass.

You were not initiated into the mystery of life. It has taken some time to shed an attachment to a detour promising to demystify life. Now, without the alleged power of your Bypass, you wonder, "What is there beyond being in control of my own life?"

The truth is difficult to hear and take in: "You were never meant to have an abundance of control over your life. You are granted only some small measure of control over your life." You didn't come to this planet to be mostly in control of anything. You came to learn about love. And it serves you to get on with the lessons.

Beyond the Bypass, you are now bonded to an endearing soul task. You are learning that so much is not about you but rather the condition of being human. Your need for control shifts, allowing for a journey by which you are touched, moved, and taught.

Your salvation is about accepting life's impermanence. Your apprenticeship reveals how to live and how to die. You know where you belong, where your heart is fed, and you cocreate a life every time you ask for help.

4

The Apprentice

We are all apprentices in a craft where no one becomes a master.

–Ernest Hemingway

Now that there has been adequate meandering and loosening of your grip on some Bypass, you may be ready to let go of your striving to become a master of living. The gift of such surrender is your apprenticeship, which is the secret to living a mysterious, insecure, and unpredictable journey.

Who is an *apprentice*? An old definition of the word is "learner of a trade." We can think of a learner as someone desiring to acquire knowledge about a craft. The craft we are focusing on here is how to be an effective person on a mysterious and unpredictable journey, with some measure of wisdom being the outcome. The knowing that supports such a learner is embodied in the ancient Hebrew word *yada*. *Yada* means bringing the fullest employment of our senses, minds, and hearts to personal experience. It implies not holding back in one's engagement with both the external world and our inner landscape. All of which is essential for an intimate epistemology.

Apprenticeship embraces a relationship with a teacher. The principal teacher is fate, and the students are those devoted to charming the universe. Those devoted to an intimate relationship with fate can be very useful guides. I remain deeply grateful for the devotees who have touched my life with their cups of experience. They knew how to confirm what was sacred, to focus on what truly mattered, and to, in the words of Sufi mystic Hafiz, "charm the universe to reveal its wonders." One such mentor recently messaged me, telling me that he felt like a shell of a man who was dying. I responded by saying, "My teacher was no shell of a man. He taught me how to speak, how to listen, how to trust my intuition, to live with more heart and welcome views different from my own." That teacher would always introduce one of his beliefs by saying, "My hunch is…" In his presence I was introduced to something every apprentice must become familiar with to confirm what truly matters: good knowing.

From Self-Loathing to Self-Compassion

Nothing plagues efforts toward charming the universe more than self-loathing. Two primary psychological phenomena thwart our attempts to loosen the grip of self-repugnance. The first is denial; the second is trying to vault our psyches into the garden of self-compassion, catapulted by positive affirmations. Ultimately, we can neither make-believe self-loathing does not exist nor decide nice thoughts will emancipate us from self-abuse.

In leaving an undesirable place, we must first be willing to acknowledge being in that place. In relinquishing something, we must first be willing to claim it before we can release it. Seeds of self-love are planted in the compost of acknowledging and claiming self-loathing.

Indicators of Self-Loathing

Unlimited Ambition – I sometimes refer to this indicator as the Sisyphus Syndrome, in reference to the Greek mythological figure condemned to roll a rock up a hill in Hades, only to watch it roll back down, for all eternity. This is not simply about having a goal to achieve. It is about expending inordinate amounts of time and energy to the point where other parts of our lives are seriously compromised. Each achievement offers temporary respite from a self-loathing that nips at the coattails of our successes, driving us feverishly toward the next goal.

Unlimited Giving – This selfless activity aims at procuring the favor of others as a boost out of self-loathing. It makes us dependent on others noticing our boundless altruism; and if they don't, they run the risk of being objects of our resentment. As a result of this exhausting process, we at least unconsciously expect to be compensated for our limitless capacity to make offerings. When that fails to happen, more resentment follows.

Self-Righteousness – This is a likely compensation for living in disdain of the self. Temporary relief comes as we elevate our character above the crowd.

Diminished Accountability – Due to the shame that often accompanies our mistakes, holding ourselves accountable can be severely challenging. Justification and explanation take the place of genuine responsibility.

Attachment to Perfectionism – Striving to have our work and decisions reflect some idealized state is another way to compensate for self-hatred. My imperfection is my greatest resource. May I return to it again and again, finding myself there. The path of imperfection is the cradle of my humanity, while perfectionism remains a violation of my humanity.

Inner Voices of Self-Ridicule – Ongoing self-admonishment is a poor strategy to keep us from making the same mistake.

Little or No Investment in Self-forgiveness – Self-forgiveness is not a viable approach when making mistakes or violating our own values.

Feeling Numb – Suppressing feelings of shame and inadequacy becomes preferable to the ache of emotional oppression, even as the rest of our emotional life freezes over. In such paralysis, we tend to fall back on numbing aids such as alcohol, prescription drugs, street drugs, gambling, sugar, and workaholism.

Purposes of Self-Loathing

Before a meaningful examination of your psychology can take place, your first action should be to put an end to self-harm. Whenever a social worker visits the home of a suspected child abuser, removing the child from harm is priority number one. Likewise, you must commit to ending self-harm through thought or action, one day at a time.

Deepening self-compassion is impossible without also acknowledging self-loathing. A willingness to know your self-loathing makes replacing it that much easier. Once you are able to identify your experience of self-loathing, your power to release yourself from it is greatly enhanced by clarifying its purpose. Below are some common purposes of self-loathing.

Loyalty to the Past – Because there are no perfect parents or other authority figures, we all have experienced some degree of emotional abuse or neglect. Self-loathing keeps us connected to historical perpetrators. We treat ourselves the way they treated us. In doing so, we postpone a much-needed separation from where we come from.

Early Expression of Love – As children, we experience the pains and struggles of our families and are determined not to make matters worse by muddying the proverbial waters with our own needs. Toward suppressing said needs, we decide we are not worthy enough to know or express them.

Remaining Risk-Averse – The more we convince ourselves of being damaged goods, the more testimony we have against taking risks. Thus, we mark ourselves as doomed for failure.

Too Much or Not Enough – We are easily overwhelmed by how little we control people's acceptance of us. Rather than face the helplessness of being chosen by others, we maintain the illusion of an effective strategy. We decide that we are either too much for people or not enough, holding on to the belief that we can control being loved by making alterations accordingly. This strategy only keeps us feeling bad for ourselves.

Indulging in Being Someone Especially Damaged – The ego is alert to myriad ways of getting its needs met. It is willing to bask in the feeling of being either positively or negatively special. Being so undesirable should entitle one to some kindness and mercy, and maybe even to being the recipient of someone's heroic attempt at rescuing or saving us. In this wretched state, we might even expect others to love us more than we love ourselves.

Desiring to improve a relationship with ourselves is akin to bettering a relationship with someone else. It would be meaningless to just start spouting affirmations without addressing where and how the relationship has been compromised. Self-love bids us to review how our relationship with ourselves has broken down, especially with regard to self-loathing. We begin by becoming more mindful of self-loathing and its alleged purposes in our lives. Thus, healing becomes possible as we learn to welcome more compassion for the self. Such is the charm we bring to lived experience.

Being Present

We have been strongly encouraged by spiritual visionaries and social scientists to focus our attention on the here and now. As is the case with many words, the root meaning of *present* is more verb than noun. One of the oldest definitions of *present* is "being there," indicating a physical experience. Before exploring how "being there" supports good knowing for the apprentice, let us examine why it is so popular to avoid being present. Such a consideration can help minimize our self-perception as spiritual failures due to some predisposition toward not being present.

Hazards of Being Present

Being present means uniting with what greets us in the here and now. It would be naïve to imagine that being present in and of itself is an emotionally fulfilling experience. We learn early on that the present may have hidden threats and dangers yet to be realized. We are shamed, ridiculed, and excluded in the present. In fact, being present holds more potential for harm than being in the past or the future.

To be sure, we can experience some post-traumatic fallout from past injuries, even though the actual event is finished. Conversely, we worry and lament over a possible future incident, even though it has yet to and may never occur. Being present offers myriad possibilities, from warm and loving acknowledgment to disdain and harm. Being present is often greeted by an undoing of our best efforts to remain in control. Rather than face the possibility of a loss of power awaiting us in the present, we tend to prefer illusions of power found in the past and in the future.

Preoccupied with the Past

Living in the past offers an attractive escape from the unpredictability of being present. With our memories in full control, we are liberated from the burden of losing power in the present. We can step away from being responsible for how we feel about ourselves now. Reminiscing about past achievements and victories massages a tentative self-worth. Insufficient closure from meaningful relationships and past experiences allows us to avoid the challenge of creating new meanings now. And so, we bask in the feel-good experiences of the past rather than face the risks of creation.

What is the most fulfilling way to inhabit the past? A connection to what has ended frees us to be present. Such a connection is woven with gratitude, curiosity, and possibly sorrow for what was lost. Visiting the past is like visiting a friend. The encounter is time-sensitive. Gratitude helps us make peace with the life we were given, opening us to what lies ahead.

The word *curious* is rooted in the Latin *cura*, meaning "care." When we are curious about our past experience, we bring care and interest to it. We hold what happened in the past with regard as a carrier of information helping us bring stewardship to being present. When a loss is heavily accompanied by grief, we might consider scheduling ten minutes per day to honor what was lost while disallowing the loss from usurping our ability to be present.

Fascinated with the Future

Anchoring our attention in the future offers several desirable escape routes from being present. It is too easy to take up residency in visioning, thus feeding our preference for imaginary realities. The future holds a special seduction when we ascribe potency to strategies aimed at generating success and happiness. Infusing a supposed power into our plans eclipses the value of simple preparation. There is also the wonder and magic of worrying. We often complain about how much we agonize over the uncertainty of future events. Yet even our worry is imbued with illusions of control: "I'm not sitting here, being present and doing nothing; I'm worrying!" Letting go of the magic of our plans and our worry means learning to surrender to the mystery of the future, knowing only that whatever happens there will be an opportunity for us to be present with it.

Letting Go of the Past and the Future

Being present mostly means letting go of our attachment to the past and to the future, both of which steal much of our focus. The following are several ways of being present.

Being Bodily – Being present is mostly a corporeal experience. It means we are aware of having a body that occupies a particular space at a specific time. We can think of our bodies as being in a particular place either instinctively or mindfully.

The first happens when we are instinctively active or emotional. One way to instinctively be in a place is by expressing deep emotions - especially grief, fear, sadness, and anger. Athletes, actors, and performers are often instinctively present. Their actions are driven by instinct, not mindfulness. It is important to note, however, that their instinctive presence does reflect some intention of being unaware of the moment. Instinctive presence can be unconsciously destructive, causing harm and pain. When that happens, increased mindfulness is advised.

The second happens when we are mindful of our bodies. We may notice internal sensations like a clenched jaw, a pounding forehead, jittery limbs, a bloated abdominal area, or shallow breathing. We may also be mindful of the different repositories in our bodies of emotional energy. Such possibilities include fear in the stomach, anger in the jaw, and sadness in the chest. Mindfulness of body also includes an awareness of our senses: vision, hearing, taste, touch, and smell.

Aside from being mindful of our bodies, we can be mindful of the stories we tell ourselves. Being mindful of the story in which we are currently living enables us to understand how we perceive our experience. Our stories can have an infinite number of themes. We may be comparing and contrasting ourselves to others, lamenting over some prior defeat, planning for a future endeavor, or wondering what to do about feeling shunned by a friend.

"Stopping the internal dialogue is the singularly most important act an apprentice must accomplish in order to unlock his or her full potential as a magical being" (Theun Mares). Internal dialogues are composed of old beliefs and old emotions. Pausing to stop the internal dialogue or story with which we are presently preoccupied enables us to be considerably more receptive to what is happening in the moment. Perhaps our receptivity to be informed in a new way is what Mares means by becoming a "magical being."

Pace – Maintaining stillness or moving slowly keeps us in place. Speed ushers us into the next moment. Moving fast, even talking fast, is a way to be constantly in the future. Fast talk easily leads to dissociation. Swift movement, typically praised as productive, likewise obstructs our efforts at being present. Slowness allows for our energy fields to align with our centers of gravity, approximately two inches below the navel. Thus centered, we can bring more mindfulness to our emotions and to how we are being impacted by our experience. We have more opportunity to be aware of how our judgments and conclusions are constructed.

We are able to use language rather than act impetuously. We lower the likelihood of harming others or ourselves in regretful ways. We must then employ a series of justifications and rationalizations to redeem our behavior. Moving slowly takes courage. Loss, confusion, defeat, and fear are all waiting there in the moment. How seductive is the illusion that we can outrun what we don't want to face or feel! A slow pace allows for more focus and attention.

Attention – An old definition of the word *attention* is "active direction of the mind toward some object or topic." As mentioned above, our attention can be focused on the inner world or the outer world. Attention directed toward the inner world can reveal the feelings we experience, our intentions, and the stories we live in. Interior attention yields mindful living. When we offer attention to the external world, we are experiencing something happening in the immediate environment with minimum distraction. When such attention has quality, we can say that some measure of attunement is taking place. We are adjusting the directions of our minds to take in the feelings, beliefs, or values we are witnessing. When attunement is sharpened, our listening is minimally burdened by our biases.

The Preferred Present

Being present means our bodies are in a particular place, slowly moving and attending to internal or external experiences. According to existential philosopher William Barrett: "It is the familiar that usually eludes us in life.

What is before our nose is what we see last." Having looked at the hazards of being present, let us now explore the benefits.

We are more receptive to being informed. Receiving more information or knowledge is a great benefit of being present. This means we hold faith in the here and now as an effective conduit for deepening our understanding of life and ourselves. We are more receptive to "what is before our nose." But when the future is glamorized, it can be very challenging to believe that the present would have something valuable to offer.

We have a greater capacity to bring discernment to our decisions. Stillness allows us to be touched and moved by our experience while having the time to explore our reactions. We limit acting prematurely and give ourselves more time. Pausing enhances discernment by allowing our perceptions greater acuity, our decisions more consideration, and our ability to track more urgency.

We can exercise some measure of control over our lives. Having some degree of control over our choices and decisions is possible only when we feel ourselves present in some particular place. We are likely to be less reactionary and more tolerant of ambiguity.

We are more available to love and be loved. Love can only reach us, and we can only offer love in kind, when being present. How is it that being loved becomes such a motivation for not being present? This is a topic for further examination.

We are more prepared to support our safety when necessary. Because safety is a prerequisite for curiosity and exploration, the ego's natural tendency is to seek safety in either the past or the future. Unfortunately, neither is an authentic resource for safety when needed. One of the first lessons in any fundamental martial arts class, for instance, is how to remain grounded and stay balanced, since falling is to be avoided at all costs when sparring. Acquiring balance and being grounded, as well as being able to flee or fight, can only happen when we are present.

Being present is not something we ultimately figure out. We become familiar with it because of our commitment to remain its apprentice. In our apprenticeship, we will experience a lack of presence again and again. This is not an unfortunate failure. It is the way of real development taking place in the context of polarity. We learn about being present by being able to recognize when we are not present.

This process is no different than the development that takes place in all polarities. We come to know freedom because of our experience of bondage, fulfillment because of knowing emptiness, being welcomed because we know what it means to be forgotten, and compassion because of issuing or receiving disdain. The only thing that matters is our compassionate commitment to the apprenticeship, not a striving toward some idyllic state of always being present. Of course, apprenticing to the unknown calls for a variety of other apprenticeships.

Apprenticing with Integrity

Contrary to popular opinion, the arduous work of living with integrity has little or nothing to do with being moral. It is not about right and wrong; it is about who you are. It is about growing up. It is about leaving home enough times to know what your personal values are, rather than to believe in something because you were told to. It is about risking knowing and living your passions, uncertain whether others will find your choices to be honorable. Above all, it means learning to bear the tension that will inevitably befall you when your values and heart's desire are polarized or when you are forced to choose between two conflicting values.

An old definition of the word *integrity* is "whole." Integrity reflects living congruently and exercising an ongoing commitment to individuate, reclaiming our uniqueness apart from social influences. You are living in integrity when your actions reflect your values and/or your heart's desire. Integrity is more of a "how" than a "what." The how of integrity is the resiliency to endure tension when your longing and your desire do not match up or when you are facing a value conflict. It is also the struggle to forgive yourself when you betray a personal longing or value.

Integrity comes easily when there is no split between your actions and values. The true ordeal of integrity comes when your heart's desire calls you to act in a way that is incompatible with some cherished value. The true substance of integrity may not be whether you choose in favor of a cherished value or honor your heart's longing, but rather to be mature enough to live creatively with such tension when they are polarized. In order to lean into the wholeness indicative of integrity, you must be acquainted with your values and passions. Integrity cannot happen when you do not know your values or what you want.

The Birthplace

Desire is the birthplace of your values. The more desire comes from the beat of your own heart, the more you can trust it as a true passion. The combination of living from your desire and attempting to support what you want determines what really matters: your values. You have more information about how you want to live, how you want to treat others and be treated by them. When values are taken seriously and mature, more is revealed about freedom, compassion, family life, love, work ethic, and the meaning of your life. But until you become acquainted with personal longings, your values cannot be born.

Acquainted with Personal Longings

Being aware of desire and being committed to living your desire is the first step toward a life of integrity. "It doesn't interest me what you do for a living. I want to know what you ache for, and if you dare to dream of meeting your heart's longing" (Oriah Mountain Dreamer). It may be that one of the most satisfying reviews of your life would be to say, "I lived my love." Finding clarity with regard to longing will eventually yield deeper awareness of your values. We will now explore what it might mean to act with integrity if your behavior is congruent with what you want, forgoing awareness of some value consideration.

What you love or desire might not easily come to you, especially when you survived childhood by keeping your longings anonymous. You figured out on some deep level that expressing desire runs the risk of being disruptive. Perhaps disruption compelled your parents to issue shame or ridicule and define you as insensitive, selfish, or burdensome. It did not take long to realize the tension that existed when you were aware of your desire and feared giving it a voice. The only way you knew how to ensure your desires were never broadcast was to gradually make them unknown even to yourself.

This pattern of "I have no idea of what I love or want" may be reinforced by friends, partners, and relatives. Such unawareness hands control of your life over to others. When your desire is anonymous, someone else's desire defines you in its place. Significant others will have one of two reactions. They will either delight in the control your confusion gives them or feel quite neglected. The latter state happens because they are not being met by your desire, nor do they feel chosen as the one for whom your desire seeks satisfaction.

Allowing yourself to know your heart's desire is a gradual process. Not knowing your desire was originally a survival mechanism aimed at preventing anyone from viewing you as disruptive and then abandoning you in some way. Keep it simple. Pause during the day; ask what you may want in that moment. Acceptable responses include the following: grab a coffee, sit, call a friend, eat, take a walk, or even admit to not knowing what you want. The key is to call desire to you, even if you cannot identify it. When you do so, you are rebuilding your relationship with desire.

Desires and No Values

For reasons of immaturity or arrested development, you can know what you want but still be unable to identify your values. I would not describe my 11-year-old grandson as living with or without integrity. He neither has enough life experience nor the internal resources to construct his own values. For now, he sees his behavior as resulting in either a favorable or unfavorable response from authority figures and peers. I encourage my grandson to know and live his desires as much as possible, because they will bring life to his values. I also support his learning how to cope with the inevitable frustration and disappointment of unrealized desire.

It is the passionately personal nature of his desires that will eventually make his values his own. Passionate desire is the birthplace of values. It is through strong desire that we begin prioritizing some action. My grandson's deep emotional and instinctual responses to life experiences will yield values that will be the hallmark of his character. Genuine values cannot be borrowed. They must come from the heart, in all its fullness and brokenness.

From Desires to Values

The bridge from desire to values is our willingness to make a cherished behavior not simply good for us but a devoted consideration of others. I call this attitude of consideration ethical engagement. When this attitude is active, we wonder who will benefit from the action we value and who might be hurt. Am I willing to make some appropriate sacrifice to support this valued action? Would I prescribe this action to others under similar circumstances?

Values germinate in desires. How values actually mature remains a mystery. Desires reflect personal tastes and preferences. We don't typically make a big deal over someone's desires if they do not impact another in a way that evokes consideration of values. What we eat, our hobbies, where we vacation, the clothes we wear, or the plays and films we enjoy are all examples of desires with likely no consideration for the role of values.

Early modeling and socialization provide opportunities to witness the kinds of values we may want to adapt. One of the key elements in the growth of a value is the desire to be your own person while seeking to belong to others. It is not clear what maturing values would look like if you lived alone on a desert island. It appears that the need to support your uniqueness in relation to others morphs your desires into values. The more seriously we take our connections to ourselves and others, the more likely our lives will be guided by what we want not only for ourselves but also for subsequent generations. Our values become the ingredients that make up our moral positions.

In both Kohlberg's and Gilligan's models of moral development, the highest level of maturation is characterized by an investment in universalizing values. Universalizing a value means going beyond yourself to an investment in the welfare of others. To universalize a value means it is viewed as beneficial for all (e.g., the preservation of life). Gilligan suggests that empathy plays a major role in deciding how a particular value will be employed. Just because you empathically universalize a specific value does not mean it will never conflict with another of your values. Such a conflict may exist between your value of preserving life and the value you place, for example, on assisted suicide. Another example is the value you place on telling the truth versus making an exception when telling the truth would create undue harm to yourself and others.

"The shortest and surest way to live with honor in the world is to be in reality what we would appear to be; ...all human virtues increase and strengthen themselves by the practice and experience of them" (Socrates). Knowing your values allows you to be at home with yourself. You likely will, if not already, have a life direction you can trust, one that allows for the development of rapport with others by giving them a clear picture of who you are. Clarity promotes trust. Even if others disapprove of what you do, they can trust that you will be who you say you are. Those who know you can take care of themselves accordingly. Internally guided by hard decisions and choices, your life's purposes become more illuminated.

The What of Integrity

The what of integrity happens when your behavior directly reflects your values and/or your heart's desire. Actions that reflect your values and not your wants are commonly viewed as honorable expressions of integrity. This esteemed position manifests for two reasons: 1) you are acting in some self-sacrificial way when you prioritize your values over your longing, and 2) you are acting from your values in a way that considers others' needs.

When you are aware of your values and your heart's desire, it is no simple deed to act in honor of your longing and not your values. Throughout history, sacrificing some value to honor the heart's longing for companionship has been a major theme in countless love stories. Such a choice is often filled with internal turmoil and external consequences.

As we have seen, the prerequisite for any act of integrity is clarity with regard to personal values and desires. Acting with integrity is easiest, of course, when both values and desires are compatible. The challenge of integrity occurs when values and desires are polarized. An important way of understanding integrity is to say that betrayal of values or heart's desire must be a possibility. When polarization is present and betrayal is not possible because your values are borrowed and/or your desire is not clear, then you are not capable of acting with integrity.

The How of Integrity

The how of integrity is the ability to hold deep knowledge of what it means to betray your values or your heart's longing. Once you are acquainted with your values and desire, a loyal bond ensues. Then life happens. You discover that some situation will only allow you to live your devotion to your values or your desire. Coming to know how loyalty and betrayal live in your inner landscape brings you to the depths of soul and the essence of integrity. I call such a knowing a sacred crisis of integrity.

Sacred Crisis of Integrity

Sometimes, living in integrity is easy, as when a woman holding the value position that abortion is unacceptable wants another child. In having the child, she is conveniently in integrity. Such acts of integrity are the most effortless to perform, since there is no tension with which to cope. There is conflict neither between her desire and her values nor between two conflicting values.

How wonderful it would be to step into integrity where your values, your heart's desire, and your action reflected a sublime wholeness. Eleanor, a 58-year-old client of mine, tells the story of bringing more heart to her values.

"I was 23 at the time and my sister, who was mentally ill, was pregnant. I have always believed that families must tend to their members. When the baby was born, I was filled with love for this little guy who belonged in our family. In some way, he belonged to me as much as he did to my sister. As I held an image of handing him over to foster care versus taking him home with us, my choice become more and more obvious. It was such a large commitment to consider. It felt so right and yet I could not imagine what I was really getting myself into. After some reflection and discussions with my husband, we adopted my nephew. He is now twenty-eight years old and a successful artist." Eleanor's heart infused her values with a decision that would expand over more than two decades.

The way of integrity is laced with betrayal. If you know your values and you know your heart's desire but they do not match up, you are being asked to betray one or the other. This crisis dwells at the very core of the human condition. As noted, the betrayal of desire in honor of some value is easily perceived as nobler than the opposite. Since your values typically have some direct effect on how you treat others, they receive more acclaim. When you choose your heart's desire, you are prioritizing yourself. The key is not to automatically decide there is something wrong with making your desire a prime concern. As Michael Meade's son once told him, "The one who comes to us intending to disturb as little as possible by not expressing desire neither deserves our admiration nor our respect." These words capture what it means to forsake your passions. They suggest that you have decided not to be fully alive, which is an insult to the self and to those who would be receptive to being impacted by your heart's desire.

A Collision of Values

Sometimes, a crisis of integrity reflects two opposing values. Maria, a 42-year-old graduate student, tells the story of her collision of values.

"I was twenty-five at the time, my daughter was five, and my son was three. My husband was actively addicted to street drugs and alcohol. I became pregnant and very much wanted to bring this baby into the world. But I didn't want to bring the child into the intense dysfunction of our family. I anguished over the decision of an abortion. I so wanted this child to be with me and her siblings, even as I realized our family wasn't a place to welcome a new child. I valued both her birth and her entering a healthy family. During the abortion I continued to weep. The attending nurse knew that this wasn't my deepest value. Her gaze was soft with empathy. I couldn't have both. Seventeen years later, I continue to grieve the loss of her."

I recall making the decision to step away from my first marriage. It entailed betraying the values of supporting a family and parenting in the context of an intact marriage. I deeply feared that I had not done enough to support the value I placed on the sustainability of a marriage. I especially felt regret and guilt over my son's intense allegiance to family life. Before his wedding, I reluctantly agreed to attend a traditional stag party that was being planned for him, but only if he would attend the one I was putting together. He agreed.

Eight of my male friends and I gathered on a friend's farm, where a permanent sweat lodge had been constructed. We began the evening in the sweat lodge, where men tolerated increased heat from water being poured over hot rocks while offering warm blessings to my son's destiny as a spouse. Following that ceremony, we assembled in the farmhouse to enjoy a meal prepared by the men. After the meal, each told a story of the joys and trials that characterized his commitment to a significant other. As my son took in these personal narratives, I noticed his undistracted attention. I imagined his soul digesting every word.

When the men were finished, I turned to Jason and said, "I'm aware of how much family life means to you. I want to make an amends to you regarding my choice to fracture our family," wondering how my acknowledgement might impact him.

Jason took a larger-than-normal breath and replied, "I do take family life very seriously, and I do feel its loss. But you've offered me a map showing me what it means not to remain too long somewhere I don't belong."

The male assembly quietly held the truth of my son's declaration, as if the pause would enable each of us to find an inner place where his words might reside for a while. In the wake of that evening, I became more sensitive to the sacredness of experiencing a crisis of integrity. Such a watershed moment reflects the deepening of maturity. It can only happen when you have some real understanding of, and devotion to, your values and of what your heart's desire is asking. Without these realizations and devotion, there cannot be a crisis of integrity and no real capacity to act in integrity or understand it.

The predicament created by a crisis of integrity is also a crossroads where you are being asked to choose in a more penetrating way. Either some value of yours or your heart's desire will be betrayed. If you do not know what it means to betray your yearnings in favor of some value, then you likely are trapped in some measure of childish narcissism. If you do not know what it means to betray some value in favor of your heart's desire, then you are likely trapped in your attempts to please others, determined never to disrupt.

A crisis of integrity can also occur when two values are in conflict and you are clear about the nature of these values. James, a 45-year-old accountant, spoke to me about such a predicament. His wife was friendly with the woman his best friend Bruce was dating. His wife asked him to keep confidential the information she was sharing with him, but some of that information had to do with Bruce being misled by the woman he was dating. James felt deeply torn by the value he placed on maintaining confidentiality regarding what his wife had revealed and the value of offering his friend the best form of support he could.

"I didn't know what to do. I didn't want to violate my commitment to my wife, and I didn't want to withhold information from Bruce that might help him strengthen how he took care of himself in his relationship. I found myself encouraging him to ask his girlfriend lots of questions. Knowing that he was being strung along, I asked him to make sure it was the right relationship for him. I just hated my predicament," explained James as he shook his head from side to side, his voice trailing off.

Mutually Enhancing

There is a way in which your values and heart's longing deeply serve one another, regardless of whether they are compatible or polarized. Your passion makes your values your own. Even if your values reflect what is commonly acceptable, the way your heart carries them will be particular to you. Enthusiasm and heartfelt devotion will be emblematic of your character. Your passion may cause a value to be transformed from an abstract precept to a life's cause or act of service. Toxic legacies are often interrupted because your heart hungers to act in support of the next generation.

Values make an equally significant contribution to that for which you yearn. Desire falls prey to what is immediate and satisfying. Values are the psychological scaffolding allowing you to have a larger vision. They prompt you to consider others and what will be sustainable. Values bring more meaning to your desire. Acting against your values can jolt you into feeling guilt, shame, and remorse. These unfavorable reactions seem to operate as a guiding system, helping you return to what is truly important.

Values are the banks along the river of desire insofar as they guide its flow. If your values solidify with rigidity, dogmatism, and self-righteousness, they may dam the stream of your desire. Values no longer emanate from the heart; now they are fear-driven. When fear replaces your heart's desire, values begin to barricade the flow of compassion, grace, and mercy. Being right replaces being forgiving, understanding, and curious about how to hold a larger vision.

Integrity Wonderings

Do you know your own values, or have you borrowed them to secure the approval of others? Can you risk being disruptive because the vigor of your passion can no longer be contained within the confines of your body? Can you withhold expressing disdain for the one who champions her or his desire? Can you remain devoted to both desire and values, knowing you will be asked to betray one in support of the other? Can you postpone personal gratification in favor of an empathic consideration for the welfare of others? Can you find some soft holding of self-forgiveness when you either banish your values or exile your heart's desire?

The Seven Sustainables

More than ever, we must be clear about what it means to create a sustainable and intimate relationship with life. Education, wealth, and fame are regularly endorsed as ways to approach life, when in reality we should be moving beyond the bankruptcy of an ego-orientated life to a point where we are doing life. This new approach to life entails being honest about the nature of fate and what it might take to create a meaningful and sustainable relationship with it. It may be challenging to see fate honestly as being about change and uncertainty. Accepting that, we can then explore what it takes to have a relationship with such a journey. There are at least seven conditions that help us sustain a relationship to the sacred as well as to mystery and change: authenticity, compassion, gratitude, integrity, simplicity, courage, and generosity.

Authenticity

A commitment to authenticity entails living a self-examining life and speaking the truth about who we are whenever possible, except when it creates undue harm to ourselves or to others. Some helpful discerning questions regarding whether we should have an authentic voice include: Is there a hidden agenda attached to what I'm going to say? Does my statement reflect my perceptions and feelings? Is what I'm going to say absent of blame and ridicule? Am I able to bring a measure of compassion to the content and tone of my message?

Becoming effective at speaking authentically means being willing to do it imperfectly. We will fall short in either the amount of truth spoken or the amount of compassion accompanying what is said. Although we are constantly changing, authenticity allows us to have an honest relationship with ourselves. It may simply mean being genuine about what we feel, desire, or believe in any given moment. Although relationships are in constant flux, authenticity offers the opportunity to be trusted, loved, and chosen by others.

Compassion

Compassion is the ability to hold sympathy for the suffering of others, for suffering we might inflict on others, and for our own suffering. As my old friend Henri Nouwen once said, "There's no truth without compassion." There are two ways we can see the importance of Nouwen's statement. The first is that we stop seeking the truth about who we are if we do not regard what we discover with compassion. It is simply too painful to constantly shame and ridicule what introspection reveals about ourselves. Without compassion we become strangers to ourselves, making our experience of change and uncertainty almost unbearable. We set ourselves up for anxiety and depression or self-medication.

The second implication of Nouwen's statement is that others will gradually avoid us if we do not soften our truths with compassion. Softening happens when the tone and content carry an implicit consideration of a differing view. Softening also occurs when our messages lack any criticism of the listener's character. Compassion allows us to get close to ourselves and allows others to get close to us. We do not need to endure the arduous challenge of facing life's changes and mysteries alone.

Gratitude

The word *gratitude* comes from the Middle French, meaning "good will." It is therefore worth asking: What happens to us when we do not notice what in life deserves good will? As in any relationship, when we do not notice what deserves good will, we fall prey to indifference, anger, and feeling like a victim. From a place of indifference we no longer have an active relationship with life. We go through the daily motions, deeply alienated from the pulse of life. From a place of anger, we protest and complain about life. A victim's position leaves us oppressed and injured by life. There is nothing in these three energies that helps us mobilize in the face of change and uncertainty.

When we are grateful for our experiences, we define ourselves as beneficiaries of life. By definition, gratitude defines us as active recipients of life's offerings. Our relationship to change and uncertainty softens as we expect to receive support, love, beauty, and learning from our lived experience. In gratitude, we hold the faith that life will make some offering to us worthy of our good will.

Integrity

Much has already been said about integrity. We revisit it here because it allows for an intimate connection with ourselves and with fate. Integrity means we are making choices congruent with what and whom we love and/or value. The what and the whom are fate's offerings and opportunities to live intimately. We inevitably fall out of integrity when we act in a way that is not compatible with what we love or value. Being in or out of integrity is a significant measure of maturation. It suggests we have diminished a childhood attachment to pleasing, that we are now acting or not acting in accordance with what we truly believe.

A commitment to live as much as possible in integrity offers us a GPS while traveling a changing and uncertain journey. Rather than attempt to pursue the unattainable by finding ultimate truth or accessing some paramount level of consciousness, we strive to remain aware of what we love and value by doing our best to reflect our principles in our actions. We all wander from the path we call ourselves. The key is being able to summon enough awareness to know we have separated from ourselves. Also of import is being able to identify the resources we need to move back to acting in accord with our values.

We have so little control over people, places, and things. A devotion to integrity keeps us focused on where we do have power. We become more effective at knowing what truly matters to us and whether we are making choices that reflect our deep concerns. It is up to us to determine whether these deep concerns are truly ours or borrowed.

Simplicity

Simplicity is critical to sustaining a relationship with change and mystery. An old definition of the word *simplicity* is "singleness of nature." It does not denote naïveté or simple-mindedness but rather single-attentiveness. Simplicity makes multitasking quite dubious. If the Industrial Revolution invited us to become intimate with machines, current technological advances only intensify that invitation. The more intimate we become with our machines, the more we see an advantage to becoming like them. We begin to jeopardize the essence of our humanity. Instincts, emotion, imagination, intuition, living in the present, and even wisdom become extraneous and insignificant. These reflections of the human condition are simply incompatible with our adoration of the mechanistic.

A devotion to simplicity or being singularly attentive offers a great deal as we cope with life's impermanence. There are several significant benefits to a life of simplicity. A kinship with simplicity reveals the generosity of the moment. Beauty, acts of kindness, joy, and simple comforts become more vivid as our attachment to grandeur diminishes.

It becomes easier to live in the moment where we are singularly attentive. Those we encounter experience our undivided attention, building trust and rapport. We come to accept what lies beyond our immediate attention rather than dwell on what is out of our control. Deepening a capacity for acceptance strengthens our ability to feel gratitude for what is rather than lamenting what is not.

Courage

A relationship with fate is like a relationship with a lover. It takes courage to endure the hard times. We can think of courage as the willingness to know and act in honor of what our hearts are called. There will be an ever-present fear, whether we are called to act or let go and surrender. Life simply will not offer us untarnished clarity and permanence.

We are called to have an ongoing relationship with risk. We are asked to take action, uncertain about the outcome. Taking a risk often takes us somewhere we have not been before. We are allowing life to touch, deepen, and broaden us. We become risk-friendlier as we understand that our real fear is not the risk we are entertaining. Rather, it is how we might treat ourselves if the outcome of a risk is unfavorable. When events do not go according to plan, many of us beat ourselves up with ridicule and self-diminishing thoughts. The more willing we are to forgive ourselves in light of some adverse outcome to a risk we take, the friendlier we grow toward risk and life in general.

Generosity

Generosity connects us to the vital life force of giving. We remain in an intimate relationship with fate when we choose to see needs around us and make some offering. Our life's purpose depends on some awareness of what we are supposed to give. A devotion to making an offering unfolds glimpses of our purpose, lifting us out of either a compulsion to consume or an insatiable emptiness.

We typically think of being generous with our money or helping out at the church bazaar. We can take generosity to a new dimension by asking: How generous am I with my attention? How generous am I with my empathy? How generous am I with offerings of acknowledgement and encouragement? How generous am I with my compassion? How generous am I when it comes to offering a welcome?

Generosity can be something we settle into consistently amid change as we remain devoted to making offerings that serve others. When change challenges the credibility of the human condition, generosity can restore faith in humanity. Much may be uncertain, but generosity continues to clarify what is truly important.

We live in a time that calls for radical honesty about the nature of life and what it means to commit to a sustained relationship with our lived experience. My hope is that The Seven Sustainables allow you to live more deeply while preparing the way for future generations. The Seven Sustainables can offer direction concerning what it means to access genuine personal power.

A Blessing for the Apprentice

Since your early days, you were destined to be an apprentice to the unknown. You learned to eat with a spoon, brush your teeth. Place was a yearning and a tenacity to possess the known. That's the way of it. You would first know the power of the known before you could find the courage to apprentice the unknown.

Your appetite for knowing fell upon people, places, and things with occasional interest in knowing yourself. You simply wanted to be a knower, which blessed your curiosity, wonder, and longing. Life would be right then, and there was certainly a measure of truth in that thinking. Besides, fate wants you to be interested in what it brings to you. However, your struggle twisted and turned as you fell into unknowing again and again.

You kept hearing the praises of knowing. It was very hard to see yourself as someone who didn't know. Not knowing would invite you to berate yourself over and over again. You would take confusion, ignorance, and bewilderment and hide them on some back shelf of the mind. However, you would be asked to endure one tenure of novicehood after another.

Then, a dawn light began to gradually push away the dark. Dawn light wants to brighten without being too disruptive. It invites vision without demanding it. Morning shadows are muted and gradually the contours of self-indictments begin to fade. Now, arriving at conclusions begins to lose its luster. The heart of the apprentice beats with a harmonious rhythm.

This new rhythm breathes curiosity. Not knowing loses its weight, allowing intrigue to create a buoyancy that carries you more gently. You know now that there was never a temple of wisdom waiting for you. You're ready to remain an apprentice to the unknown, as you do the only thing that can be done: allow yourself to walk the wisdom path, paved with mystery.

Preoccupation with its destination is of no service. There is no place to arrive. There is no temple of wisdom preparing to greet you. Living the wisdom path as an apprentice is the destination.

5

Power

*Be not the slave of your own past—plunge into the sublime seas,
dive deep, and swim far, so you shall come back with new
self-respect, with new power, and with an advanced experience
that shall explain and overlook the old.*

–Ralph Waldo Emerson

Awful! Awful! Awful! Such is our exclamatory reaction to abusive power, especially as depicted in popular media. Power gets a bad rap. It is all too easy to succumb to its seduction, remaining unconscious about the price paid for despicable abuses. A compensatory reaction is to disavow any interest in having power whatsoever. In doing so, however, we limit power to a web of abusers, victims, or denial.

We spend much of our lives caught up in issues involving power without naming what is going on or how to acquire more knowledge about it. It behooves the apprentice to remain vigilant about the status of power in her or his life. When such attention is lacking, we struggle to allow fate to remain informative, regularly getting distracted from the path of genuine personal power.

Remaining devoted to learning about power keeps our apprenticeship to the unknown alive. Fate continues to teach us when we identify what is in our control and take the risk to initiate action. Rather than allow fear to keep us enslaved to the past, we "plunge into the sublime seas, dive deep, and swim far." Such a dive enhances and broadens our experience of fate. We come to know defeat, close calls, and triumph. We have regular exposure to the known and unknown alike. And perhaps, one day, we make peace with the hidden ignorance accompanying all that is known.

As we shall see, a tedious scrambling for protection ensues when too much power is given away, accompanied by a crippling dependence on dominating others to feel good about ourselves when too much power is grabbed. We will also explore the differences between Socio-Economic/Political Power versus Personal Power.

We begin with an ancient definition of the word *power*: "ability to do." It is sometimes difficult to distinguish what we want to be able to do from what we are actually able to do. Our explorations inevitably find us relinquishing too much power or grabbing more than our just due.

From the time we emerge from the womb, we are instinctively attempting to reproduce the kind of bond we experienced in utero. We are constantly exploring what we are able to do in relation to caregivers in terms of consumption, elimination, and rest. At around 18 months of age, we become quite interested in what we might be able to do on our own. Our capacity to impact our external environment becomes intriguing. British pediatrician and psychoanalyst Donald Winnicott describes a normal child's intrigue with power: "The normal child, if he has confidence in mother and father, pulls out all the stops. In the course of time, he tries out his power to disrupt, to destroy, to frighten, to wear down, to waste, to wangle, and to appropriate."

Our exploratory efforts typically include falls and bruises, as well as disruptions of our parents' nervous systems. We become enthralled not only by the fact that events are happening to us, but also by our possession of a will that can make things happen. In the estimation of Erich Fromm: "To create life is to transcend one's status as a creature that is thrown into life as dice are thrown out of a cup." Our "ability to do" moves us away from objecthood to personhood.

Of course, nothing gets the ego's attention more than noticing that we are a cause and not just an effect. We are able to manipulate objects, making them roll, smash, topple, and remain stationary. Early on in our development, we are fascinated with, and glean satisfaction from, exercising power, delighted by our newly found efficacy. Yet none of it is so rewarding as learning how to engender love.

Deciding how to get love from others is a curious endeavor. It may be through our innate propensities, combined with sensitive reads of family dynamics, that we commit to such decisions. In any case, our quest for love is ultimately about how much in the way of will guides our choices. Because a perfect expression of will eludes us, we explore different ways of being able to get the love we want.

Here are some examples of what we are able to do when it comes to love. A child witnesses a parent feeling overwhelmed by caring for six children. The child very likely begins to underestimate what she or he is able to do. The child does not want to add to the fray. Willfulness gets constricted in an attempt to ease the parent's burden. Receiving love is about suppressing needs and desires in favor of adaptation and compliance. Such a child steps into adulthood with too little will, confused about her or his "ability to do."

Another child may grow up in a single-parent home with one younger sibling. The child figures out that the parent could benefit from a surrogate partner and attempts to step into that role. Of course, this means the child will need to pretend she or he is able to meet the expectations of the adult role. The parent might even bless the child's attempts at adulthood. Receiving such favor encourages the child to continue masquerading as an adult. By adulthood, such a child is habituated to compensating for feeling confused and limited by inflating the ego. Limits are denied and overlooked; one's abilities are hyperbolized. This kind of aggrandizement, initially driven by a desire to love and be loved, is often accompanied through an exaggerated sense of competency.

By age 13, I became my mother's surrogate father in response to my perception of her arrested development. On some preconscious level, I understood life as much as I needed to. I decided to make others happy; I could easily take care of myself and make important decisions without undue worry. In order to maintain these illusions, I compensated by beefing up my pride, concealing vulnerability, and coping through abuse of alcohol, all the while believing this puffed-up version of myself was who I really was. It would take some serious work on my part to see that my illusions and compensations were born out of love for my mother.

Such examples of early power explorations can be useful metaphors for the apprentice. They represent the countless factors influencing our attempts to clarify how we want to exercise our "ability to do" or understand our relationship to power. Power is directly related to loving and feeling loved. Our early strategies aimed at making love happen accompany us into adulthood. The hope is that we will become increasingly conscious of our relationship to power as we notice how we carry it.

Grabbing Too Much or Giving Too Much Away

Once we name power as an "ability to do," we can begin to define some basic needs and desires. Primary among them are safety, shelter and food, education, strengthening of individuality, and meaningful connections to others. All of these serve a grander desire for a purposeful life. We don't learn about power because we carry it in some perfect way. We learn about power because we either grab too much of it or give too much away. It is worth noting that the most valuable lessons about power take place in a relational context. In order to remain open and receptive to fate's teachings, the apprentice must be clear about her or his relationships with power.

Giving Too Much Away

Giving away too much power means we underestimate our "ability to do." When giving too much away, we prove our overvaluation of being accommodating, understanding, deferential, compliant, adaptive, and nondisruptive. The giveaways are the things we tell ourselves to justify this type of action: "I won't bring too much attention to myself." "I'll support you." "I'll remain receptive to your wishes." The key to understanding our tendency to give too much power away is to know it as an attempt to garnish power. Other giveaways include nonverbal requests that render us immune from unfavorable feedback in favor of safety, respect, acceptance, love, and cooperation. Of course, giving too much power away means others have an inordinate amount of influence and control over our lives, which they enjoy or exploit.

An immense opportunity for learning about power presents itself when we are not getting desired outcomes by being obsequious. That is, instead of feeling supported, safe, and accepted, we feel exploited, used, and violated. The latter feelings alert us to the possibility of learning about power. When grabbing too much power, we tend to rely on the complaints of others so that a possible power agenda gets our attention.

When lessons of power are at hand, fate has likely rendered us victims of circumstances out of our control. But if we allow ourselves to get caught in the perpetrator-victim paradigm, we will never gain clarity with regard to how much power we have given away.

It is easy to ridicule ourselves for giving too much power away, as if mistreating ourselves enough means we will never repeat that mistake in the future. Learning flourishes when we resist shaming ourselves for allowing someone to take advantage of us. The key is to see there are only two ways to understand power, and that giving too much away is one of them. We must forgive ourselves by seeing the surrender of power as a natural and human way to address early survival needs.

Learning to Reclaim Power

The good news is that because we are the ones who gave power away, we possess the ability to reclaim it. Others cannot keep what belongs to us. There are several things to be aware of when learning how to reclaim power.

1) Bodily Cues - The first is identifying bodily cues with regard to how someone's choice is affecting us. We might sense abdominal tightness, shallow breathing, and a clenched jaw, to name a few. The more we allow these inner sensations to get our attention, the more they will inform our discernment as to what is going on.

Some years ago, I was addressing a large audience of folks who had grown up in alcoholic systems. I was talking about the importance of paying attention to bodily cues that can compel us to feel disturbed or troubled. The congregation quickly wanted to know how to represent their bodily nudges in a clear and cogent fashion. I suggested letting go of trying to express their experience so perfectly. I offered several possible responses: "I feel disturbed." "Something isn't quite right." Or even, "That feels like shit," at which they chuckled.

Sometime later in my lecture, I was having trouble with the sound system. Someone hired by the facility came in to help. His initial attempts to fix it yielded a loud screeching sound, to which the entire assembly yelled, "That feels like shit!" I embarrassingly smiled, attempting to reassure the gentleman that we were not members of some anti-establishment group and, shrugging my shoulders, indicated that the group had gotten a bit out of hand. As the technician exited, I pointed out that they sounded ready to begin trusting their sensory-motor responses to their boundaries being tampered with or violated.

2) Energetic Boundaries - The second way to address our bearing of power is to pay attention to how far we might be living outside our bodies. Acting at a distance from our cores ruptures our energetic fields, resulting in a loss of balance and lack of necessary boundaries.

Sophia, a 38-year-old second-grade teacher living with her partner and two children, was sitting with me for her second session. During her first session, she had already shared with me her desire to work on developmental trauma. As she spoke now, sitting some eight feet away, I could feel her energy field about an arm's length from me. Although we were in the early stages of developing a rapport, I decided to offer some feedback about her energy.

"Sophia, I'm experiencing your energy drifting somewhere about two feet from my body. Try closing your eyes and pulling your energy back into your body, imagining it resting about an inch below your navel."

She closed her eyes and opened them about a minute later. I had a strong sensation of her energy being retracted. I explained that she obviously understood my request and was able to reclaim her energetic field, and asked how she felt being more anchored in her body. She reported feeling fine and began to gently sob. She went on to explain that maybe her energy had been communicating to others that she was more available to them than she was to herself. Her downward gaze suggested to me a realization of what her extended energetic field had been conveying to those around her.

"I think I understand how I was sexually abused several times and emotionally taken advantage of many times. My energy has been communicating a kind of giveaway, like 'Here I am. What would you like?'"

It took Sophia several sessions before she was able to stop admonishing herself for giving so much power away. She came to understand there are only two ways to learn about power. Her early training set her up to learn about power by giving too much of it away. Her mother's strong narcissistic tendencies had taken up an especially great deal of psychic space. Sophia had learned to love by giving up her psychological space, which meant suppressing her own needs and desires. Her paradigm of love also included the suspension of verbal boundaries.

3) Verbal Boundaries - Our willingness to set up verbal boundaries is a significant way to hold and reclaim power. It requires us to say "No" and "Yes" authentically, reflecting what is desired or valued. Sophia was learning that she attributed a considerable amount of magic to her understanding of love. She decided that if she eliminated boundaries, then her presence would send the following messages: "I'm here only to support you." "I have no expectations or demands of you." "I won't obstruct you in any way." "Helping you get your needs met is my priority." Only after multiple instances of being used and abused did Sophia become willing call her paradigm of love into question. She was initially shocked that making such a large offering to others would not yield favorable results.

4) A New Way to Love - Switching from a boundary-less way of loving to loving with effective boundaries can be challenging. When the former way to love carries so much magic, we find it hard to believe others will feel loved or that we will get love when we exercise boundaries. We must be willing to be an apprentice to a more mature way of loving, a larger way of loving that welcomes discernment about where and where not to open our hearts. It also entails learning to limit betrayal of self and others, and to cooperate and collaborate. As part of this new curriculum of love, we must give and receive with reverence. Learning about love is a lifelong endeavor regardless of our early love lessons.

5) Trust is Earned - Trust is not given because someone looks attractive or acts polite. Trust is earned. People earn our trust in our belief that they will treat us kindly and tell us the truth. They do not need to do it perfectly to gain our trust, but they must do it with consistent kindness and honesty. The more discerning we are about where to place our trust in the name of someone who has earned it, the less likely we are to give power away so arbitrarily.

Learning to Stop Grabbing Too Much Power

Learning to inhibit our tendencies to grab too much power is considerably more difficult than stopping ourselves from giving too much away. The problem is that the ego relishes in believing it is governed by a manifest psychological destiny. And so, its borders continue to reach toward the distant horizon, reveling in new acquisitions. Unlike the internal cues of feeling violated, used, and abused, indicative of giving too much away, the internal cues of grabbing too much indicate that only something delightful is happening. Let us now pause and take serious inventory of our grabbing tendencies:

1) Feedback from others - Getting feedback from others is a critical intervention. Unfortunately, it is common for grabbers to surround themselves with either other grabbers or those who give too much power away. Both groups collude with those who grab too much power. Other grabbers applaud their comrade's ability to raid power, while those who give too much power away are perfect prey for grabbers. But if grabbers get enough unfavorable feedback from significant others, they may begin to examine their own relation to power. The feedback they receive will likely need to be accompanied by logical consequences, leading to some loss for the grabber. Remember there are those who very seldom grab too much power, others who do it part-time, and the extreme group who indulge in it at every opportunity.

2) Bottoming Out - Sometimes bottoming out is the only possible interruption of an obsession with grabbing too much power. Attempting to procure too much power may be a compensation for feelings of helplessness. Unless there are dire consequences to face, such as the loss of a job or marriage, it is unlikely that extreme grabbers will change their ways. Change depends on several factors: accepting significant consequences, having enough internal resilience to face the helplessness and vulnerability that replaces lavish inflationary attempts to garnish power, and viable external resources who can support the transition.

3) New Paradigm of Self-Love - It is critical for those who grab too much power to learn about authentic self-love. Grabbers rely on conquests to feel good about themselves. We need to take the time and receive adequate support if we are to integrate an inwardly focused scaffolding of self-appreciation. This transformation replaces the glory of triumph with presence, empathy, compassion, and self-nurturing.

4) Apprenticing to Humility - Grabbing too much power gets us caught in distortions of who we really are. A spirit of arrogance distances us from others and ourselves. An injection of pride accompanies each conquest. We are temporarily removed from knowing our limits or endure some extended estrangement from clearly knowing where we begin and end.

The key is to remember you will find yourself either giving too much power away or grabbing too much. It is likely that we will prefer one to the other, wandering down the other path on occasion. I have heard folks who give too much away proudly declare their displeasure over being a grabber. It may be that the preference of giving too much away reflects the alleged goodness of being a victim.

While virtue of victimhood is the result of not wishing to harm others, self-made victims ignore the job of taking care of themselves by expecting others to do it for them. Victims tend to collude with the perpetration of grabbers. We can only grab what is available to us. Victims are also prone to self-righteousness and are resentful of grabbers who exploit their poor boundaries. Victims run a high risk of eventually acting out in some cruel way as a compensation for excessive self-sacrifice.

My recommendation is to suspend allegations of who is better or worse. We were all groomed to have a propensity toward either giving too much power away or grabbing it in excess. Instead of admonishing ourselves or getting caught up in who has greater claim to virtue, let us see both positions as the only ways to learn about power. We must remain an apprentice to power, knowing there is no way of getting it absolutely right. There is only the dedication to learn.

All expressions of power are contextual. In one context we might give away too much, while grabbing too much in another. It is a lifelong project to remain mindful of our "ability to do." Self-awareness of this ability greatly determines the apprentice's relationship to life and how learning will happen.

Here are some questions that may help guide the discerning process: What is it about this situation that can help me identify my "ability to do"? Is there someone to whom I give away too much power? Is this situation asking me for more entitlement to speak or to create more space for the voices of others? How will I feel about myself if I don't have a significant impact on others in this situation? What do I want from my participation in this situation? Do I have something to prove?

Two Categories of Power

Power falls into two mutually exclusive categories: Socio-Economic/ Political and Personal. In an extroverted society, talk of power is typically indicative of the former. Until emotional intelligence and spiritual growth are given their just due, Personal Power will likely continue to be disparaged or ignored.

Socio-Economic/Political Power – There are three determining factors for Socio-Economic/Political Power: 1) education, 2) income, and 3) occupation. Prevailing forces like class, race, ancestral legacies, and cultural trauma can deeply impact the availability of these three factors. Some form of struggle is required to navigate these impediments. Socio-Economic/ Political Power is not conveniently delivered, even when legislation supports it. It is a power that must be taken. This means engaging in external as well as internal struggle. It may drive you to leave a neighborhood overrun with violence or create a coalition aimed at generating jobs for gang members. It may involve numerous levels of networking with others who are deprived of Socio-Economic/Political Power. It may call for active support of candidates who believe in the cause of those less privileged by prioritizing food, shelter, medical care, and safety.

Poverty and race are strong determining factors of who is likely to be disenfranchised in regard to extroverted forms of Socio-Economic/Political Power. When speaking of access to education, income, and occupation, people of color carry less privilege than white, heterosexual men. Those of us who carry more privilege should be aware of it and how we live it. That said, I do not recommend that the privileged engage in an ongoing recompense driven by guilt. The privileged do not necessarily choose their status or station. The key is to identify how we can best support those living with less privilege.

We must not view even a genuine desire to be supportive as simply altruistic. There are plenty of non-altruistic reasons to be supportive that are more trustworthy. Our involvement with those different from ourselves opens us to a much wider range of learning opportunities. Our apprenticeship with the unknown gets a significant boost as we expose ourselves to different customs, values, beliefs, and aspirations. We get a better handle on our biases and how they impact personal choices. We might even gain a new perspective to enrich our lives. When we are less insulated from what is unfamiliar, we allow differences to bring depth and breadth to our collaborative efforts.

By lending a hand to those less fortunate, we stop relying on social and economic hierarchies to bolster self-worth. Such hierarchies are houses of cards when it comes to genuine worth, precariously perched and prepared to topple. Being a resource for those less privileged pulls us beyond a false sense of diversity. The ancestors of most white, heterosexual men were likely disenfranchised when disembarking from Ellis Island.

To be an external resource for those less privileged is to prioritize inclusion that supports the educational, occupational, and financial mobility of women and people of color. We find one good example of such mindfulness in the work of Marc Benioff. He is the CEO of the tech company Salesforce, overseeing some 30,000 employees. In 2018, *Fortune* magazine placed his company at #1 on its "100 Best Companies to Work For" list. During an interview with a *60 Minutes* television journalist, Benioff admitted to feeling shocked when his Director of Human Relations suggested their company might have some significant gender inequities pertaining to promotion and salary. Benioff prioritized an audit to determine the veracity of these allegations. When the audit showed there were indeed significant gender differences, Benioff authorized managerial staff to immediately address the unfair practices in his company.

Benioff's response to gender inequity shows how white men can use their privilege to promote the privilege of others. Sexism, like racism, can be either systemic (institutional) and/or psychological. Educational, religious, and other social institutions are sexist and racist, which means they operate under assumed norms and/or unconscious biases. Psychological sexism or racism is a conscious intention to subjugate women and people of color.

Like any man, Marc Benioff was an institutional sexist. He firmly believed he had created a cooperate culture that supported gender equality and yet had failed to do so. His reaction to his unconscious sexism is as good as it gets. It is important not to lump institutional biases with their psychological counterparts. Because we have all gone through some form of conditioning, each of us carries institutional biases. Those possessing privilege as well as the less fortunate harbor gender and racial biases. The hope is that we become more willing to analyze how these biases impact others and ourselves.

Personal Power – Personal Power has none of the allure of Socio-Economic/Political Power. CNN is not likely to interview someone because they hold a good deal of Personal Power. It may be that we are attracted only to the measurability of one's bank account, education, career, and political influence.

A core definition of the word *personal* is "private," which itself means, "to be removed from the rest." Personal Power flourishes within the privacy of our inner worlds. We can bring our Personal Power to the marketplace, where it is challenged and tested, but it will be constructed elsewhere. The following are some ingredients of Personal Power:

1) **Dedicated to a self-examined life** - Only when we believe we are worth knowing and worth caring for are we able to create a life of substance. The self can be immeasurably elusive. It cannot be contained. Living intimately begins when we bring curiosity and heart to ourselves. Authentic self-examination includes an inventory of our strengths and of what is fragile or wounded. It further includes a willingness to be accountable for our actions and offering just recompense where appropriate.

2) **Dedicated to compassion** - An old definition of the word *compassion* is "a suffering with another." Compassion is the connective tissue of humanity. We neither allow our suffering nor the suffering of others to separate us. We may be prone to massaging our own psychological suffering—be it self-loathing, shame, or loss—by scapegoating others. We hold others responsible for our plight or disparage them in order to gain temporary relief. But how much more can we learn from our experience when we refrain from being divisive! Through compassion, our suffering finds its own meaning, no longer asking others to mitigate it for us. Following the Dalai Lama's twenty-year captivity and torture suffered at the hands of invading Chinese, his personal physician was asked how he endured. He explained that the Dalai Lama remained mindful of the fact that the persecutors inflicting pain on him must themselves be in great pain.

3) **Dedicated to integrity** - Integrity is the ability to identify what we desire and what we value, and to act in accordance with one or both. Integrity is self-loyalty. When guided by our values and heart's

desire, we create the most intimate relationship with life possible. Nelson Mandela deeply valued bringing peace to his beloved South Africa. Even when imprisoned by his enemies, he was determined to embody that value to the fullest. As Mandela himself once said, "If you want to make peace with your enemy, you have to work with your enemy. Then he becomes your partner."

4) Dedicated to the soul's task - Such dedication moves beyond what is deemed appropriate and socially endorsed. It opens oneself to being beguiled by some deeper calling. Viktor Frankl remained faithful to his soul's task while in a concentration camp: "We had to learn ourselves and, furthermore, we had to teach the despairing men, that it did not really matter what we expected from life, but rather what life expected from us." Being confined and removed from all remnants of Socio-Economic/Political Power did not deter Frankl from enhancing his Personal Power. He remained loyal to the task life presented.

There is certainly some credibility to Abraham Maslow's theory regarding a hierarchy of needs, where food and shelter become prerequisites to self-actualization or personal power. And yet, as cited in the above stories of three courageous souls, an act of Personal Power can transcend our socio-economic and political situation. A higher order of power is available to all of us. We need not be spiritual or political leaders suffering from brutality to access Personal Power.

A dedication to living a self-examined life begins when we give pause and focus inwardly. So much of who we are awaits our acknowledgement. A friend recently shared: "I know you're wondering why I remain in the relationship I'm presently in. I want you to know that I stay because I'm afraid to be alone." I acknowledged his awareness and the courage to speak a difficult truth.

A dedication to compassion is not necessarily the act of a canonized saint. It can be done while standing seven-deep in an extended checkout line that has come to a standstill because a woman is meticulously counting her food stamps. Instead of taking it as an affront to your schedule, use the opportunity to interrupt your quiet mockery of her financial status. Or, maybe you could let go of the quiet disdain you feel for the person directly in front of you carrying an extra fifty pounds.

In such situations, it is helpful to ask yourself: Do I know my heart's desire? Do I live my heart's desire? Am I clear about my values and realize when I act either in accord with them or against them? Do I allow myself to see times when I rationalized taking some action that was incompatible with my values?

The soul's task comes into focus when you hold yourself accountable for your behavior. It is difficult to see your way to what life is asking of you when you are scrambling to look good. When you do not know how to carry your mistakes and shortcomings, you do not know how to live. You are pretending to be something you are not, that life is something it is not. Life is an endless opportunity for fumbling. It requires you to be honest with yourself. Do that, and you will grow closer to hearing what life is asking of you.

Personal Power and the Oppressed

When it comes to Socio-Economic/Political Power, it is clear who has it and who lacks it. Those who are privileged tend to be unaware of their privilege. Because we do not prize Personal Power, we either fail to identify who has it or come to recognize it because some exceptional endeavor has been attained outside the framework of Socio-Economic/Political Power (Viktor Frankl's story being a quintessential example).

Personal Power is typically rooted in loss. We may experience loss of care and attention due to parental abuse. We may experience loss of freedom at the whim of a domineering spouse. At least those who face Socio-Economic/ Political oppression receive some measure of entitlement to address their injuries. We do not perceive a woman who has been a victim of domestic abuse as less of a woman because she seeks help.

So, who are the oppressed when it comes to Personal Power? The answer should be obvious, but often is not: white, heterosexual men and men of color are oppressed with regard to Personal Power. They are not entitled to be victims. They are given little or no permission to be sexually, physically, or emotionally injured. They risk jeopardizing their manhood by seeking help. The only time they are allowed to be victims is in the context of combat. Even then, their homecoming may not be all that hospitable.

When asked about the heroism of Senator John McCain, President Donald Trump responded, "I prefer soldiers who engage in combat and who are not captured," referring to McCain's capture and subsequent internment in a POW camp. Although the comment would be deemed a significant act of impropriety by most value systems, it reveals our darker assessment Personal Power: praise only for the victor, disdain for any man not victorious, and indifference toward any man who is honest about being vulnerable and wounded.

So what happens when we preclude a segment of our population from being emotionally wounded and in need of healing? First, that group is relegated to perpetrator status. They are only viewed through the lens of Socio-Economic/Political Power, free to enjoy and exploit their privilege. Below are some examples of what happens to white, heterosexual men who are victims of diminished Personal Power.

Their emotional maturity is interrupted. They no longer know who they are emotionally. They either express anger violently or internalize it as depression. They get stuck in denial when addressing losses and are never sure about how to move on. They have a shameful relationship with fear, which prevents them from being honest about the objects and nature of their fear. Denial of fear leads to overcompensation via reckless behavior or withdrawal to gain some semblance of safety.

They experience internalized oppression. No one needs to tell them they need to stop feeling vulnerable and in need of support. They readily subjugate themselves, striving to prevent any indication of emotional intelligence that would jeopardize their cherished manhood.

They compensate by attempting to access inordinate amounts of Socio-Economic/Political Power. Unable as they are to step into genuine Personal Power, they offset this loss by attempting to obtain excessive amounts of Socio-Economic/Political Power. Misled into believing this is the only kind of power available to them, they are easily driven by greed and workaholism. Falling prey to the prospect of endless acquisitions, and in demonstration of their economic prowess, they lose sight of what truly matters.

They have no permission to ask for emotional support. When an emotional life has little or no meaning, any need for support is irrelevant. Street drugs, alcohol, prescription drugs, and even workaholism become active substitutes.

They are unable to interrupt toxic legacies. When a man does not know who he is emotionally or where he comes from, he tends to reproduce whatever dysfunctional patterns characterized the lives of his ancestors. Addiction, domestic violence, gambling, acting out sexually, and a range of other self-sabotaging behaviors get passed on.

They are confused about how to exercise authority. Men are often confused about how to exercise their own authority. Should they adopt a nonchalant attitude or go all-out when it comes to offering supervision? Those impacted could be employees or even their own children. The challenge is learning how to draw boundaries that simultaneously support the purpose of the group while empowering everyone within it.

They are disabled in regard to sustaining an apprenticeship with the unknown. When feelings of insecurity and vulnerability are not permitted, pretense becomes a default method of navigating life's challenges. Leading with pretense denies our experience with fate. Learning is significantly stifled when we are dishonest with others and ourselves about what happens to us as we make our way.

In order to learn and heal, all socio-economic and racial groups must see themselves as both victims and perpetrators. We violate our humanity when we eliminate being either a perpetrator or a victim from our identities. To be fully alive means we will harm and be harmed. Seeing ourselves as the harmed, we are able to begin healing and identifying with others who have been harmed. Accepting that we also inflict harm, we diminish self-righteousness and lessen divisiveness.

White, heterosexual men will not loosen their tenacious grip on Socio-Economic/Political Power until they feel a loss of Personal Power. Feminists devoted to non-divisiveness or unity consciousness readily understand that such men have been perpetrators and that they are victims of Personal Power.

When heterosexual women carry a significant father-daughter wound, they easily lose faith in the possibility of being loved by men. They stop calling the men in their lives to love and emotional intimacy. They settle for being emotionally needed by their male partners, thus colluding with the man's tenuous degree of emotional intelligence. Instead of colluding, women should risk giving men a reason to emotionally grow up.

Power is always with us. It serves us greatly to increase mindfulness about our lived experience of power. Here are some questions that can help maintain a power focus: Do I remain vigilant of what is and isn't in my control? Am I aware of to whom I'm inclined to give power? If I carry socio-economic and political privilege, am I willing to learn about inherent disparities? If I carry such privilege, am I willing to explore it as compensation for a lack of Personal Power? Am I willing to consider that people of color and white women often live with internalized oppression with regard to Socio-Economic/Political Power? Am I willing to acknowledge that white, heterosexual men and men of color live with internalized oppression regarding Personal Power?

The more honest we are about how power lives with us, the more we can mitigate the intensity of distractions while we meander.

A Blessing for Power

There came a time when stretching your limbs to the far reaches of your crib was simply not enough. Curiosity reached a crescendo, calling you to discover just how much your body was capable of, and what your explorations might reveal about the world. Inevitably, you would pull a lamp down onto your head, trip over a rug, and successfully launch a projectile not designed for flight. These were just some of the calamites befalling the young apprentice dedicated to understanding Power.

There would arise endless Initiations into Power along the way. There is no arrival at the ideal place of Power. There are only adjustments and corrections to make along the way. We can only live the questions of Power. What are my gifts and strengths? Who benefits from the employment of my gifts? Am I mindful of either making an unnecessary advance or being excessively yielding? Am I able to be mindful about an attachment to domination? Am I able to see that I'm living in someone else's story?

There are two teachers of Power. The first is abuse, or grabbing too much power. This teacher's lesson can be difficult to learn. The ego revels in controlling as much as possible. It almost feels godly. Such is the robustness of its seduction. Yet there are prices to falling prey to this seduction. The grip of isolation will tighten as others avoid you. You'll likely live the distortion that you are actually powerful. Truth is the power given to you out of fear.

The second teacher is abdication, or giving too much power away. This teacher has a stealth quality whereby the abdicator might be viewed as a good person rather than someone who abuses power. Learning from his teacher becomes very challenging, as you fail to see that abdication betrays the Power life has given you. Being an abiding student of abdication means reclaiming Power that belongs to you. Find the

*courage to risk, to fail, to be lost, and, most of all, to forgive yourself,
however many times it takes.*

*The apprentice of Power is a genuine apprentice to the unknown.
Sadness, guilt, and remorse are all aroused in response to being
mindful of your lived experience of Power. You are asked to be mindful
of whether or not you're giving too much away or grabbing too much.*

*Learn to hold Power with reverence. Power allows you to live
your mind and heart. It allows you to be generative and creative.
Power moves you to love and forgive. Power allows you to create a
relationship with yourself and others. Just as it did when you first crept
and crawled, it reveals where you begin and end.*

*Remaining an apprentice to Power is a wonderful way to befriend
fate. Moving away from domination and abdication, you entertain
an abiding connection with fate. You will need to forgive yourself
continually for not getting Power right. Only then can you allow fate to
get you right with endless opportunities to live mindfully.*

6

Triumph Over Defeat
and Victory

Greatness lives in one who triumphs equally over defeat and victory.

–John Steinbeck

I f wisdom is about remaining an apprentice to the unknown, then befriending the fool within is necessary. As Carl Jung observed: "The greatest and most important problems in life are all in a certain sense insoluble. They must be so because they express the necessary polarity inherent in every self-regulating system. They can never be solved, but only outgrown." Careful attention to Jung's words may help us uncover the role of the fool when sustaining an apprenticeship with the unknown.

"The greatest and most important problems in life are in a certain sense insoluble." Assume that some of the "greatest and most important problems in life" include issues such as justice, freedom, security, love, power, healing, and peace. These problems are shrouded in ambiguity, with no clear direction and conclusion. Yet they are what make life worth living. Jung employs the term "insoluble" and not "insolvable." While the former does infer the latter, it also reflects Jung's preference for alchemical notation. We can assume Jung is suggesting that when considering a polarity such as conflict and peace, neither energy will conveniently merge with the other and be dissolved.

Jung goes on to suggest that these problems are insoluble because they "express a necessary polarity." We can think of polarities as opposites. For example: independent/dependent, trust/distrust, willfulness/surrender, stability/transformation, peace/conflict, freedom/restriction, mine/yours.

These polarities are organic, reflecting both the evolving and regressive attitudes of our lived experience. It behooves an apprentice of the unknown to learn to outgrow polarities. Otherwise, major portions of fate will go dismissed or ignored.

For example, dependence/independence will be a necessary polarity in any committed relationship between two people. Too much dependency leads to enmeshment or sacrifice of individuality. Too much independency leads to alienation, eroding any significant emotional connection. The perfect balance of dependency and independency cannot be solved. The best that can happen is that both participants in the relationship ask how this polarity can best be currently lived. Variables such as childcare, job demands, illness, hobbies, and travel can influence how this polarity is approached. Obviously, there may be two different views to the question.

Jung concludes by saying, "they can only be outgrown." An apprentice to the unknown will need to outgrow polarities to maintain a viable relationship with the unknown. Let us look more closely at what it means to outgrow and not outgrow a polarity.

Not Outgrowing a Polarity

It may be helpful first to look at what it means to not outgrow a polarity—in other words, when both ends of a polarity are not equally accepted. Acceptance of opposites can be quite challenging. Below I outline several obstacles that can inhibit the acceptance of a polarity.

Anxiety created by ambiguity – The ego prides itself with arriving at an alleged certainty. There is no certainty when working with polarities. Inner variables such as changing values, beliefs, and desires will impact the balance of a polarity like dependent/independent. External variables such as climate, illness, loss, relocation, and organizational downsizing also impact how a polarity can be lived, accompanied by some tension due to lack of certainty. The tendency will be to massage the anxiety by making one end of the polarity inappropriate or unacceptable. The result is that we unnecessarily struggle, trying our best to make the chosen energy work for us. Attempting to eliminate one aspect of the polarity takes the places of curiosity, resiliency, and learning. Our apprenticeship to the unknown will be suspended.

Shame – Sometimes, when we deem one of the polarities bad, we feel shame the more we approach it. Betty, a 42-year-old mother of three children and working full-time in a hospital as a lab assistant, once related to me how she shamed her needs and her dependency on others to love and allegedly be loved.

"I've been married for nearly twenty years and I can't remember asking my husband for anything," Betty recounted assertively, glancing downward.

"It sounds like you've come into this awareness about your refusal to make requests," I added.

"Yes, it's recent. I started wondering why I resented Tim so much, when he is a very loving man," she explained as her eyes moistened.

"I'm hearing that you have both appreciated and resented Tim," I explained.

"I have no right to resent him. It became clear in the wake of the psychological work I've been doing, that I shamed my needs as a child. I saw my mother as overwhelmed with her job and attending to my three younger siblings. There was no way I was going to add to her load by depending on her to get my needs met," she admitted, with a sense of pride for having taken care of her mom.

"Sounds like you decided that being self-sacrificing was the way to go as a child supporting your mother, and that your marriage to Tim is asking for more," I proffered.

"Yes, he's a good man, but expecting him to read my mind, while I struggle not to depend on him, does nothing for our marriage," Betty explained, leaning forward and raising her voice.

Betty came to understand that her needs and depending on Tim were not shameful. She began to slowly "outgrow" the dependent/independent polarity by interrupting the old pattern of shaming her needs. The more she took the risk to depend on Tim for her emotional needs, the more she outgrew the polarity.

Denial – Denying either the value of one component of a polarity or that we are feeling the impact of both components is quite common. For instance, the betrayal/loyalty polarity is often treated with denial, driven by fear, guilt, and shame. Once the polarity is acknowledged, a great deal of tension may arise.

Outgrowing Polarities

Outgrowing polarities does not mean that somehow we move beyond them, as if transitioning from a tricycle to a bicycle. We do not transcend polarities as if our lives conveniently escape their influence. Polarities are forces thrusting and jostling us in different directions. Their tension challenges us to find balance and stability, especially when they seem to possess equal strength.

The title of Dr. Anthony Wolf's book on adolescent psychology—*Get Out of My Life, but First Could You Drive Me and Cheryl to the Mall?*—captures the dilemma of working with the dependent/independent polarity. Ultimately, outgrowing a polarity means having a creative relationship with the tension created by the polarity in question. Such a relationship is a shift in values characterized by greater acceptance, resiliency, and curiosity. This kind of relationship with tension ultimately diminishes it. Exemplary processes of outgrowing are poignantly depicted in the myths of Parsifal's search for the Holy Grail and Odysseus's return home. In each we encounter a hero led off course, meandering for a time before resuming his original quest.

Parsifal

Parsifal, following his father's death, spends his childhood living with his mother in a forest cottage. His mother, as the first woman to charm him, has his primary loyalty. As recounted in *The Grail Legend* by Emma Jung and Marie-Louise von Franz, "Like so many fairy-tale heroes, [Parsifal] grows up in a forest. With its plant and animal life, its twilight and its restricted horizon, the forest aptly illustrates the as yet barely conscious condition of the child."

There is much to be said about Parsifal living in "twilight and its restricted horizon" in the forest. An old meaning of the word *twilight* is "half-light." Parsifal lives in a light that precedes greater light and comes before darkness. He has yet to come into the greater light of consciousness or the ordeals and perils affiliated with substantially larger darkness. Because of living in half-light, it will be difficult for Parsifal to see his strengths and weaknesses, what or who deserves his devotion, a vision of his own purpose, and how to best manifest what he loves. Deeper darkness might include a confrontation with his destructive nature. It would likely involve some exposure to death and suffering through acts of ignorance.

The "restricted horizon" may suggest a reduction in his ability to envision future possibilities and learn from evolving experiences. There will be little motivation to seek what lies over the horizon, since he has no experience of a horizon. It implies a preoccupation with his immediate experience of being a son. A son, at the very least, is obedient and emotionally connected to a parent. Parsifal's parent is Herzeleide, a mother whose very name ("Heart's Sorrow") reflects the loss of her husband and two sons. Parsifal lives in her psychic orbit, pulled away from excitement and adventure to shield her from further grief.

Parsifal's mother will likely ask her son to take the place of her dead husband, which calls him to a role he is ill-equipped to fill. Such a request morphs into strong feelings of inadequacy. Yet Parsifal must also remain a son, allowing his grief-stricken mother to continue in her role as such. Both invitations will weigh heavily on a son, impeding his development.

Parsifal is far removed from making peace with at least two important polarities: naïve/experienced and innocent/understanding. Oblivious to the inherent tensions therein, he knows only naïveté and innocence. His limited life experience disallows his mature understanding. Our story therefore begins with a son nowhere near ready to outgrow these two polarities, since he has yet to experience their tension with self-awareness.

Because Parsifal is significantly undersized, he is unable to learn from life as an apprentice to the unknown. He does not know what it means to meet fate with his desire or make choices reflective of his own values. He is ignorant of what is and is not in his control. As one excessively susceptible to accepting advice from authority figures, he cannot live on terms set either by himself or by life itself. While dwelling in his mother's cottage, he knows obedience but not curiosity and wonder. And so, when a forest encounter thrusts him away from home and into the world, he takes a step closer to the man he is meant to be.

One day, while meandering in the woods, he hears horses and the clamor of arms, and quickly decides that devils must be approaching. Suddenly, he sees five knights whom he believes must be angels. His initial perceptions reflect a dichotomy of good and evil characterized by naïve consciousness. The plumage adorning their armor and horses mesmerizes him. Upon learning they are knights who received their armor from none other than King Arthur, he is determined to acquire his own finery. Thus, he is more enamored with the alluring apparel of knighthood than he is with its attendant virtues of chivalry.

As superficial as his motivation is for becoming a knight, his enchantment with knightly accoutrements is enough to lure him away from home. We are, however, given several indications that riding down the road at a full gallop does not guarantee a swift departure from childhood. His mother crafts a riding garment for him that is unfit for courtly presentation and is more a statement about where he comes from than where he is headed. She also instructs him to be courteous to all women and to avoid asking too many questions.

One way to understand his mother's instruction is as a warning against disrupting others with his desire and curiosity. Such maternal bidding will inhibit a son's capacity to be passionately involved in lived experience. Fearing the risk of being excessively disruptive, the son errs on the side of passivity, compliance, and inhibition.

We see further evidence of his being undersized in his self-referencing. Apparently unknowing of his own name, he instead refers to himself by the terms of endearment—bon fils, cher fils, beau fils—his mother used to identify him. Robert Bly has suggested that it will take a man, if he is lucky, a lifetime to sever his mother's psychic umbilical cord, thus claiming his own name and his own adult identity, which lies beyond being a son.

Parsifal makes his way to Arthur's court, where he has an unexpected encounter with a so-called Red Knight. Covetous of the Red Knight's horse and armor, he is invited by the Red Knight to come take it. He is knocked to the ground but throws a dagger, killing the Red Knight and acquiring the knightly attire and weapons he desires. The act of killing the Red Knight creates tension between his naïveté and experience. Inflicting a lethal blow introduces him to a dangerous part of himself. The story tells us that he never kills another knight, but in his triumph sends them to serve King Arthur instead.

Significantly, he dons the Red Knight's armor over the shirt his mother tailored for him. This suggests a need to keep his mother's offering close in secret while outwardly presenting his knighthood to the world. Might the arrangement of his attire symbolize his continued attachment to "twilight and its restricted horizon"?

Parsifal's travels take him to Gournamond, his godfather, who mentors him in the arts of chivalry and battle. He impresses on Parsifal that he should not seduce (or be seduced by) a fair damsel and yet insists that he search for the Grail Castle and, upon entering, ask: "Whom does the Grail serve?" Again, he is advised to distance himself from any erotic connections, just as his mother told him to remain courteous to all women. Both instructions prove to be a double-edged sword. On the one hand, if he follows them, carnal urges are guaranteed never to impede his quest. On the other hand, his desire is not being given full permission to live.

When finally arriving at the Grail Castle, he only needs to ask, "Whom does the Grail serve?" and the king and kingdom will be healed. His maternal directive now undermined, he grows mute, unable to give voice to the very question that will bring about restoration.

Parsifal's Triumph Over Defeat

An Old French root of the word *defeat* is "to undo." What is Parsifal being asked to undo as he leaves the Grail Castle in defeat? Surely, it is his loyalty to the maternal mandate in fear of his own curiosity. Said loyalty makes him more susceptible to questioning whatever others keep hidden. Tension between loyalty to his mother and to himself is inevitable. He must therefore come to know the tensions between the polarities of naïve/experienced and innocent/ understanding. If he is ever going to triumph over defeat, he will need to outgrow these polarities.

Outgrowing the Naïve / Experienced Polarity

Parsifal never loses a battle. Rather than kill his combatants, he sends them back to serve King Arthur. An old meaning of the word *naïve* is "native disposition." Parsifal's consistent triumph over adversity suggests an evolving repertoire of fighting skills and, by extension, life experience. We can interpret his mother's insistence that he avoid posing questions as her caution against excessive disruption. By not killing his opponents, he avoids being overly disruptive. His "native disposition" reflects a higher value of service to the king over random carnage.

Parsifal's "native disposition" is to be dutiful to his mother. His wound is an enmeshed relationship with his mother, a serious impediment to his ability to be independently self-conscious. His maternal wounding is not simply unfortunate; it leads him into fervent devotion to duty by living his gifts for fighting, protecting, and serving.

The story of Parsifal suggests that triumphing over defeat means paying attention to our gifts and how they might serve. Defeat has the power to turn us away from life, shrouded in cynicism and self-pity. Our gifts or strengths may be the connective tissue of life, even when we are temporarily separated from our own Grail.

Parsifal's naïve/experienced polarity is a common one. Here are some questions that can help us outgrow it in our triumph over defeat: How does my naïveté or my roots restrict my experience? What injury, and what gift, was bestowed upon me by this restriction? What are my strengths and what experience will best develop them? To what form of service are my gifts or strengths calling me?

Parsifal faces a quandary of how much he can rely on his experience to inform him, entitled to draw conclusions while remaining curious. He will come to know the tension inherent in the ego's claim to experience while striving for humble acknowledgement of those elements of his character that remain raw and green.

Parsifal curiously prepares himself to return to the Grail Castle during his years of meandering, serving the king, the poor, and the disenfranchised. The quest culminates when he returns to the Grail Castle and asks, "Whom does the Grail serve?" Although he is clueless regarding the whereabouts of the Grail Castle, he appears to be up to what the Grail is all about: service!

Outgrowing the
Innocent / Understanding Polarity

In order for Parsifal to triumph over defeat, he must outgrow the innocent/ understanding polarity. A root meaning of the word *innocent* is "harmless or unwounded." To be innocent is to be unconscious of one's wound. He outgrows this polarity as he gains more understanding of his wound and how it restricted his curiosity, as well as how it allowed him to serve dutifully. His healing happens the more he engages his curiosity, enduring the possible disruptions or failures that ensue as a result.

He encounters Blanche Fleur, a maiden who requests his help to liberate her castle from a besieging army. Curiosity compels him to oblige by dueling the army's second-in-command. He wins the duel, is then victorious over the first-in-command, and sends both knights back to serve the Round Table of Arthur. Such conquests engage his curiosity, which translates into the discernment and understanding he requires to be victorious. He will need to be curious about his strengths and his limits, as well as those of his opponents.

Coming to know and feel these tensions forges character. Without them, Parsifal would remain a child. Tensions are creative because they inform a personal belief system. They are the veritable pulse of one's values, devotion to a particular cause, and purpose in life. Knowing how to carry the flames of doubt, despair, shame, and confusion, along with those of confidence, satisfaction, clarity, and faith, all make significant contributions to the forging process.

Parsifal comes to know both the tension and eventual acceptance of these polarities by attending to his knightly obligations and eventually rightsizing himself. He begins to "outgrow polarities" as he becomes more conscious of the contribution made by the opposites on either end. His outgrowing process deepens as his vision broadens enough to appreciate how each end of a polarity plays a significant role in enriching his ability to be conscious. He triumphs over defeat by integrating his native disposition of filial duty, which translates into his lifelong service to King Arthur.

Parsifal leaves the Grail Castle, having been defeated by failing his mission, and meanders for twenty years, dutifully slaying dragons, saving fair damsels, lifting sieges, and protecting the poor. He is now conscious of the tension inherent in these polarities. His many victories will move him out of being undersized.

Undersized to Oversized to Rightsized

In the course of our psychological development, we do not move from being undersized to rightsized. It simply takes too much to undo undersizing, which we can describe as naïve, falsely modest, reticent, callow, deferential, and disempowered. Parsifal's knightly successes jostle him out of being undersized toward being oversized. The psyche naturally compensates, searching for balance by shifting from undersized to oversized, which we can describe as arrogant, shameless, overbearing, entitled, and smug.

Triumph Over Success

The great gift of defeat is that it allows us to triumph over success. Without defeat, it is too easy to remain oversized, held in the grips of an ego overly impressed with itself. When we are taken hostage by such an ego, the truth of who we are remains hidden. In Parsifal's case, he carries the knowledge of having failed to access the Grail. Even though he does not know the whereabouts of the Grail Castle, he remains devoted to the quest of arriving there, ever an apprentice to the unknown. He attends to his duties without succumbing to the lure of some Bypass.

"Parsifal has had the arrogance beaten out of him by twenty years of fruitless searching, and he is now ready for his castle" (Robert Johnson). Parsifal's "fruitless searching" allows him to triumph over success. As one "ready for his castle," Parsifal is becoming rightsized. This entails being *humble* (the word itself comes from the Latin *humus*, or "earth"). Connection to the earth denotes balance, stability, and presence without inflating the self as something one is not. It means accepting we are flawed human beings, stumbling toward enlightenment.

Rightsizing asks us to be authentic, living with compassion for ourselves and others, holding ourselves accountable, and being honest about strengths and shortcomings. It also denotes being sensible, realistic, and gracious for what we have received with a devotion to serve. More than anything, rightsizing reflects a shift into being conscious of who we are and what life is requesting of us.

Parsifal's last trial before returning to the Grail Castle is to resist the seductions of Kundry. In response to her erotic overtures, he will need to exercise his own values. He moves beyond the advice of his mother and godfather regarding the treatment of women. He is neither caught in the quandary of supporting what she allegedly desires nor obedient to childhood instructions. Instead, he responds with compassion, deciding that his abstinence would serve both of them. We can imagine the tension experienced by a young, virile male as a gorgeous female demonstrates her sensual receptivity to his potential penetration.

He is depicted as remaining loyal to his own beliefs, regarding her with compassion. His passion is to be directed toward the fulfillment of his quest to bring healing to the kingdom of the Grail. Does this last temptation suggest that the kindness shown to Kundry reflects his values and not a maternal imperative? Does his resistance to the seduction suggest a maturation that transcends the erotic? He does not innocently offer the female what she appears to desire. We might say that he is passionately claiming his soul's task to be a healer by treating Kundry as something more than the fulfillment of sexual satisfaction.

The story of Parsifal captures a central theme of meandering. It is not simply about learning lessons but is a time to be honest about the tension between the polarities that move us. Parsifal learns about tension by spending twenty years attending to his knightly duties. During this time, he outgrows polarities by making peace with their tensions. Parsifal must learn to become sophisticated without sacrificing his simplicity, knowledgeable without forgoing innocence, and experienced without forfeiting some level of naïveté.

Simplicity, innocence, and naïveté at first glance seem to impede living a conscious life. It is critical, however, to see them as essential to maintaining a relationship to the unknown. As qualities of the fool (Parsifal's name, in fact, means "Pure Fool"), they prevent us from taking up residency in what we know, the power of our experience, and the seduction of our sophistication.

Parsifal's first visit to the Grail Castle issues him a major defeat. He cannot ask the question, "Whom does the Grail serve?" as it would mean leading with his curiosity in betrayal of his mother. However, there are numerous ways to understand what it means to be ill-prepared for a Grail experience. There is the fear of failure, to be sure, but there is also the fear of success. There can be a nagging sense of not being deserving of such a sublime and fulfilling experience, of how others will perceive us differently due to a Grail experience.

Robert Johnson makes reference in *He* to an early Grail experience for which a youth is not prepared: "Most men can remember a magic half hour sometime in their youth when the whole world glowed and showed a beauty not easily described. Perhaps it is a sunrise, a glorious moment on the playing field, a solitary time during a hike when one turns a corner and the whole splendor of the inner world opens for one. No youth can cope with this opening of the Heavens for him and most set it aside but do not forget it."

I had such an early Grail experience at seventeen during a high school basketball game. We were playing one of the best teams in New England, a perennial regional champion. It was the third quarter and we were down by ten points. I proceeded to make five baskets in a row. The last hoop came as I drove to the right side of the basket about fifteen feet away. I came to a two-foot stop, jumped straight up to shoot, and found a large defensive hand some six inches above the apex of my release. I was forced to change the trajectory of my shot to avoid being blocked. The ball seemed to go straight up with little or no chance of finding its way to the basket. Surprisingly, I heard the snap of the net, indicating a score. The opposing coach jumped to his feet to call a time-out.

Our coach huddled us up and explained that our opponents were going to adjust their defense to a box-and-one, which entails four players playing zone and one player defending me, man to man. He further instructed my teammates to continue passing me the ball, setting a pick for me or clearing out to give me room. We returned to the court to find the opposing team adopting the very defense our coach had predicted.

Like Parsifal, I had been groomed for this situation over the past ten years. I knew the player defending me would likely overplay me. All it would take was a fake in one direction and I would be clear to move toward the basket in the opposite direction. Instead of taking charge, however, I passed the ball to my teammates over and over again, never initiating an offensive move toward the basket.

I spent hours over the years reviewing the timidity that gripped me in that game. Johnson's suggestion of not being ready has helped relieve the shame of my defeat. Fifty-three years would pass before I once again found myself in a Grail Castle moment. Of course, I had no idea there would be another opportunity to visit the Castle. Thankfully, I felt called to psychologically work with men and spent forty years refining my skills to help them grieve their losses, tap into reliable sources of personal empowerment, and deepen their capacity to engender authentic emotional intimacy.

In February of 2018, I traveled to Spain to work with ten men I did not know. The work was to take place over two days and be focused on the archetypes of masculine maturation. I arrived feeling ill yet assured of being in the right place doing the right work—work that I had been trained to do over four decades. The men and I built a container to hold their losses, their dreams, and their gratitude for what life had bestowed upon them. Each man stepped into the story of a broken heart seeking some renewal of its capacity to love and be loved. It was not until I was jetting toward home over the Atlantic that I understood I had just made my second visit to the Castle.

I recalled Robert Johnson's words regarding how overwhelming one's initial visit to the Castle can be. So much of a boy's inner world is lined with unseen forces, calling the boy somewhere he has never been and for which he is unprepared. It is a form of victory, success, or accomplishment he simply does not know how to carry.

Now, outside of Barcelona, I was doing what I was meant to do, guiding men toward touching and welcoming some part of them that longed to come home. I had been serving men and now I felt the Grail serving he who serves. I was glad to be living so intimately with regard to my purpose. The key to purpose is to gain some consciousness about what life is asking of us—holding the faith that life can get us right.

Consciousness and the Grail

The word *conscious* comes from the Greek word *syneidos*, meaning "to know." Knowing implies a deeply intimate connection with our lived experience. It also involves being open to diverse perspectives. Parsifal remains deeply devoted to King Arthur's vision. He is committed to deconstructing the old maxim that "might makes right," supporting the weak and the poor, and protecting the vulnerable from danger. Parsifal remains loyal to his calling while being ignorant about the whereabouts of the Grail Castle. He does not allow self-pity or humiliation to sabotage his knightly vocation.

So long as the Grail Castle is shrouded in mystery, Parsifal remains an apprentice to the unknown. He continues allowing his service to deepen and broaden his consciousness of life and self. He lives his gifts, his athletic ability, his understanding of injustice, and his devotion to something larger than himself. Because he comes to understand his devotion on a soul level, the Grail Castle once again becomes available to him. Only now can he ask, "Whom does the Grail serve?"

Robert Johnson captures Parsifal's maturation: "When Parsifal learns that he is no longer the center of the universe—not even his own little kingdom—he is free of his alienation and the Grail is no longer barred from him." We can interpret the words "free of his alienation" as a kind of knowing, an intimate learning. Parsifal knows that the Grail (Cup of Christ) serves he who serves.

Parsifal's Lessons for the Apprentice

There is at least a little Parsifal in each of us, male and female alike. The energy of Parsifal can show up as naïve, innocent, deferential, codependent, passive, confused, or obedient. Several Parsifal lessons can support an apprentice with some of his characteristics.

Addressing a Parsifal Wound – A Parsifal wound is to a great degree the over-involvement of a parent in the apprentice's psyche and life. The parent calls the child to his or her own needs and expectations without referencing the child in his or her inner world. The parent may need the child to remain a child to prolong the top-down relationship. Like Parsifal, the child is asked to take the place of a partner made unavailable by death, illness, divorce, or emotional inaccessibility. When a child is called to replace a spouse, it is only natural for the child to experience deep feelings of inadequacy due to confusion over stepping into that adult role. In order to cope with this premature call into adulthood, the child grows convinced of needing to try harder to meet the parent's expectations. Cut off from instinct and imagination, the parentified child is driven to please. Healing happens for the Parsifal wound only when the child begins to claim his or her own desire and a mentor focuses on the development of the child's gifts, as did Gournamond. The acknowledgement and development of personal gifts begins to shift the young person's identity from being someone's child to being in the world with a purpose.

Encountering a Hermit – "Because he did not ask about the Grail, [Parsifal] no longer understands himself and is cut off from the source of his inner being. The hermit who helps him on his way therefore personifies a tendency towards introversion and towards a renunciation of the world as a first exercise preparatory to solving the Grail problem" (Emma Jung and Marie-Louise von Franz). The image of the hermit can be translated into both internal dynamics and external experiences. As Emma Jung and Marie-Louise von Franz point out in the above passage, a relationship with our inner being is a necessary preparation for worldly endeavors. The hermit within us is not distracted by worldly events. We are able to explore our inner terrain, becoming familiar with our wounds and the medicine those wounds are asking for. We begin to understand how important it is to be conscious of where we come from to know where we are going. Our self-examination must highlight our gifts. Continuous self-examination, of course, will be challenging. In the words of Saint Augustine: "Men go abroad to wonder at the heights of mountains, at the huge waves of the sea, at the long courses of the rivers, at the vast compass of the ocean, at the circular motions of the stars, and they pass by themselves without wondering." We will ultimately serve from both our gifts and our wounds. It is, of course, extremely helpful for the hermit to show up as an actual person who knows how to navigate the inner landscape. As in the case of Parsifal, such a guide points to the darker sides of our personalities, shortcomings, and failures. Until we can hold our inner world in panoramic view, defenses aimed at keeping us looking good will distort our perception. Thus, we cannot know who we are or what life is asking of us. The external hermit can also offer compassion, pointing us in the right direction.

Remaining Curious about What Polarities Need to Be Outgrown – Several polarities accompany a Parsifal wounding: dependent/independent, domesticated/wild, naïve/experienced, innocent/understanding, compliant/rebellious, submissive/contentious. In order to continue welcoming the mystery of fate, the apprentice will need to see the value offered by each of these polarities. Expanding our values is necessary to outgrow a polarity. The apprentice will need to outgrow the rigidity binding him or her to a particular value while rejecting its opposite. An 85-year-old woman recently came to my office willing to submit to outgrowing the dependent/independent polarity: "Following my stroke, I can't do for myself like I once could. I was always strongly independent and saw dependency as weak and a burden to others. Now, I slowly understand that dependency allows me to admit and accept my limits. It also gives those I love an opportunity to give. But most of all, I'm learning to receive, a life lesson I've avoided only too long."

Daring to Be Disruptive – Parsifal steps into spontaneous disruption when he kills the Red Knight. Avoiding disruption keeps the apprentice externally referenced. Such referencing means living close to the expectations of others, the rules and guidelines given to us. Compliance restricts a sense of wonder that desires to walk away from convention. The apprentice is asked to risk the disfavor of others, not as a way of being flamboyantly provocative but rather as a way of honoring the inner directives of instinct, imagination, and intuition.

Learning to Focus on Rightsizing – In the course of our psychological development, we do not move from being undersized to rightsized. In one version of Parsifal's story, after completing the task of posing that all-important question—"Whom does the Grail serve?"—he learns the Grail King is his grandfather. The Grail King explains that he will die in three days and that Parsifal will reign in his stead. The story ends with the Grail King's funeral and burial. What can we say about a Grail experience leading to kingship?

Parsifal has a second Grail opportunity because he has attended to his business of being a knight. He has lived his gifts in service and performed the duties aligned with his life's purpose. The second Grail opportunity is simply what he was destined for and now possesses enough maturity to step into. His destiny is born when he meets fate with the choice to serve.

His crowning is deeply symbolic of a capacity to access more of the archetypal energy of the king. There are a number of characteristics indicative of newly awakened sovereignty. There will be more clarity about where one belongs and how one's gifts will best serve. There is sharper insight regarding the need for help and how to best access it. There are fewer disturbances regarding self-worth, replaced by a deeper feeling of being settled with regard to one's personal value. There is a renewed enthusiasm about the gifts of others and a heightened investment in blessing them. Authority is held with more stewardship, and with less of a propensity for abusing or abdicating authority. Purpose has more clarity, being held with a soulful understanding of one's personal values and how they might serve others. Living wisely manifests through one's devotion to serve. In such devotion, the Grail will serve us.

Odysseus

Odysseus's story begins quite differently from Parsifal's. Unlike Parsifal, powerful men, along with a god, influence Odysseus's childhood, as he is the great godson of the god Hermes. Odysseus bears an early wound of abandonment. Such an emotional injury morphs into a counter-dependence characterized by extreme self-reliance, resistance toward asking for help, seeking perfection, denying weakness and vulnerability, intellectual arrogance, an aversion to emotional intimacy, and difficulty relaxing and taking rest.

His grandfather Autolycus names him: "Just as I have come from afar, creating pain for many—men and women across the good green earth— so let his name be Odysseus … the Son of Pain, a name he'll earn in full." Unlike Parsifal, who has a commiserative relationship with his mother's grief, Odysseus will eventually create a grief of his own.

Being away from home does not significantly challenge him throughout the ten years he spends fighting a war on behalf of Menelaus, who wants to reclaim his wife, Helen, after she runs off with Paris. It would appear that Odysseus was highly attached to being victorious at Troy and is not prepared to leave for home without a triumph. An obsession with winning ignites his cunning and cleverness. The result is the offering of a wooden horse to the Trojans as an alleged token of Greek defeat—one that proves fatal for its recipients.

Whereas Parsifal's vision of the horizon is restricted by a thick forest, Odysseus grows up on an island where the horizon is visible as far as the eye can see. Possibilities live close to his soul. Parsifal finds belonging at the hearth, while Odysseus likely lives with a growing restlessness for adventure.

Both heroes are described as athletic. Parsifal's strapping physique develops from his romping around the forest, climbing trees, and jumping over streams. His strength is a reflection of being a natural child. Odysseus's sturdiness, by contrast, is the result of his early entrance into the world of men. He becomes proficient in archery and enjoys hunting with his dog. He is gored by a wild boar, leaving a scar on his leg. He possesses an uncanny ability to solve problems and outwit his opponents, and is an eloquent speaker. His story begins with being oversized and working with a set of polarities quite different from those of Parsifal.

Odysseus is clever, bold, and cunning. Not until he departs for home, following the Trojan War, will he come to know the tension inherent in the polarities that hold these character traits. These polarities include clever/unknowing, bold/timid, and cunning/honest. In order to outgrow them, Odysseus must go from being quite swelled and oversized to undersized before he can arrive at some semblance of being rightsized in between those two extremes.

In Homer's *Odyssey,* Odysseus is scheduled to reach his home of Ithaca in a matter of months following the Greek victory at Troy. The voyage will take him a full decade of meandering to reach his destination. His lack of gratitude to Poseidon for his victory at Troy ensures he will encounter numerous obstacles along the way. He battles the Cyclones, struggles with the Lotus-eaters, fights the Cyclops, resists the witch Circe, and succumbs to the influence of Calypso. Calypso's charm brings much healing to the war-weary adventurer. The power of her seduction is something he could never have given himself.

Once stranded on Calypso's island, his crew dead and ship destroyed, he can no longer employ the cleverness that helped him win the war and overcome the ensuing trials he faced. Now, he kneels on a beach in deep sorrow for his defeat, having no vision of how to return home. He has come to know the tensions between being cunning and honest, bold and timid, clever and ignorant. His suffering is honest; he cannot boldly and cleverly make his way home. We can assume his heart has been opened to a longing for home. He rejects Calypso's offering of immortality, even though she warns that human difficulties are the alternative.

Triumph Over Success

Odysseus comes to Calypso's island the hero of the Trojan War. He devised the plan of presenting the Trojans a wooden horse as a token of their apparent victory of the Greeks. He employed his cunning and cleverness by having Greek soldiers occupy the horse's interior in the hope that the Trojans would be seduced into taking the horse within the walls of their city. The rest is history.

He spends seven years on Calypso's island, not only indulging in her erotic overtures, but as Jean Houston has pointed out, also nurturing the emotional wounds of a protracted war. We can assume that his psyche softens while in relationship with this Earth Mother. If nothing else, he grows more honest about the helplessness of his situation and loosens his grip on being clever, realizing he has no clue about how to get home. By the end, he has learned to embrace his timidity, becoming a bit less bold. Being timid would diminish his willfulness, allowing him to be touched and moved by Calypso's offerings of nurturance, support, desire, food, warmth, and shelter. He may even have begun learning to be grateful.

His defeat ushers in the death of an arrogance that denies his limits. In their place is born an openness to receive help and honor fate as something larger than the sum of his cunning and cleverness.

Triumph Over Defeat

At this point in the story, Athena, Goddess of Wisdom, implores her father, Zeus, to allow her to help Odysseus. Zeus reluctantly grants her request. Hermes is sent to inform Calypso of Zeus's order to help Odysseus build a raft for his immediate departure. Although she is not happy about Zeus's bidding, she complies.

It appears that divine intervention is offered to Odysseus when he embraces defeat and drops into deep sorrow for his inability to go home to Ithaca. We might see Athena's intervention as a metaphor for support and power coming from someone or somewhere outside of ourselves. Coming out of denial over being defeated may be the initial essential ingredient for triumph over defeat. Kneeling in the depths of sorrow and helplessness, Odysseus opens himself to being helped.

From this we can glean some understanding about descending into the depths of defeat as an opportunity to achieve our original goal, as in the case of Odysseus. Either that, or we accept the inevitability of defeat, which allows us to let go of our original purpose, bringing our intentions and attentions in a new direction. Thus, defeat possesses the power to point us toward where we belong.

For example, I have worked with dozens of alcoholics who felt deeply defeated by their relationships with alcohol. Some lost jobs, marriages, friends, and, almost always, a connection with their emotional and spiritual lives. Very few modified their relationship to alcohol and became social drinkers. Most decided to remain sober one day at a time. These sober individuals allowed their defeat to alcohol and their sobriety to point them toward a new experience of belonging. Rather than the belonging they allegedly felt on a bar stool, they now attended the games and concerts of their children. They found belonging in genuine friendships to which they could bring joy and sorrow.

Two Fools Moving Out of Distortion

Both Parsifal and Odysseus must experience defeat. Defeat opens the door to outgrowing polarities that have held them in distortion. Just as Parsifal's childlike innocence must die, so must Odysseus's glorification of his cleverness. The former is then able to construct his own values, the latter to receive help as he relinquishes a compulsive self-reliance.

Parsifal's story begins with innocence and naïveté, distanced from the values of experience and understanding, while Odysseus's story is founded on boldness and cleverness, disparaging of timidity and unknowing. Trapped by the tension inherent in their polarities, we can understand their foolishness as the inability to hold the best version of the truth about themselves and about life. Parsifal does not understand the value of experience and how much there is to know; Odysseus does not see the worth of timidity and unknowing.

Both narratives may be conveying that our stories inevitably begin in distortion, living to some extent as a fool. Yet it may be naïve for us to forget that Parsifal is the only knight who can access the Grail, if only because he begins with a pure heart, disinterested in manipulation and personal gain. He is destined to understand and embody the Grail's ultimate message of service. By outgrowing his polarities, his pure heart will be maintained as he integrates naïveté and innocence instead of allowing them to dominate his psychology.

Distortion takes the apprentice hostage when he refuses to outgrow a polarity. Odysseus is held captive to the limits of boldness and cleverness, thus devaluing the contributions of timidity and unknowing. Timidity suggests shyness and recoiling—qualities that interrupt Odysseus's impetuousness. Timidity allows us the opportunity to pause for thoughtful consideration. Unknowing interrupts our presumptuousness, opening us to more curiosity about ourselves and what life may be requesting, which is critical for any apprentice to the unknown.

Both characters face a final erotic temptation. Parsifal must resist the sexual overtures of Kundry while Odysseus, traveling in the land of the Phoenicians, must forego an erotic encounter with the virgin Nausicaa. Why this final test in both stories? Are we being informed about the power of the erotic to extend our meandering? Does the restraint of these heroes imply they no longer need confirmation of personal worth? Does the longing to complete their quest now occupy a larger place in their hearts? Does not succumbing to temptation suggest that both men no longer need to depend on a woman for compassion, grace, and acceptance? Does their resistance demonstrate some level of ownership of these qualities? There is much to reflect on with regard to the erotic's power to distract and what it means to diffuse its potency.

Parsifal and Odysseus face severe defeat, as if to remind us of its inevitability. The key is how we carry defeat. It may be that the single most significant aspect of meandering is allowing defeat to help us outgrow some polarity rather than fall into the depths of victimization, self-pity, humiliation, or cynicism. Defeat may ask us to refine our relationship to fate.

Parsifal fails to ask the right question on his first visit to the Grail Castle, then does what he does best: plays the role of the noble knight. Parsifal's refinement makes him larger, capable of exercising as much of his curiosity as he chooses, therefore able to ask the healing question, "Whom does the Grail serve?"

As Odysseus says to his son Telemachus, "It is no hard thing for the gods of heaven to glorify a man or bring him low." Odysseus acknowledges that the gods influenced both his victory and his defeat. His refinement is letting go of an inflation of self, helping him to be rightsized. We can say that meandering is about rightsizing the soul. We must either let go of some childhood script that diminishes us or let go of self-inflating hubris. It is the Parsifalian fool who, despite being uncertain of his or her direction, is willing to participate in life, committed to serving. The Odyssean fool, on the other hand, is the one convinced he or she possesses all that is needed to guarantee success.

Odysseus's Lessons for the Apprentice

Healing an Odysseus Wound – There are two natural defenses in response to an abandonment wound. The first is codependency, where we fuse with another person in the hope of preventing separation. The second defense is counter-dependency, where we inflate our autonomy. The hope is that our expansive identity excludes the need to depend on others, thus eliminating any possibility of being rejected. Of course, it means that emotional needs related to others such as love, acceptance, guidance, and intimacy are thwarted. So will an enduring acceptance of self be eliminated. Healing counter-dependency will greatly depend on some form of crisis, following which the papier-mâché scaffolding of the psyche tumbles down. Sorrow and helplessness are the medicine of this injury, as is the willingness to accept help. In order to remain an apprentice of the unknown, accepting the help needed to deconstruct the ego's inflation is critical.

Allowing Passivity to Bring Us Closer to Ourselves – Parsifal leaves his mother's cottage to discover the world. Odysseus leaves Ithaca for the world to discover him. Odysseus is obsessed with glory but seems confused when it is given by those who hold him in adulation. Glory must be sought again and again, thus condemning the seeker to restlessness and striving. While with Calypso, Odysseus has no opportunity to seek glory, he is unable to prove himself by indulging in some form of conquest. It is his opportunity to become more introverted and move closer to his inner world, at last grappling with his vulnerability, his limits, his suffering, and his longing for home. At this point in the story, his contrived confidence begins to crack, so that Athena is moved to help him return home. An apprentice with an Odysseus wound will need to pause, learning through vulnerability, suffering, and longing. These are powerful, humbling energies that allow for a more authentic view of the self and a clearer account of life, as well as greater permission to relate to the unknown with a faith that more will be revealed.

Remaining Curious about Outgrowing Odyssean Polarities – As we have seen, Odysseus is caught in the polarities of bold/timid and clever/unknowing. A counter-dependent reaction to an abandonment wound places the apprentice in an adversarial relationship with the unknown.

Like Odysseus, the apprentice will need to experience serious defeat before ceasing to wave banners in honor of cleverness. When that happens, a stifling humiliation accompanies the defeat. A root of the word *humiliation* is the Latin *humilis*, meaning "on the ground." Humbling ourselves in this manner, our face becomes hidden. A face provides the uniqueness of our identities. We see the world with our faces and our faces allow us to be witnessed. To some degree, we are our faces, and so to "lose face" in humiliation is to lose identity. The apprentice will experience the death of excessive pride, slowly birthing a face that can tolerate the tension of relating to the unknown. An old definition of the word *bold* is "swift." We can therefore understand boldness as the intention to swiftly impact life rather than tolerate the slowness that allows life to impact the apprentice to the unknown. Excessive boldness interrupts life's capacity to teach.

Committing to Be Rightsized – Triumph and glory can easily seduce the apprentice into remaining inflated, oversized. The ego naturally basks in its hierarchal status, content on living the delusion that it is immune to feeling inadequate. The way down is typically measured by how high we insist on going, as attested by Odysseus's journey. Rightsizing is not easily chosen by a psyche organized around boldness and cleverness. It calls for a major defeat and openness to help. It can be extremely difficult for the apprentice suffering from an Odysseus wound to even recognize the need for help and who might be able to offer it genuinely. Was it possible for Odysseus to know that he was not simply a captive on Calypso's island, but rather there to receive much-needed care for his war wounds? The apprentice must become more mindful of the need for help and who can offer it, as well as how to move beyond any resistance to receiving it. If there is any glimmer of hope that being bold and clever will come to the rescue, then there will be no rightsizing. If feeling the humiliation of defeat does not subside by attending to the excessive pride generating it, then the apprentice will continue feeling like a victim. As a victim, life remains the enemy, incapable of guiding the apprentice toward more reliable versions of the truth about the self and life. Victims stop drawing new conclusions, and without new conclusions, there is no way of believing the unknown will reveal more.

The Challenge

It is challenging to accept the inevitability of defeat. The ego's intolerance of defeat, accompanied by an acculturation that equates defeat with inferiority, all adds to the challenge. We are taught to do whatever it takes to avoid defeat. In being defeated, we do not simply lose; we are losers deserving of self-inflicted shame. Once wrapped in a shroud of shame, our essential goodness remains just out of reach. The ego recoils, warning us that defeat must not recur. A natural response is to either become risk-avoidant or bang on our chest, determined to overcome impossible obstacles. In either case, defeat loses its capacity to teach and unearth deeper truths.

The challenge is learning to accept that, as apprentices of the unknown, we will make choices we are not prepared to make. We will get distracted, lost, and seduced. How easily we forget our kinship with the unknown! Although we need to have dreams and aspirations, we are not here to do something with or to life. We are here to allow life to do myriad things with and to us.

Although fate wields a great deal of control over us, we are not here to simply be life's victims. We are here to have our love and our desire meet life in passionate engagement. Our purpose is to have a real relationship with life and its mystery. Of course, to have an involved relationship with life's immensity guarantees defeat. It is simply too tall an order for us to have our way at any given moment. We are left with three options: remain deluded about the inevitability of defeat, get defeated by having an intimate relationship with life, or get significantly defeated by choosing an unlived life. If we choose the first, it will be helpful to become more mindful of the sacredness of defeat.

We have explored what it means to make peace with various polarities. In her book *Becoming Wise*, Krista Tippett reminds us of Jung's heartening to outgrow polarities: "We are so achingly frail and powerful all at once, in this adolescence of our species. But I have seen that wisdom emerges precisely through those moments when we have to hold seemingly opposing realities in a creative tension and interplay: power and frailty, birth and death, pain and hope, beauty and brokenness, mystery and conviction, calm and buoyancy, mine and yours." Only when we "hold seemingly opposing realities in a creative tension and interplay" do we allow life to get us right, opening the door to wisdom.

A Blessing for Triumphing Over the Tension of Polarities

Fate calls you to make peace with its immensity. To find the resiliency and courage to transform tensions of opposites into contractions of labor, birthing yourself again and again. These polarities will come relentlessly, leaving you susceptible to choosing one and attempting to discard the other: innocence & experience, power & vulnerability, despair & hope, passivity & activity, dependence & independence, and clarity & mystery will be some of the visitors.

You begin to birth yourself by being mindful of your "native disposition," your origin. Such mindfulness is the tension of opposites. If you come from a Parsifalian beginning, then there is little or no presence of a father and a great deal of mother. Your natural inclination is to lean toward the hearth and not distant places. You know a strong maternal loyalty, and home is the cradle of your vision. Your polarities include naïveté & experience, submissiveness & contentiousness, innocence & understanding.

Triumphing over naïveté & experience means that a certain purity of heart maintains, while you allow yourself to grow closer to fate by acquiring experience. Triumphing over submissiveness & contentiousness means you have the ability to honor your limits while being able hold your ground and advance your strengths. Triumphing over innocence & understanding means you allow innocence to open you to the immensity of fate while allowing your curiosity to shed some level of understanding.

Opposites accompanying an Odyssean origin include timidity & boldness, cleverness & unknowing, independence & dependence. You triumph over timidity & boldness when you see how they slow you down, offering you a pace that accommodates reflection and acting with discretion. Triumph also means accepting boldness as a way of bringing yourself forward, notwithstanding the inertia presented by doubt.

Wisdom does not come to those who are satisfied with only one component of a polarity. Wisdom demands a whole story, not a partial one. Be aware of the seduction to praise independence and discard dependence in favor of some relief from the tension of these opposites. Living wisely means knowing and accepting that fate will be requesting that we carry some form of tension.

Of course, fate's magic and magnitude are revealed in the polarity of victory and defeat. These are fate's most powerful energies, and they constitute the most challenging training ground for the apprentice. Remaining unaware of how to creatively carry victory & defeat makes living wisely nearly impossible.

You are neither victory nor defeat. Parsifal carried defeat by not lamenting his failure. Like him, you can get on with your duties, attending to your soul's task rather than drown in self-pity. Parsifal does not succumb to arrogance and self-aggrandizement by destroying each foe. Rather, he sends his defeated opponent back to serve Arthur—a cause bigger than himself. Find your Arthur!

Odysseus learned to triumph over defeat & victory. Find your Odysseus within you, and you have the power to triumph over victory by acknowledging the will of the gods playing some role in all of your achievements. Triumphing over defeat by kneeling in the sand of Calypso's island, lost in deep sorrow, with no hope of finding home. With your cunning and cleverness being of no use, may you be similarly blessed by Athena's compassionate assistance.

7

Confirming What Truly Matters

All things are filled full of signs, and it is a wise man who can learn about one thing from another.

–Plotinus

It was a Monday morning, the day after I attended a Matthew Fox workshop. Normally I would still be glowing from having been in the presence of a man who devotes his life to the pursuit of the Sacred. But as I left my office, heading toward the kitchen, I felt a tremor that I realized was an aftershock from the weekend. Fox has suggested we consider holding a single breath as sacred. In that moment, I did not know how to attribute sacredness to such a simple act. Yet the more I approached my kitchen, the more I wondered whether I truly wanted to hold such an act as sacred. This single troublesome thought limped into my mind, somewhat veiled.

I poured a glass of lemonade. The second sip made my esophagus spasm. I could not breathe. I was home alone and immediately realized that I could not depend upon anyone to help me. I proceeded to bellow out a series of sounds, accompanied by a range of bodily gyrations. The clock was ticking. I became more frantic and swung open the front door of our home as if I intended to go somewhere. The moment I reached the front steps, my esophagus returned to normal, allowing the passage of air.

I sat there holding vigil, as if the steps had somehow restored life to my lungs. Of course, I was profoundly grateful for that single breath. As Plotinus predicted, there would be signs. Was my spasming esophagus a sign? Was this what I needed to go through to learn how not to dismiss the banal as sacred? Would I be able to hold the sacredness of a single breath the way I did in that moment? Was I learning the way of the fool who needs to return again and again to some lesson that eludes its own obviousness? Or had my institutional, religious upbringing debilitated my ability to long for contact with the Sacred? Did I need to struggle for air just to allow myself to be touched by the Sacred? At this point, it may be helpful to remind ourselves of some old meanings of the very word *sacred*.

Some Old Meanings

It is too easy to think we have moved beyond using terms like "the Sacred." Perhaps you have been disillusioned by clergy members who professed being above all things lecherous and perverse, only to discover them acting out sexually in a number of devious ways. Or maybe you have grown weary of religion's inability to offer authentic psychological scaffolding. Too much fire and brimstone scorches us emotionally. It may be that no matter how disappointed we have been with our religious experiences, our longing for the Sacred flows freely through our DNA. Our first old definition of the word *sacred* tells of an intimate connection: "to confirm or ordain what truly matters." Such is the ongoing invitation to the apprentice who remains devoted to confirming what truly matters.

This lofty yet modest undertaking of confirming what truly matters exists in an unyielding paradox. In the words of Emerson: "To the poet, to the philosopher, to the saint, all things are friendly and sacred, all events profitable, all days holy, all men divine." Let us look at the notion of "confirming" from two different perspectives. **First, there is the process of confirming, which includes the exploration, inquiry, frustrations, dead ends, and abiding care of continual seeking. Second, there is the confirmation, a conclusion that some value or principle holds the station of truly mattering.** Emerson's suggestion that everything is sacred points us to the first view of "confirming" as the quest for what truly matters.

John, a 52-year-old trainer and consultant, had been working with me for some time when he came across Emerson's quote and was racking his brain over it.

"I think I've got it!" John exclaimed, his right fist clenched and pumping upward to signal his accomplishment.

"Well then, tell me what has gotten clear for you," I responded.

"It has a lot to do with that idea of psychological ecology we spoke about a few weeks ago. I understand that all my experiences, friends, foes, victories, and defeats can be viewed as raw material, helping me, guiding me in the direction of the Sacred," John explained.

"Yes, I recall our discussion. But I'm wondering if anything happened that made Emerson's quote more lucid for you."

"Oh yeah. Do you remember that group I told you about that had a few members eager to scapegoat me?"

"Yes, I do. I recall that it was painful for you," I added.

"Well, it was hurtful. One guy who wanted to apprentice with me influenced some folks in my training program. I refused to let him in. He spread the word that I had it in for him. The truth was that I kind of liked the guy but that he simply wasn't ready for such a rigorous level of training," John explained.

"Sounds like some people believed this fellow," I suggested.

"Yes, several people believed him, dropped out of the training, and actually attempted to persuade others not to join."

"I remember how hurt you felt about being misrepresented. How has such a painful experience helped clarify Emerson?"

"I began to see how subtly I've invested in others being responsible for my worth. I received enough admiration and respect from people to distract myself from being clear about what I was doing about self-worth. Once rumors and stories misrepresenting me began circulating, I felt defeated, hurt, angry, and vindictive. I wanted justice! I finally came to see and accept that the situation was asking me to take much greater responsibility for my personal value. I began to understand how even my foes were helping me confirm what really matters," John explained, his cheeks and eyes softening and his tone carrying the assuredness of satisfaction.

As John left my office, I was aware that his story had moved me closer to understanding confirming what truly matters as an act of devotion rather than the making of any specific decision. I also understood a bit more about Plotinus's suggestion that the world "is full of signs" guiding our commitment to confirm what truly matters. Examples of such signs include sudden loss, illness, defeat, victory, depression, anxiety, conflict, feeling loved, feeling forgotten, betrayal, and a deep sense of belonging. We can think of these signs as the Sacred eagerly seeking our attention.

160   *Paul Dunion*

I recently received such a sign when the static of tinnitus in my right ear grew louder—a significant irritation for someone highly introverted like me who takes solace in silence. As I shaved on the morning of my 71st birthday, I felt scorn and condemnation for my failing organ. Suddenly I made eye contact with myself in the mirror, only to realize how attached I was to generating static in the first place.

My days were filled with cognitive perseveration, excessive rumination, analysis, visioning and projecting, judging and wondering. I decided that my tinnitus was a sign asking me to be much more discerning about what to fill my head with and to hold faith that more will be revealed. I immediately felt relief, letting go of a measure of urgency to figure it all out.

Jacob of the Old Testament received his own sign in the form of a nightlong wrestling match, calling him to confirm what truly matters. Such a process is never supposed to be easy. Confirming what truly matters reflects one of the most profound wrestling matches of the human condition, as fate will surely announce what it deems important. We create meaningful relationships in the hope they will last. But then we find ourselves feeling betrayed, if not also betraying someone we love or even ourselves. A second root meaning of the word *sacred* is "to sacrifice." Could it be that when we confirm what truly matters, we will be asked to sacrifice something as a matter of course? Perhaps moving in that direction necessarily involves conflict and sacrifice.

Jacob's Story

Around the middle of the 8th century BCE, we find one of the first written accounts of wrestling quite literally with the Sacred:

"That night Jacob got up and took his two wives, his two female servants and his eleven sons and crossed the ford of the Jabbok. After he had sent them across the stream, he sent over all his possessions. So Jacob was left alone, and a man wrestled with him till daybreak. When the man saw that he could not overpower him, he touched the socket of Jacob's hip so that his hip was wrenched as he wrestled with the man. Then the man said, 'Let me go, for it is daybreak.'
But Jacob replied, 'I will not let you go unless you bless me.'
The man asked him, 'What is your name?'

'Jacob,' he answered.

The man said, 'Your name will no longer be Jacob, but Israel, because you have struggled with God and with humans and have overcome.'"

(Genesis 32:22-31, New International Version)

Who is He?

In this portion of Jacob's story, he has treated his twin brother, Esau, deceitfully and with manipulation, and now fears Esau's revenge. The name *Jacob*, in fact, means "supplanter" or "heel catcher," the latter in reference to the fact that he was born grabbing hold of Esau's heel. We need not demonize Jacob for these qualities. His story shows us that deception is issued not only to us but also by us. We are the ones who deceive ourselves.

This story further suggests that the ego will invariably refuse to live life on life's terms, employing deception and cunning whenever possible. We are told that Jacob prays a fervent prayer, asking the Lord for help. This plea for divine intervention stems from his fear of an inevitable defeat at the hands of his brother, resulting in a nightlong wrestling match. Why does this wrestling match ensue? What is its purpose?

To Wrestle or Not to Wrestle

Our wrestling opponent comes to us by way of fate. It is therefore no coincidence that the word *fate*, as we have already explored, was originally defined as "will of the gods." We might expand that notion to include the will of others (as permitted by the gods) and even the diseases and other destructive forces of Nature. Deciding we must surrender to fate may be a naïve spiritual axiom. St. John of the Cross reminds us that what we desire will not always line up with fate or the will of the gods when he writes, "No man of himself can succeed in voiding himself of all his desires in order to come to God." And so, we wrestle. There may be a spiritual motivation to discover who we are by bringing our desire to bear against the forces of fate.

The word wrestle comes from the word *wrest*, meaning "to twist." If you have ever wrestled someone or witnessed wrestling, you will know it involves various limbs twisting, intertwined and entangled any number of ways. Unless the wrestlers are engaged in mortal combat, this form of contact is distinctly intimate. It is one contorted embrace after another. The goal is not to conquer but to explore the contours and edges, the strengths and weaknesses, the beginnings and endings of each combatant. There is neither victor nor loser in this dynamic encounter. Is Jacob's story asking us to remain in a dynamic encounter with fate to confirm the Sacred?

Jacob wrestles throughout the night. How is he to know whether his opponent is his brother seeking revenge or one of his brother's men, a drunken goatherder or some manifestation of the Sacred? Such is the metaphorical power of Jacob's nocturnal brawl. As we raise our curiosities and wonderings about what truly matters, we inescapably become entangled with assumptions that are obscure and ineffable.

Whether our opponent is a drunken goatherder or the Sacred, we wrestle all the same. So long as we bring open hearts and minds to the brawl, we may discover some aspect of the Sacred in the drunken goatherder. We struggle with fate, with all that is out of our control, all the while attempting to determine what is truly important. We never begin such a clash knowing the true nature of our opponent. We only come to know our contender by the robust nature of the encounter. The drunken goatherder may be someone who once helped us or in some way reminds us of who we are. It is all too easy to dismiss who or what does not possess style and appeal.

Let us examine some possible examples of real-life wrestling with fate. Do we dare attempt to heal a relationship after being betrayed? Do we choose to abort a fetus in order to preserve a way of life for ourselves? Do we withhold a secret, not knowing if disclosure will enhance or damage a relationship? Do we remain in a job that pays well but is a constant source of emotional depletion? Do we remain stressed by keeping a disabled child at home, knowing that institutionalization will likely result in diminished care? Is it possible to recover faith in life after the death of one's own child? Is it possible to find love after being deeply hurt? How do pacifists decide whether or not to employ violence when they fear some political or military force will inflict immense harm to their children and their children's children? All these acts of fate call us to wrestle with uncertainty and ambiguity, hopefully in the direction of the Sacred.

Most wrestling takes place in a few minutes and ends with combatants rolling over in exhaustion. Jacob's skirmish lasts throughout the night, suggesting that clarity requires resilience and stamina. Time and time again, we believe we have a grip on what truly matters, only to notice it slipping away as the altercation moves to a new level. Each twist and turn of feeling and thought moves us away from, or closer to, what truly matters. All the while, we wonder whether we have our hands on a drunken goatherder or the Sacred.

Jacob's story may be telling us that we discover the Sacred only by our willingness to wrestle long and hard. Wrestling suggests intimate contact. We show up with our desire and engage what others bring to us, as well as what Nature advances. In our quest to touch and be touched by the Sacred, we wish neither to destroy nor be destroyed. We intimately allow ourselves to get twisted up with fate. We lose ourselves tumbling with life. We deepen our intimate connection with fate as we grow curious about what this twisting and tumbling is all about.

What is fate asking of us? We are curious about sacrifices to be made, blessings we might seek. We inquire about the lessons trying to reach us as a result of our wrestling with fate. Yet we must bring enough of ourselves to the encounter, along with the discernment to know when enough is enough and shift into surrender.

It may be that, in the mayhem of the wrestling, you roll to the edge of a deep ravine, holding on for dear life with one hand. Suddenly, your opponent pulls you to safety. As you lie there, gasping for breath against a constricted chest, still bracing for a disastrous plunge, you notice that your savior is a drunken goatherder. In that moment, the chasm between the profane nature of the goatherder and the Sacred swiftly closes.

The Honoring

The honoring of a relationship is marked by a curious and compassionate involvement, accompanied by resilience – In any relationship, we can ask: Is there too much of me in this relationship? Is there not enough of me? These are the only questions to which we can remain mindful and corrective. There is no perfect level of participation. The same holds true of our relationship with fate. If there is not enough of us in the relationship, then we have restricted our participation, which does not reflect an honoring and a gratitude.

We feel victimized by fate when we believe our only recourse is to restrict our participation. This feeling of victimization is often joined by self-pity and cynicism, both of which erode an intimate connection with fate. If we bring an inordinate amount of our wills to bear upon our experience, then we are negating the power of fate. Fate finds ways to address our arrogance, cunning, and narcissism, all of which we uphold as ways to avoid fate's immensity. Fate appears to remind Jacob of its size by wounding his hip, giving him a lasting memory of their relationship.

Jacob's fortitude and resilience are acknowledged as his opponent decides he cannot overpower Jacob. I appreciate the man's understanding of his inability to simply overpower Jacob. Rather, he wishes for the engagement to remain intimate, with no excessive use of power. Such a choice may be what confirms his opponent's sacredness. He does, of course, permanently injure Jacob's hip. Jacob's gait is forever marked by this intimate engagement with fate. Are we being reminded that to be born into the human condition is to be injured by fate, and that this injury will, of course, eventually kill us?

Jacob refuses to let go of his adversary until he agrees to bless him. An old definition of the word *bless* is "to make sacred via sacrificial offering." What to make of Jacob's wrestling ending with a request for blessing? Is it possible the request itself is what sanctifies whatever we have been pulling and pushing against? To be sure, Jacob could have ended the wrestling with a fit of accusations and complaints. Instead, he makes a request for blessing, thereby sanctifying his life. What might such a request imply and what can we take away from this story to benefit our own lives?

Acknowledging that *fate* ("will of the gods") possesses a power worthy of reverence – Jacob's request for blessing suggests he knows his fellow combatant has the power to ordain the sacredness of his life in a way he cannot. I must continually return to acknowledging the sacredness of a single breath, how it blesses me and all it provides for me. My gratitude for a single breath is a way to bless the breath. Jacob's request is also itself a blessing of his adversary. In both cases, Jacob and I have set out on the path of deconstructing arrogance.

Deconstructing arrogance – We are all prone to self-inflation. It happens in moments of passion, anger, exuberance, or enthusiasm. Inflation turns into arrogance when driven by fear and employed as a psychological defense. Jacob's reliance on his cunning suggests the presence of arrogance.

Deconstruction of arrogance informs Jacob about his limits. He can then have a more honest relationship with himself and better assess what he is capable of bringing to his relationship with fate. He does not defeat his opponent, because by having his resilience confirmed, his limits are also demonstrated. Arrogance delivers too much of ourselves into our encounters with fate. It arms us against being informed and touched by life in general, and specifically protects from the will of others. We can bring an overbearing amount of our intentions, beliefs, and accounts of our achievements to whatever life presents us. Arrogance severely disables the apprentice's receptivity to the unknown.

Some time ago, I was having coffee with an old friend, passionately explaining some new insights I was exploring. Suddenly my friend raised his hand in an unequivocal gesture, directing me to stop.

"I'm finding you to be extremely formidable!" he exclaimed, igniting my curiosity about his reaction.

"I've never been described as formidable. Can you say more about what it is that has you experiencing me as formidable?" I added, knowing my friend's feedback would be valuable.

"Well, you sound like you really know what you're talking about. You're laying down some heavy concepts, and you set a very rapid pace of delivery," he offered, his tone neither mitigating how overwhelmed he felt nor in any way condemning my demeanor.

I realized I was laying myself on too thickly for our meeting, burdening our connection in the process. I was dancing too fast to support a mutually engaged rhythm. There was simply too much of me at that table. My friend struggled to find his own vision beneath the weight of my inflated exuberance. If he could not find himself, then I certainly would not be able to find him. Had he not spoken up, I would have kept on as I had been, coffee mug in hand, deluded into believing some kind of meaningful exchange was taking place. This was not the first time the volume of my voice eclipsed any attachment to an authentic encounter with a friend. Nor, I imagine, will it be the last.

Unfortunately, when arrogance is infused with charisma, a simple articulation or gesture can become quite impressive. When that happens, it is highly unlikely that the speaker will receive the kind of valuable feedback offered to me by my friend. Arrogance divides. When employed as an unconscious defense, it separates us from others and from ourselves. We are ignorant of the need to be larger than our actual size, set apart from the fear that there will not be enough room for us as we relate to others, as well as from the fear of our own limitations. As arrogance swells, occluding our vision with alleged self-importance, we lose the ability to experience others as they are. We no longer know whom we are encountering. Our inflation further prevents us from feeling any genuine empathy as we distance ourselves from our hearts, caught in waves of irrepressible rhetoric.

The defense of arrogance intensifies when we live convinced that downsizing ourselves will render us unnoticed, forgotten, and hurt. In order to deconstruct the unconscious use of arrogance as a defense mechanism, we must become mindful of our fear. We must learn to feel the fear, speak the truth of the fear, and, little by little, learn to be present so that we may be seen, heard, and remembered. Healing arrogance allows us to live more genuinely. **Intimacy with fate is impossible if we encounter it disingenuously, as through excessive inflation. Such intimacy calls for resilience and a capacity for surrender as we open ourselves to an encounter with the Sacred.**

Jacob's story is about resilience. He is an apprentice of surrender. His resilience, born of arrogance and boldness, is challenged by his nocturnal brawl, which informs him that being bold and knowing when to surrender are more than enough to support his relationship with fate. All of which is epitomized in his balancing of blessing and sacrifice.

Blessing and Sacrifice

The image of Jacob's injured hip shows that fate blesses us by asking for sacrifice. It is not to be taken personally. It is just the way of it. Being able to declare what truly matters depends on our relationship to what is sacrificed. Upon receiving his blessing, Jacob is told, "[Y]ou have struggled with God and with humans and have overcome." A superficial understanding of overcome would be an act of triumph over some external force. A deeper meaning might be the encouragement to bring as much of ourselves as we can muster to lived experience, overcoming timidity or excessive yielding. Also, overcoming the temptation to descend into self-pity when fate brings us to some undesirable place, as well as overcoming the temptation to turn against fate. Another expression of overcoming would be moving beyond a self-preoccupation that would have us forget about gratitude and a request for blessing from that which is larger than us. Jacob's adversary changes the meaning of his name to Israel, or "he who struggles with God." We can understand struggling and prevailing to reflect Jacob's resilience, remaining intimate with fate, resulting in contact with the Sacred.

Wrestling with fate is a deeply intimate act, characterized by a rich level of involvement, challenging us to decide if we are engaging a drunken goatherder or the Sacred itself. The nature of our encounter with fate determines its quality. A drunken goatherder, for instance, herds his goats across our campsite, destroying much of our equipment. We choose to focus on his carelessness. But imagine we trip and fall into a ravine with no way of signaling for help. That same drunken goatherder stumbles across us, struggling against the disorientation of his intoxication, and manages to pull us to safety. Now we stand there, gazing into the eyes of our savior with a gratitude that transforms the goatherder into something born of the Sacred.

Our entanglement is reflected in our use of verbs in the language we have been exploring. **Confirming, sacrificing, wrestling, prevailing, and blessing all denote action. Another action is surrendering to the Sacred when we have exhausted our internal resources.** As in any relationship, both sides thrive when we avoid turning against ourselves or against fate. Jacob's story suggests that a request for blessing needs to be accompanied by resilience and surrender in equal measure. Otherwise, we fail to honor our willingness to be involved. We fail to honor the will of the gods, cloaked in mystery though their will may be. Our resilience allows us to wrestle and request a blessing that ultimately sanctifies fate and our own lives within it.

Being Bold

Remaining an apprentice to the unknown calls for boldness. Fate will come calling with its challenges and upsets. Unless we are bold, we run the risk of becoming excessively yielding, believing the only way to meet fate is by avoidance and/or adaption, sacrificing the power of our wills. Such a path condemns us to be chained to infantilism. Attempting to avoid fate excludes the necessary wrestling that may grant us an encounter with the Sacred.

It is vital to distinguish arrogance from boldness. Arrogance is an inflation of ego, driven by fear. Its aim is to secure the high ground before someone usurps desired terrain and leaves nothing for us. Arrogance has no clue where true north is. Lost in its hunger for inflation, the arrogant self struggles to understand what it means to be submerged in ignorance. Trust ceases to exist.

A root meaning of the word *boldness* is "confidence." But even that can be misleading. Very often in our culture, confidence implies excessive self-reliance, cockiness, an inordinate amount of bravado. It may help to shed some of our swagger by recalling the old Latin definition of the word *confidence*: "with trust."

Being bold entails acting with trust. Trusting ourselves and trusting fate. Again, old meanings are helpful. The word *trust* can denote "a willingness to enter into a covenant." It may be that we learn to trust ourselves only when we are willing to enter into a covenant with ourselves. The following are certain types of agreements on which we might build such a covenant.

Self-Trust

Self-trust involves holding two distinct beliefs about ourselves. First, we allow ourselves to know what matters to us and what we desire. This level of self-trust calls for a certain degree of courage since giving voice to what we believe may disrupt the status quo.

Although my father and I had a turbulent relationship during my adolescence, I recall a time when I was 15 that reminded me my father was more than I had considered. He often frequented the local VFW, where he took great pleasure in telling stories about his days in the service while enjoying several cold draft brews. It was a Wednesday evening in early December, the chill offering new invitation to step out into the bite of twilight, with snow predicted by dawn. I was in my room pretending to do homework when I heard the kitchen door open. It was my father, returning from the VFW. Instead of his usual loud entry, I heard my mother say, "What's wrong, Bill?"

As I made my way downstairs, I anticipated his response to my mother's curiosity, but none came. When I finally reached the bottom of the stairs, I stepped into a heavy silence, the weight of which seemed to push down on my chest and shoulders. The atmosphere only thickened as my father passed by me, his upper body bent forward as if he were straining to hold himself up. I knew what drunkenness looked like, but this was something else entirely.

I thought it best to refrain from asking my mother what was going on. I was unsure of how much she knew anyway, since nothing had been said. I decided to wait until morning, after my father had left for work, to express my curiosity.

"What happened last night?" I asked, rushing through a bowl of cereal before catching my bus to school.

"Your father decided to speak out against the war in Vietnam down at the VFW. It was a crazy thing to do," she added, thrusting each dish she was washing into the sink with increasing vigor.

"Maybe he really believes we shouldn't be in Vietnam," I suggested.

"That's great! Maybe he does, but why does he have to let everyone know about it at the VFW?" she objected. Dishwater flowed over the side of the sink. Her apron looked like it needed to be wrung out.

"I don't know. That's where he usually lets guys know what's on his mind," I pointed out, feeling a bit protective of my father as I imagined the reactions from other Vets.

"That's great! Let folks know what's on his mind without thinking about how they might see him and his family members," she protested.

"Well, I'd better get going. I don't want to miss the bus," excusing myself in the hope of making it out of the kitchen without being unfavorably impacted by my mother's torrent of emotion and water.

Years later, I would come to understand my father's boldness better and his idyllic perception of the VFW as a forum for the exchange of diverse opinions. I also gained a better understanding of what it means to risk ties with folks who hold views different from our own.

The second portion of our covenant with ourselves is the commitment to treat ourselves kindly. Trust for ourselves strengthens when we interrupt self-incriminating broodings. Overattachment to stories of personal shortcomings is unkind. Kindness liberates us from perfectionistic aspirations. Striving for perfection guarantees deep feelings of inadequacy and constitutes an assault on our essential humanity.

A pledge to treat ourselves kindly entails commitment to self-forgiveness. The covenant is about reclaiming our goodness when we have made a mistake or acted contrary to our values. A violation of our values incurs feelings of shame and guilt. When I take up residency for a protracted period in shame, a colleague often asks, "Do you believe you should've been larger than your mistake?" Of course, the answer is "Yes."

Her question creatively penetrates the wall of shame separating me from my worthiness. Arrogance has me believing I should have been larger, postponing my ability to feel good about myself. Living boldly becomes more of a genuine alternative when we take seriously the responsibility of self-forgiveness.

I recently had the opportunity to witness expressions of boldness in my office. Jed had been working with me for a year and was in the middle of a divorce. He expressed concern over his 15-year-old daughter and the impact the divorce may be having on their relationship. He requested a session with his daughter, which I was more than willing to accommodate.

A week later, he and his daughter stepped into my office. "Paul, this is my daughter Lisa; Lisa, this is Paul," the introduction went. Lisa shook my hand, her head tilted down and away from me.

I was aware of Lisa entering a strange space, with little or no reason to trust me, other than the fact that her father spent time with me regularly. Jed took the lead, explaining why he had invited her to the session and what he hoped to accomplish, which felt like a good way to initiate our meeting. Having no idea how much Lisa would be willing to participate, I kept my expectations as low as her posture.

"How do you feel about our relationship lately?" Jed asked.

"Well, not just lately, but I have felt distant from you for a long time," Lisa responded, lifting her chin to face her father.

I was struck by the lack of hesitation in her response, as if she had been waiting for the opportunity to speak her truth.

"Can you tell me how long it has been that you've been feeling distant from me?" invited her father, the furrows of his forehead deepening and his upper torso leaning forward.

"I watch you interact with Stevie [Lisa's younger brother]. You ride bikes together, swim, skateboard, play baseball, and hike. You get excited about hanging out with him. You look forward to it!" asserted Lisa, the volume of her voice making it clear how much she was saying about her father and herself.

I was hearing a declaration that had been germinating long after it should have come forward. I decided to let it sit and be held by a silence, honoring the depth of heart that Lisa had offered. I then turned to her, noticing a single teardrop on her right cheek, and asked, "Do you feel forgotten by your father?"

Lisa turned to her father. "I feel forgotten by you," she quickly disclosed, more tears following the first.

"Can you tell your father again what you just said?" I added.

"I feel forgotten by you, I feel forgotten by you, I feel forgotten by you!" tears flowing over the banks of any resistance with which she may have entered the officed.

I knew I was hearing the bold voice of a teenager, risking the unknown reaction of her father. I was also hearing the voices of the hundreds of women who had sat in my office before, feeling forgotten by their fathers yet never boldly declaring that displeasure directly. It was a sacred moment for the three of us.

Jed shared his regret with Lisa, letting her know that he wanted her to feel heard, seen, and understood by him. There was no rationalization or justification for how he might have contributed to his daughter's feelings of neglect. He simply and boldly offered acceptance of her experience. After some initial resistance on Lisa's part to how they might spend more time together, they made plans.

As the session ended, Lisa stood, squared her shoulders, and made direct eye contact with me, saying, "It was good to meet you." In those words, she conveyed something much larger than a cordial gesture.

I returned the acknowledgement, thinking silently to myself, "You spoke for many today," hoping the fullness of my respect for her might channel itself through our handshake. Like anyone acting boldly, Lisa chose to enlarge herself, risking exposure of a significant personal truth in the process. She was likely scared of being criticized or unheard. Yet her fear was not driven by a need to impress or usurp the moment before someone else grabbed it. Boldness carries a significant level of heart and therefore courage.

Lisa's father also expanded beyond the defensive fortifications of his ego. He boldly accepted Lisa's truth, attempting neither to offer a self-serving account of what had happened nor to talk her out of her reality. In lamenting her experience of feeling forgotten by him, he moved into exploring possible remedies for their situation. On some level, he was humbly accepting the limits and challenges of being a father. Humility calls for such boldness. It means letting go of an inflated story about our strengths and abilities that denies our limits.

A Covenant with Fate

Living boldly means living in a covenant with fate. Our first task is to suspend parental projections to the will of the gods. It is too easy to decide that fate is either a good or bad parent. The next step is to avoid get snared into believing that fate will treat us kindly if only we can be good children. This kind of pseudo-agreement ruptures our relationship with fate's mystery, so that when tragedy strikes, we are left despondent in the depths of bad faith. But if we refuse to fall prey to infantilism, obedient to Daddy fate, then we will have a more creative relationship with suffering and tragedy. Let us, then, explore what it means to remain in a covenant with fate.

Including the Dark

Thomas Moore reminds us to integrate tragedy or darkness: "To integrate it is to co-opt it into the light. The real task is to live in, and with, the darkness, appreciating its unredeemed value and loving its irreversible qualities. What is needed is a view of life that includes the dark." When fate offers insecurity and unpredictability, it will be critical to our covenant that we address what it means to create "a view of life that includes the dark."

Fate makes only one promise: endless opportunities to heal and learn. We include the dark only when we acknowledge and accept this promise of fate. Opportunities to heal and learn are characterized by brokenness and getting lost. The ego recoils from either prospect. It wants no suggestion that might undermine the well-constructed charade of its self-importance. When we deny our wound, we reject fate's offering of a chance to heal and learn. We violate any possible covenant with fate.

We are often called to endure a significant amount of pain before we can accept some emotional injury. The ego must come to its knees, struggling to hold its worth as a wounded entity.

Jane, a 44-year-old physician's assistant, came to see me about some recent losses. She was leaving a relationship in which she felt deeply neglected and betrayed. She was also grieving the loss of an older sister with whom she had a deep connection. I initially believed we would be working on those two losses. But in light of her perpetual smile and posture, which suggested an exuberant invitation for engagement, I decided there must be a deeper wound asking for our attention.

"I experience you as very *on*," I offered, thinking that after three sessions, we had developed enough rapport to welcome that kind of feedback.

"What do you mean by *on*?" she asked, her tone suggesting that curiosity had outweighed her fear.

"I experience you as working very hard, unnecessarily hard, when you're with me," I added.

"Working hard at what?" she questioned, her curiosity building.

"Well, I guess working hard at impressing me, attempting to demonstrate that you're likable, maybe that you're a good client, or maybe just soliciting my approval." I wondered what she would do with that information. To my surprise, she immediately generalized my feedback and said, "I'm always working this hard."

Her response told me she was ready to explore how hard she worked when relating to others. She confirmed her readiness by asking, "If I wasn't on so much, then what would it look like to be *off*?" Her voice softened, shoulders dropping back into the seat as her breath became more measured.

I began by describing what I just witnessed as subtle characteristics of being off. She seemed to understand and wanted to offer an account of her origin of being on. She explained that when she was 14, she feared her shyness would lead to invisibility. She was afraid of going unnoticed, so she amped up her displays of sensuality in a strategic attempt to become more seductive. Her physical attractiveness ensured she would be noticed and convinced her this was the way to go. She acknowledged taking her game plan into adulthood and wondered about its implications.

"When you lead with an exuberance of sensual energy, your strategy is present, but you're not. You're not available to really be seen, joined, and loved," I offered, as she quietly wept, seemingly feeling the pain of her losses.

Jane was learning about a grief that stretched far beyond the recent losses of her sister and her boyfriend. She was coming to terms with having lost herself in the dense fog of her dramatic displays. She was now learning about living her sensuality in more non-strategic and grounded ways.

Our work reached a new level when I suggested that she was not in my office to relate to me, but to have a relationship with herself in my presence. For Jane, having a relationship with herself in anyone's presence became her mantra for being off. I once again felt the honor of being in the presence of someone who was renewing her covenant with fate.

A Blessing for the One
Who Wrestles with the Sacred

Let Jacob's namesake show you the way to the Sacred. He is the supplanter, and therein lies your invitation to what truly matters. Come to know the wrestling that goes on between self-deception and authenticity. That very tussle constitutes the birth of the Sacred.

Welcome your shame, your fear, your need for revenge, and your vulnerability. Your ego will gladly knock you down in deference to self-deception rather than some radical sense of honesty. Let the brawl begin. You fight with Jacob's blessing.

There will be much pushing, pulling, squeezing, and twisting as you seek what truly matters about who you are. Much along the way will be disguised as the Sacred. As you become more honest about yourself, so you become more honest about what happens around you.

You have exercised a bold covenant, initially consummated with cunning and now with a reverence for what visits you. And so you gain a devotion to both your interior world and the world around you.

Like Jacob, you are no longer called the deceiver. Now, you are the one who struggles with the gods and with humans and have overcome. You have overcome a dissuading timidity, overcome a pride once preventing you from asking for blessing from those acquainted with what truly matters.

8

Knowing and Unknowing

An apprentice needs a teacher who himself has charmed
the universe to reveal its wonders inside his cup.

–Hafiz

I came to my knees, again and again. Sometimes, collapsing under a torrent of helplessness; at other times, after spending an inordinate amount of time and energy blaming myself and/or others. I found gratification in cursing the gods. The tension generated by the knowing/unknowing polarity was crushing me. My challenge was not a simple matter of ignorance. It was about finding a way in which I could trust and on which I could depend.

The power of this polarity descended on me in an exorbitant fashion when my daughter Sarah was diagnosed shortly after birth with a rare neurological disorder. We would discover that, although she was quite intelligent, she would be nonverbal and unable to control her bodily movements. Sometimes the roles we play have an unforgiving demand for knowing. How could we know how to best support Sarah and her siblings, as well as our marriage? Who were the most effective external resources? How would we know the kind of education that would best serve Sarah? How would we know when we had done enough? What would it take not to institutionalize her?

My relationship with alcohol inflated what I actually knew, disabling the power of curiosity, wonder, and acceptance. When a counselor confronted me about my drinking, I found myself again in the grips of a polar tension. How could I really know whether alcohol was an actual problem for me? And even if I did admit it to be a problem, how was I to go about addressing it? How could I know how to identify who would serve as genuine resources? How would I know how to cope without alcohol? If I chose sobriety, would it be appropriate to return to controlled drinking? Only with the help of folks willing to support me was I able to trust responding to these questions while remaining genuinely curious about their outcomes.

Another bout with the depths of knowing/unknowing would come years later when the decision of what to do with a twenty-five-year-old marriage came bearing down on me. I was faced with the challenge of feeling deeply committed to healing a marriage while also devoted to my best understanding of the relationship I wanted to be in. What kind of knowing would allow me to step away from years of devotion? Had I done everything possible to heal the marriage? How could I know it was right to stop asking my spouse to participate in a relationship that did not serve her? Was I simply being too self-centered?

Of course, it would take countless episodes of bewilderment before I could address the tension permeating this polarity of knowing/unknowing. My principal learning has been and continues to be: Do not attempt to carry the tension of the knowing/unknowing polarity alone. Learn to identify those who can help and seek them out. Even with good help, being able to discern what constitutes good knowing calls for a willingness to create a personal epistemology.

Good Knowing

The prefix *episteme* comes from the Greek meaning "knowledge" while the suffix *ology* means "study or learning." A personal epistemology is no different than a personal morality, spirituality, or work ethic. When constructing a personal morality, it is paramount to clarify and distinguish between the values of others and those we can rightly call our own. The guiding values of our personal moralities inform the way we live. Personal spiritualities give direction to life choices.

Here are some focus questions for constructing a personal epistemology: Am I willing to be honest about when I'm pretending to know something? How do I feel about making a significant change in regard to what I decide I know? How do I feel about myself when I do not know? How do I feel about myself when others know I don't know? How do I feel about holding some belief distinctly different from what is commonly believed? How do I decide what's valuable information when drawing some conclusion about what I know? How do I feel when others agree with what I decide I know? How do I decide that some belief needs to be held fervently? How do I feel about the level of curiosity I live with? Am I willing to be a servant of truth? Am I willing to devotionally seek the best version of the truth?

It does not serve us to be cavalier about how we go about knowing, for this is the cornerstone of our belief system. It means caring about how knowing takes place for us and wanting to learn about how we decide on knowing. If we are going to reconcile the knowing/unknowing polarity, then we must be willing to construct a personal epistemology. Coming to know the knower is the first step toward good knowing.

We live in a time when our understanding of good knowing has slipped into crisis. Existential psychologist Rollo May reminds us that we are condemned to an approximation of the truth. That is not to say that universal or absolute truth does not exist, only that the human condition limits us to our best version of the truth. It is therefore important to ask ourselves: How do we respond to the unavailability of absolute truth? How do we remain loyal to our questions?

"I beg you, to have patience with everything unresolved in your heart and to try to love the questions themselves as if they were locked rooms or books written in a very foreign language. Don't search for the answers, which could not be given to you now, because you would not be able to live them. And the point is to live everything. Live the questions now. Perhaps then, someday far in the future, you will gradually, without even noticing it, live your way into the answer" (Rainer Maria Rilke). As apprentices, we are always learning how to live our way into the answer.

Narcissism and Nihilism

Two examples of the current crisis against good knowing are narcissism and nihilism. Both are increasingly popular responses to the elusive nature of absolute truth and inhibit our ability to "live our way into an answer." **Narcissism prevails when we decide we are entitled to believe whatever we want.** Of course, whatever we want is usually defined by what serves the needs of the ego at any given moment. Because the ego is obsessed with looking good, we contort ourselves into a position that underpins that very obsession.

As the self-serving position grows stronger, any implication that said position may be detrimental to others or to the earth itself is dismissed. **Nihilism abounds when we decide there's nothing actually truthful to know.** When ultimate truth is dismissed, narcissistic liberties are unleashed. As Ken

Wilber would have it: "Nihilism and narcissism bring evolution to a traffic-jam halt." Thus, any devotion to genuine inquiry is interrupted.

One such liberty is the exaggeration of data to inflate the achievements or knowledge of the speaker. I suggest that when exaggeration is used as an expression of deception, it is a lie. Exaggeration helps the speaker look good, avoids accountability for a mistake, and diminishes the listeners. It is a sad day when leaders randomly employ exaggeration for the purpose of deception. Of course, exaggeration need not always deceive. The following are some examples of non-deceptive exaggeration.

Exaggeration can be used as a figure of speech with no intention of misleading: "It was as hot as the Sahara Desert." "I just know she'll never talk to me again!" "I must've gotten every question on the test wrong." "I've told you a million times what I want for our anniversary." None of these exaggerations is an accurate account of what actually happened but is a way of emphatically getting one's point across.

Imaginal Exaggeration

I was raised by Celtic storytellers, all of them masters of imaginal exaggeration. These men regularly interfaced their imaginations with concrete descriptions of personal experience. They believed wholeheartedly that any account of human experience worthy of being heard needed to be told from a vision of enchantment. Their tradition taught them that there were "thin places" where the temporal and the eternal sat side by side. They also believed in a "thin veil" between empirical reports of experience and the imaginal. Only when I was well into adulthood did I come to understand their artful use of exaggeration.

I have heard exaggerations described as hyperbole, which gives them a kind of sophistication. Exaggeration is not hyperbole. Hyperbole is a literary device aimed at enhancing the reader's visual experience of the written word. An example from Mark Twain: "I was quaking from head to foot, and could have hung my hat on my eyes, they stuck out so far."

Several aspects of imaginal exaggeration, as I experienced it, are worth noting. It was seldom employed to deceive or bring admiration to the storyteller. If ever he got lured into self-aggrandizement, he risked incurring the possibility of those gathered swooping down with an onslaught of references to the speaker's blunders and miscalculations. Everyone thought twice about bringing undue attention to some alleged competence. Speakers were well-versed in the afternoon's protocol, which was to help the audience live a more charmed life.

My grandfather, my father, and his brothers naturally conversed in the language of imaginal exaggeration, which had several purposes. Primary among them was to level any ideology or belief claiming sacrosanct status. Stories were typically woven with lavish outpourings of irreverence. No pretense could withstand the blitz of their disparaging remarks.

The second purpose of imaginal exaggeration was to entertain. Their stories regularly generated endless hilarity. Yet the entertainment meant more than the laughter it inspired. Each story reminded these men that their socioeconomic status would not relegate them to the junk heap. Politicians, bankers, and clergy were sure to experience a downsizing when these men gathered. The entertainment of this form of storytelling was also aimed at reducing the gravitas of life. Participants left each gathering more tolerant of jobs they believed did not reflect their innate skill set, even as they felt stung by the feeling of deserving more.

Imaginal exaggeration expressed in narrative allows the apprentice to lighten a connection to what fate brings. One's condemnation to some approximation of the truth is softened. We may live more easily with the best version of the truth we can muster, without needing to make outlandish claims of being in possession of something absolute. Imaginal exaggeration allows the apprentice to play, creating novel meanings and joy in response to the grueling nature of the unknown.

The How and What of Facts

We know we have drifted a long way from good knowing when we hear talk of "alternative facts." Such talk also suffers from narcissism and nihilism. There are no alternative facts. There are only alternative opinions. Facts are victims of an unfortunate dichotomy. Either they are exalted to the status of truth or reduced to mere opinion. When the former occurs, we dismiss the uncertainty that accompanies all facts. The finished product is "contrived certainty." When reduced to mere opinion, we create a factual free-for-all in which nihilism wins out over reliability and credibility.

Stuart Firestein, a noted neuroscientist, describes a fact: "Observations, measurements, findings, and results accumulate and at some point may gel into a fact." In saying as much, Firestein is describing the how of a fact. The key is to avoid being cavalier about the nature of observations, measurements, and findings. Good knowing means remaining curious about the nature of observations: Are they methodologically consistent? Are the observers diverse enough? Have they conducted their observations enough times to warrant a reliable predictability? How do measurements take place? What measuring devices are actually employed? Can anyone reproduce the measurements? Are there observers with different findings? What questions do the findings suggest?

The gelling is the what of a fact. The gelling includes some level of consensus, a level of comfort with the process or the how, a degree of confidence in the predictability of the findings, and a willingness to make decisions based on those findings. Here are some widely held facts: The sun offers light and energy. The moon orbits around the earth. Approximately 71% of Earth's surface is covered by water. Earth was formed around 4.5 billion years ago. Approximately eight million metric tons of plastic are dumped into oceans annually. Considering the latter, we can see that facts do not always compel us to make smart decisions.

Apprentices to the unknown are asked to remain mindful of the seduction of branding a fact with certainty. When a fact is branded with certainty, apprenticeship comes to a standstill. The apprentice falls prey to the ego's desire to deny or ignore ignorance. Good knowing is interested in what opinions are deserving of our attention and what facts seem commendable, while continuing to welcome the unknown.

The hard work of good knowing lies in our commitment to understand the one seeking knowledge, cognizant of hidden ignorance. Remaining curious, holding positions previously demonstrated as trustworthy, and boldly formulating new and evocative questions is far from easy. Let us look more closely at the hard work of genuine inquiry that is suspended and possibly brings evolution to a "traffic-jam halt" when we decide we can believe whatever we want.

The Hard Work

"The unexamined life is not worth living" (Socrates). I understand this Socratic claim as a warning against the dire consequences resulting from our refusal to examine the lives we create. To examine our lives, of course, is to know ourselves. Such a commitment offers intimate welcome to countless expressions of our characters. This welcome must be extended to what is decent and praiseworthy, as well as to parts of us deemed unfavorable and unscrupulous. **All that we are contributes to how we see and impacts how we respond to what we see.** We have suffered abuse, neglect, rejection, defeat, and success. All of these color our perceptions and our conclusions. As William Barrett avers: "We must be free for the truth; and conversely, to be able to be open toward the truth may be our deepest freedom as human creatures."

"Free for the Truth" – We might understand such freedom as the capacity to understand our experience in different ways and the ability to engender curiosity and intrigue. A root meaning of the word *wounded* is "to bump into." Since there are no perfect families, we either bump into too much, encountering parental abuse, or into too little, resulting in parental neglect. Unless we come to know the wound and the healing it asks for, we cannot free ourselves from defending against reinjury.

When we become entrenched in protecting ourselves against further harm, our defenses block pathways to inquisitive exploration. We are left with a distortion of truth, settling for something considerably less than the best version thereof. In the throes of distortion, we are unavailable to accept the best version of the truth. Below are seven defenses and their distortions:

1) **Dissociation** is a common defense we learn at home and various social institutions. Dissociation is a natural way to cope with the fear of being hurt. Emotions and internal sensations are translated into ideas and concepts. It is so much more vulnerable to have our hearts broken than it is to have someone disagree with us. The price for dissociation is the dismissal of deep feeling, which can inform us through instinct, intuition, and imagination. Dissociation prohibits us from being inspired by our body's wisdom.

2) **Rationalization** involves making up justifications and excuses to soften a hard truth. Say, for instance, that someone's mother is an alcoholic, but that instead of defining her disease, reference is made to her hard work and devotion to the needs of her children. Thus, rationalization inevitably leaves us with a distortion of the truth.

3) **Denial** is the first cousin of rationalization and is considerably more potent. Any expression of reality that feels excessive is simply

wiped out; it doesn't exist. Denial tends to spread into other areas as well. Families who deny a drug addict in their midst will likely also deny the abuse inflicted when that addiction is not met. Denial eliminates the possibility of being informed by whatever is denied, thus causing a significant distortion of reality.

4) Projection occurs when we ascribe to others whatever is challenging to accept about ourselves. We perceive others as petty, insensitive, and uncooperative to cleanse ourselves of those same characteristics we unconsciously continue to exhibit. Thus, we seriously limit knowing ourselves, fail to understand the origins of our darker attributes, and curtail the possibility of personal transformation.

5) Reaction formation is acting contrary to how we really feel, a compensation for whatever we have difficulty accepting about ourselves. We act with excessive bravado when we are scared, with domination when we feel insecure. A distortion is easily created, as we actually believe we are the compensation, which alienates us from the truth about who we are. Another example would be speaking out against gays when we feel called to own our own gay identity.

6) Idealization is the wearing of rose-colored glasses. Reality is dressed up to be more appealing. Again, the price is that we cannot learn from our experience because those proverbial glasses distort what reality actually is.

7) Anonymity protects us by concealing our deepest thoughts and feelings. It is difficult for others to hurt what they cannot see. We easily forget our inner world when trying to prevent some cherished part of our personality from accidentally stumbling into view. Estrangement from our deepest feelings and needs eliminates the inner landscape as a resource for learning. We cease to live a self-examined life. We never completely eliminate these defenses. The psyche insists on caring for us by protecting us with familiar forms of defense. Good knowing depends on our willingness to remain vigilant about the use of these defenses, and to consider softening them when protection is no longer necessary. A personal epistemology is strengthened when the apprentice pays attention to the activation of these defense mechanisms.

Trusting the Knower – Trusting ourselves as knowers depends on holding two beliefs: that we will be kind to ourselves and that we will be committed to allowing ourselves to know the truth of what happens around and within us. Kindness to self becomes critical as we inevitably hold erroneous opinions and make one mistake after another. When we do not fumble with compassion, we strain to see and admit our blunders. Learning is taken hostage by ridicule and shame.

When our egos become obsessed with exercising immunity against making mistakes, we disable needed discernment. Distinguishing reliable from unreliable data becomes increasingly difficult. Identification of sound information loses its credibility. Thus, our challenge is to hold confusion and ignorance with kindness. Such kindness gradually morphs into a humility that replaces the esteemed status of knowing with the overriding importance of curiosity and inquiry. An ancient meaning of the word *curious* is "full of care." An authentic care for learning, discovery, and inquiry replaces the ego's exhibition of what it allegedly knows. Such a shift is a dramatic change in values, reflected by our apprenticeship to fate.

Receptive to Penetration and Insemination – Good knowing is dependent on allowing fate to penetrate our defenses. Penetration is risky. Fate is not a highly compassionate mentor, but more like a Zen master pushing toward the integration of a lesson. Good knowing is much less about IQ and more about being penetrated by fate. We allow fate to confuse us, hurt us, defeat us, betray us, love us, be kind to us, and at times forget us. In this richness of experience lies the raw material for creating a life of full participation. Allowing ourselves to be penetrated and inseminated by fate leads to germination and eventual birth. When that happens, we are creating and cocreating who we are. New views, beliefs, and choices are being born.

The Intimate Apprentice

We can think of an apprentice as a learner, as someone desiring to acquire knowledge of a craft. The craft we are focused on here is how to live wisely as a person on a mysterious and unpredictable journey. The hope is that some measure of wisdom might be the outcome. The type of knowing that supports such a learner is embodied in the ancient Hebrew word *yada*, an essential component to any personal epistemology. As mentioned in chapter 4, yada refers to bringing the fullest employment of our senses, minds, and hearts to our experience. Essentially, yada implies not holding back. It denotes an intimate engagement with both the external world and our inner landscape.

Existential philosopher Søren Kierkegaard, for one, understood this notion of an intimate engagement. His insistence on the subjectivity of truth reflects the essence of yada. Where truth was once treated as a *what*, for him it was a *how*. The how of truth is subjectivity. It is the willingness to remain devoted to our senses, intuitions, past experiences, imaginations, emotions, beliefs, curiosities, and the views of others. It is the ardent patience and honesty needed to support our confusion and ignorance. The authentic apprentice takes the how of truth very seriously before offering cavalier pronouncements of what is true.

Attunement accompanied by resonance is a trustworthy how of truth. It is the way of yada. Attunement happens as we adjust to whom or what we are presently engaging. It means letting go of the prior focus of our thoughts, feelings, and actions. Curiosity drives attunement: Who is here now? What do they want? What is their intention? What are they feeling? What are they doing?

Attunement sets the stage for resonance. The word *resonance* comes from the Latin *resonare*, meaning "return to the sound." Thus, resonance is a kind of echo returning us to the sound we hear. When we hear an idea that moves and inspires us, we slip into resonance insofar as our voices, bodies, and eyes convey a connection to the idea. We communicate appreciation, excitement, and/or agreement with the idea.

When we hear someone express an emotion, we slip into resonance by conveying empathy or sympathy. The word *empathy* comes from the Greek meaning "in the suffering or feeling." Empathic resonance plugs us into the feelings being expressed to us. We might, for instance, become teary-eyed when listening to someone else's sadness. *Sympathy* translates to "with the suffering or feeling." I recently told a woman that I felt sad about the recurrence of my Meniere's disease symptoms. She responded sincerely by saying, "I'm sorry to hear that." She was expressing sympathetic resonance. She was not feeling my sadness but acknowledging the unfortunate nature of my experience.

Emotional resonance can take place through art, animals, landscapes, bodies of water, and among all forms of vegetation. Such resonance means we are moved and struck with awe by our encounters with Nature. It yields reverence for the world. This is why native peoples might perceive a river as their brother. Resonance is how we charm the universe.

Unfortunately, there are those who would prefer to sustain a narcissistic perspective about knowing. A friend recently explained how some politicians choose a self-indulgent interpretation of Kierkegaard, whereby the notion of truth is understood as being subjective in lieu of subjectivity itself. It is challenging for me to hold back my disdain when hearing such a sophomoric interpretation being used to support rationalizations, especially in regard to a thinker who has impacted my life for some fifty years.

Raja Selvam, a somatic psychologist, speaks of "embodied cognition." He explains how neuroscience has furthered our understanding of the relationship between mind and body. He places behavior, cognition (thought), and emotion in a dynamic relationship, each capable of influencing the others, with emotion having the greatest impact of the three. We come to understand our thinking if we are honest about our emotions, able to see how our actions influence how we feel and think.

I recently was in conversation with a person who described a group he was participating in as very fulfilling. I noticed a desire emerging in me to criticize (behavior) the group. I was aware (thought) of feeling betrayed (feeling) by a member of that group and still carried anger and hurt (emotion). My stubbornness reminded me that my feelings of betrayal had nothing to do with the person with whom I was speaking. I decided to listen (behavior).

There have been times in the past when I was less aware of the emotions and thoughts giving rise to a certain behavior and proceeded to criticize and gossip rather than withhold caustic language. The more we practice paying attention to the how of a given truth, the more options we have. Compassion is one of those options.

If apprenticeship means having a relationship with a teacher, then our principal teacher is fate. Those who have devoted their lives to an intimate relationship with fate can also be very useful guides. I remain deeply grateful for the devotees who have touched my life with their instruction. They knew how to confirm what was sacred, what truly matters. But the apprentice must also become familiar with good unknowing.

Good Unknowing

Good unknowing calls for an amiable relationship with ambiguity. Ambiguity is a lack of certainty. Whenever we experience a lack of certainty, we may undergo doubt, confusion, indecision, suspicion, insecurity, unease, and anxiety. Not one of these conditions is amenable to befriending ambiguity. Jungian psychoanalyst James Hollis suggests that we are more inclined toward a "contrived certainty" rather than face the challenges presented by ambiguity. Obviously, "contrived certainty" will not support the emergence of good knowing. "Contrived certainty" is, however, a way of coping with unwanted emotional states. When lacking certainty, we feel inadequate and anxious. When we are not facing uncertainty or unknowing, we slip into complacency, losing interest in remaining an explorer. As Firestein tells us: "Questions are more relevant than answers. Questions are bigger than answers. One good question can give rise to several layers of answers, can inspire decades-long searches for solutions, can generate whole new fields of inquiry, and can prompt changes in entrenched thinking. Answers, on the other hand, often end the process."

I was initially convinced that "contrived certainty" was nothing more than a way of coping with the tension of anxiety. All certainty is contrived because all inquiry remains incomplete. Firestein suggests that we have an attachment to answers because ignorance is embarrassing.

Good Ignorance and the Explorer

One way to view answers, especially practical ones, is as remedies or solutions to concrete problems. The ego delights in viewing the self as a repository of answers or solutions. In the process, we become overly attached to solutions and to seeing ourselves as capable of pulling out the right one at any given moment. Take, for instance, what happens to me when I am riding my bike and someone asks me for directions to a place I know well. Despite the interruption to my ride, I am glad to offer assistance. Immediately behind that feeling, however, is an ego gratified for being the guy with the right answer. Suddenly I am back in grade school, beaming because I correctly answered a history question.

This kind of egotistical indulgence in being right is not such a big deal until we become overly attached to generating answers rather than growing into them with curiosity. We are encouraged to have solutions and remedies throughout childhood. Parents reinforce what we allegedly know and schools give us good grades for regurgitating the good answers we are fed. Such is our formative induction into the allure of answers. The seduction never goes away completely.

We become mesmerized by the comfort and satisfaction afforded us by our concrete remedies and solutions. As technology advances, so does our screen time, discovering practical solutions to everything from how to treat a tick bite to purchasing tickets for the first civilian space flight. When certainty eludes us, we can no longer identify ourselves as having the right answers. When our identity is shaken, our self-worth is weakened: How can I be okay if I don't have a fitting answer? How can I be deserving of love? Who will want to affiliate with me? Such worries make us feel anxious. In the words of Todd Kashdan: "Anxiety, when it isn't balanced with curiosity, intensifies the need for closure and certainty, which plays out in every sense of who we are (our identities) and how we connect with others (our social roles)."

As already noted, an ancient meaning of the word *curious* is "full of care." We care about what fate presents in the way of others' choices of others as well as natural events beyond our control. We also care about how we will respond to these events, employing discretion and discernment to guide our wills. Caring about how we respond to what is and is not in our control is like responding to a friend or lover. It is fundamentally an act of heart. We remain interested in who our friend is, receptive to knowing more about him or her. Opening our hearts typically carries a level of risk and vulnerability. Below I examine how we can best support our capacity to care, or the resilience needed to cultivate more curiosity and support the tension that accompanies good unknowing.

Seven Steps to Increased Emotional Resilience

Just as being fully alive offers countless opportunities for exercising emotional resilience, fate faces us with the unknown. Resilience compels us to act with fullness of care, ever curious about life. A root meaning of the word *resilient*, in fact, is "to rebound."

Whenever the unknown of life weighs down on us, we succumb to despondence, anxiety, and despair. Emotional resilience makes no attempt to deny these experiences, but is the ardent energy helping us to move back toward the light. Resilience is the ability to recover from the sting of life, moving back in the direction of faith, trust, and acceptance. The goal of resilience is not to feel good, but to return to an abiding rapport with life, driven by curiosity.

We will now look at seven steps that help increase emotional resilience while supporting the growth of curiosity and good unknowing.

Step 1) Reframing the Nature of an Answer – The word *answer* once meant, specifically, "to respond as with a letter." We can receive our own letter from fate regarding the intentions and values of others, socio-economic conditions, political situations, choices of spouse, and the countless expressions of Nature. We answer such letters from fate with our curiosity, beliefs, desires, and hopes, all while awaiting more information. Resilience is strengthened as we let go of anxiety and accept it as part of the experience of waiting to be further informed. Recalling Rilke's suggestion that we "live our way into an answer," we must respond to what fate presents with curiosity every single time.

Step 2) An Enriched Capacity for Forgiveness – There will be little chance to rebound if we cannot forgive others or ourselves. A colleague of mine offers a helpful intervention whenever I struggle to forgive myself: "Do you believe you should have been larger than the mistake you made?" Her question immediately reminds me that any resistance to self-forgiveness likely reflects my aversion to being ordinary. When I am able to hold the value of being an ordinary person, I take at least one step in the direction of self-forgiveness.

As an apprentice to the unknown, you will make mistake after mistake. Such a pattern does not necessarily indicate ignorance but rather a willingness to remain curious and exploratory. Kornfield reminds us that forgiving others calls for giving up all hope of having a better past. Such relinquishment primes us to accept the ordinariness of having had a checkered past. Being mindful of such a past reflects the human condition, as does our living with some approximation of the truth.

Step 3) Feeling and Speaking Emotions – When emotions are neither felt nor given voice, you run a risk of anger turning into shame while fear drives our choices farther and farther away from love. Repressed emotions make it very difficult to rebound from those instances in which we are convinced we should have known better. You are feeling the bite of shame separated from love or of fear garrisoning against life. In either case, you are stuck, unable to engender curiosity.

Step 4) Remaining Self-Accountable – When we hold others accountable for our experiences, they, and not we, hold the power to rebound from arduous times. We are self-accountable when we measure what happens to us by our intentions and choices. As authors of our experiences, we possess the power to liberate ourselves from a victim's orientation toward life.

Step 5) Attend to What's in Your Control and Let Go of the Rest – Attempting to influence or change what is out of our control depletes energy and cements our wills in place. Our capacity for mobility and rebounding dwindles. We remain pinned under quixotic visions of all we allegedly can do, removed from what is real. In letting go of what is beyond our control, we free internal resources and enliven personal empowerment.

Step 6) Depersonalize Your Experience – The unknown of fate is not mostly happening to us or because of us. It is happening because it is the way of the journey. If you can accept life as mysterious, insecure, and unpredictable, then you will be less likely to denigrate your life. You will free yourself from the shackles of victimization, flexing with more grace as mystery's strong winds blow in your direction.

Step 7) Ask for Help – You cannot walk this life alone, especially as an apprentice to the unknown. The journey is simply too big and unmanageable. It will inevitably overwhelm you. The key is not to be compulsively self-reliant but to develop a keen discernment of viable resources. Strength is not about how much you can know on your own. It is about housing a sharp discretion between the well that is dry and the well that is full. Strength is also about knowing how to receive genuine help, how to walk to and drink from the overflowing well of enrichment. The apprentice must learn to receive that bounty.

Emotional resilience is difficult when our institutions continue to be dishonest about the formidable nature of life. All formulas alluding to the right education, religion, or occupation will never insulate us from the vulnerability and confusion of being alive. There will be no ultimate triumph over life as it constantly asserts its immensity and potency. Facing such forces as war, catastrophic illness, financial collapse, natural disasters, unplanned endings to significant relationships, and death can leave us psychologically drained.

Without emotional suppleness, we lose faith in life, in God, and in ourselves. It is naïve to think we can always find our way back to full participation in life. If you disagree, try telling that to parents who have experienced the death of a child. The best we can do is recover gratitude for the gift of life, remaining in a dialogue with fate, energized by curiosity. Such a dialogue will inevitably allow us to live with good knowing by reclaiming our own goodness.

Servant of the Truth

Remaining a servant of the truth greatly supports good unknowing. We can neither possess the truth nor arrive at some ultimate conclusion. We are condemned to live with an approximation of the truth. The apprentice is asked to make peace with its elusiveness. Remaining a servant of the truth will offer the apprentice the chance to lean into true north, staying close to the wisdom path. Let us think through what it means to remain in the service of the truth.

To Remember – A Greek translation of the word *truth* is "to remember." As servants of the truth, we are asked to hold two important memories. The first is to look inward. Ever-present seductions train our focus on others, avoiding the hard work of introspection. But if we are willing to take on the arduous task of self-inquiry, then we will discover the nooks and crannies of the soul. Laying claim to our arrogance, false modesty, resentments, need for revenge, deceitfulness, vanity, and greed requires courage and mercy.

The second focus of memory is to recall the immensity of truth. Such acknowledgment requires humility. The ego adores "contrived certainty." Every time we are urged toward certainty, we have opportunity to bow to "hidden ignorance" and good unknowing, returning to our charge as stewards of truth.

Suspending "Right and Wrong" – As a servant of the truth, the apprentice is asked to suspend thinking in terms of "right and wrong." Holding fast to this dichotomy brings us dangerously close to "contrived certainty" by separating us from the unknown. We also do well to let go of it while talking to others. Any insinuation that I am right and the other person is wrong can be highly divisive. In no time, the person identified as wrong launches an all-out defense of his or her position. Such maneuvering only ignites further verbal trickery. The typical outcome is a severe interruption of learning and creativity.

The speakers are no longer servants of truth. They are merely custodians of the ego's need to be superior. The only time that "right and wrong" can be dutifully applied is when we are called to take a moral position in the face of such unconscionable behaviors as genocide, embezzlement, and debauchery.

A Supple Grip – Servants of truth hold their positions with great suppleness. They are called by fate into continual wonder. Suppleness allows the servant to be penetrated and inseminated by some new vision. It may be necessary to wrestle our grip on such a vision out of the ego's tenacious hands. The ego gets drunk on the notion of arriving at the truth, possessing it with pride. Holding our positions with suppleness, by contrast, readies us to be further informed. We refuse to prematurely shut down our receptivity to further instruction. Then again, all forms of shutdown are premature. There will be times we will want to shut down either because the ego is convinced that enough has been learned or because we have become significantly disillusioned about important beliefs.

Resilient About Bad Faith – The servant of truth is asked to be steadfast in her or his faith that more will be revealed. Such a request is not exceptionally difficult when our experience matches our beliefs about love, hard work, loyalty, and kindness. Bad faith ensues when our experience fails to support those beliefs. Loved ones declare that they no longer love us, we get bypassed for a much-deserved promotion, or we discover that a spouse is having an affair with our best friend. We might even stop trusting God due to the death of a child.

Bad faith can be double-edged. When trusted beliefs are not faring well because of some new demand of fate, we may find it difficult to believe more will be revealed. We cannot imagine fate will be kind enough to offer information regarding the true nature of our work, our life's purpose, where we truly belong, and how to restore broken relationships. There is much healing in being able to declare, "I'm in bad faith." Nothing supports our service to truth more than acknowledging we have lost faith in truth. "I don't believe in you" is an intimate statement. It can also be healing to be heard and understood by those who have also found themselves in bad faith. Last but not least, it can be extremely healing for us to welcome someone whose faith has been lost.

Serving Another's Truth – We are not simply servants of absolute truth, but also in the service of truth as it appears in many tattered fashions. One of the greatest tests for the servant is to encounter a friend or relative whose truth seems harmful to themselves and/or others. We may either try to convert them to a new perspective or write them off completely. Neither option supports healing and creativity.

I am reminded of the myth of the princess who became a chicken. In a wealthy kingdom lived a king whose daughter one day decided to become a chicken. The king feverishly put out a proclamation for a worthy knight to restore his daughter's humanity. But the King was intolerant of failure. The knight who accepted the task of restoring the princess to her natural state risked a beheading if he failed.

The princess walked nakedly around on all fours, pecking at crumbs scattered about the castle. Many brave men responded to the king's offer of his daughter's hand and the future crown if they succeeded. Yet the numerous heads floating in the castle's moat bore evidence of considerable failure to restore the princess to her senses. The king grew weary and despondent as he watched his daughter pecking about the kitchen floor.

Finally, a simple farm boy approached the king, requesting a chance to restore the princess to her womanhood. The king warned the young lad of the price of failure. The boy was not deterred. He entered the kitchen of the castle, undressed, and walked around on all fours. The princess joined him, pecking at the crumbs left over from the previous night's meal. After a day, the boy suggested that he and the princess stand and partake of the delicious cake on the counter without sacrificing their poultry natures. The princess agreed and they stood upright, enjoying the cake. As evening approached again, the young lad suggested they consider getting dressed in order to avoid the chill of the night. He assured the princess that clothing would not violate their "chickenhood." She agreed. The boy continually and gently invited the princess to restore some small aspect of her humanity, until she completely returned to her full self. As these stories go, the two lived happily ever after in the castle.

This fable offers an important lesson regarding what it means to serve the truth of another, moving into good unknowing. Foremost, it tells us not to initially force the other into our truth, lest we lose our heads—a meaningful metaphor, if ever there was one, symbolic of confusion, resentment, helplessness, bitterness, and defeat. Rather, we are encouraged to attune ourselves to the other's truth by making small, gentle invitations to our own. Unlike the princess's response to the boy's invitations, there is no guarantee our offerings will be favorably met. Sometimes, folks need to remain chickens. It may be too frightening to stand upright, eating from the table and enjoying the fruits of personhood. In that case, we must be careful to not permanently join the princess in being a chicken. The hope is that we can always make haste, exiting the castle before we lose our heads.

Remaining a servant of another's truth involves compassionate detachment, or letting go, which means we do not continue to insist that the other eat cake or put on clothes. We are not supposed to betray ourselves by becoming a chicken. We might let some time pass before returning to the castle in another attempt at gentle offering.

Intimate with Truth – As we recall the old Hebrew term *yada*, along with Kierkegaard's notion that truth is subjectivity, it becomes clear that the wisdom path must be traveled intimately. We are not simply objective voyeurs inquiring about what is true. Only a deep longing for the truth and a tolerance for uncertainty place us in an intimate relationship with both the face truth reveals and the one it keeps hidden.

Sufi mystic Hafiz suggested we need teachers who "charm the universe to reveal its wonders." How do we have a charmed relationship with truth? As in any other working relationship, we must not attempt to dominate truth by pretending we can possess it. Nor should we quit and walk away because we cannot have it all. We must remain curious. Thus do we care about what is true. As in any significant relationship, sustained curiosity says, "I want to know as much as possible about you."

Charming the universe means bringing song or rhythm to our lives. An old meaning of the word *rhythm* is "movement in time." We can understand movement as literally meaning singing, dancing, playing, reciting poetry, drawing, writing and telling stories, and engaging in meaningful ritual. These kinds of movements allow us to live closer to the pulse of fate as full participants.

We can also understand the idea of rhythm as moving in response to fate touching and moving us, again and again. We do not gain immunity to loss, fear, or excitement. We invite fate to continue instructing us. The apprentice moves in response to the new teaching that may either affirm our thinking or undermine some old cherished belief. As Friedrich Nietzsche puts it: "And those who were seen dancing were thought to be insane by those who could not hear the music." May you find yourself among the dancers.

A Blessing for Knowing and Unknowing

Time and time again, change births some new known. Like the breeze gently touching your cheeks, quickly leaving to be replaced by some new wind. Come to remember your attachment to being a knower, all its promises of achievement and worthiness of commendation. It will take a while to appreciate the fleeting nature of what you hold as known.

Good knowing stays honest about the seduction of certainty. Such clarity reveals the allure of certainty, a promise of security, confidence and contentment, an end to the restless search for Truth. Yet Truth holds no warmth or welcome for certainty.

As you become less inclined to submit to the temptations of certainty, you may acquire a passion for charming the universe. Now, you live an endearing relationship with Truth, signified by the sacred knowing that you cannot possess Her. You find some satisfaction in flirtation, letting go of any expectation that consummation will result.

Curiosity, wonder, and awe move you into an intimate relationship with the ephemeral nature of Truth. Let the boundless nature of who you are be your beginning place: Where do I come from? What do I love? What are my gifts? What does life ask of me? What service is required of me?

An enchanted relationship with Truth asks for a passionate investment in seeking it, while finding the grace to live in Her mystery. Use all of you! Listen, taste, touch, see, and smell what is revealed to you. Exercise your intuition, instinct, and reflection. Bring your curiosity to others, allowing for different views to arouse.

Let Truth hear your cry: "I want to be with you!" Some gentle silhouette of Truth may appear. Allow your imagination to tell a story, playfully engaging your experience. Let some exaggeration move you toward joy and lightness. Tell Truth of your gratitude for all the people, places, and things creating opportunity to bring you closer to Her.

Most of all, make many mistakes. Mistakes are at the heart of good unknowing. Allow each to give testimony to your servile devotion to Truth. Mistakes ask you to let go of disdain for the unknower in you. Now, you may offer mercy for the flawed human you are meant to be, stumbling toward enlightenment.

9

The Aging Apprentice

How many loved your moments of glad grace,
And loved your beauty with love false or true;
But one man loved the pilgrim soul in you,
And loved the sorrows of your changing face.

–W. B. Yeats

When something natural is shunned, denied, and fought against, it can be extremely difficult to accept it as natural. So it is with aging. Our Madison Avenue culture offers endless reminders that aging is simply unfortunate. It follows this indictment by selling us products aimed at prolonging a youthful appearance. We are discouraged from having an informed and accepting relationship with aging. Such urging distances us from ourselves and hampers fate's attempts to instruct. The aging apprentice can bring a healing salve to the relationship by answering one simple question: What is aging asking of me?

Recalling Emerson's words, "there are no masters," when it comes to journeying into the unknown, we realize that apprenticing is fitting at any age. In fact, the older apprentice has likely made enough ego modifications to allow for more penetration and insemination by fate; therefore, they are more receptive to being informed rather than being the informer. Such receptivity renews our relationship to fate and to ourselves.

I recently turned 72 and found myself easily seduced by numerous ego-oriented aging questions: What can I do to look ten years younger? Why can't the hair on my head grow like the hair in my nose and ears? Why can't I swallow pills as easily as I did fifteen years ago? Can I have just one night when I do not get up to pee? Can I stop the young men at the gym from holding the door open for me and when I thank them, not that I am thankful, stop them from saying, "You're welcome, sir." Could it be possible to drive comfortably at night when it's raining? How about maneuvering out of a parking spot at the grocery store with ease?

Many of these changes associated with aging have to do with how we either present ourselves to others or navigate the twists and turns of the physical world. A request of aging may be to loosen our attachments to efficacy. We will be asked to shift our gaze away from our finest physical skills and intellectual insights. Now it may be time to spend more time focusing inwardly.

Revisiting Odysseus

Halfway through his journey home, Odysseus encounters Teiresias, the blind prophet at the border of Hades. Teiresias speaks of a journey Odysseus must take in old age. He will carry one of his most well-crafted oars and travel inland until he reaches a people who have never seen the sea and know nothing of ships. It is foretold that he will meet a stranger who redefines the oar as a "winnowing fan." Odysseus is instructed to plant the oar firmly into the ground and offer a sacrifice of a ram, a bull, and a breeding boar to Poseidon. Making "ceremonial offerings" to all of the gods, he is told that he will return home and die gently in Ithaca.

Homer does not offer the narrative of Odysseus's last journey, but Helen Luke does in her book *Old Age*. In her retelling, the oar takes on death and birth in kind. The following passage, spoken by Teiresias, captures the oar's transformation:

"Do you not know that your travels, your achievements and failures, the gains and losses to which your winged ship carried you were all forging for you a 'winnowing fan?' Now that the harvest is gathered and you stand in the autumn of your life, your oar is no longer a driving force carrying you over the oceans of your inner and outer worlds, but a spirit of discriminating wisdom, separating moment by moment the wheat of life from the chaff, so that you may know in both wheat and chaff their meaning and their value in the pattern of the universe."

The stranger reiterates the words of Teiresias. This denied part of Odysseus who has been hidden behind his thirst for conquest and love of the sea can now, on firm ground, show himself. The stranger repeats Teiresias' blessing regarding Odysseus' worldly adventures: "Do you not know that your travels, your achievements and failures, the gains and losses to which your winged ship carried you were all forging for you a 'winnowing fan?'"

Although Odysseus engaged fate heroically, his travels were driven by passion, devotion, and ambition. He lived his life fully, deciding moment by moment what mattered to him and what did not. His willingness to decide what matters and to encounter fate passionately at every turn allowed him to develop a "spirit of discriminating wisdom."

The story of Odysseus's aging tells us that a prerequisite to wisdom is the willingness to show up in our lives, utilizing our instinct, intelligence, and intuition to respond to what fate delivers. The suggestion here is that we are better off living boldly, even if that means coming across as one possessed by pride and excessive ambition. The "spirit of a discriminating wisdom" would most likely not evolve in the life of one who was excessively yielding, compliant, and withdrawn from encounters with fate. Such a person would forfeit an intimate relationship with fate and, by extension, with the unknown. Odysseus, for his part, lived with a "driving force."

The oar, once a symbol of his nautical prowess, represents the "driving force" of his masculinity. That "driving force" is now to be transformed through several stages into the "spirit of a discriminating wisdom" symbolized by seeing the oar as a "winnowing fan." It may be helpful to look more closely at the transformative stages of our own "driving force."

Stage I: Becoming more conscious of the nature of your "driving force" – Examples include: to explore, to be victorious, to accumulate wealth, to gain recognition, to create, to teach, to build, to heal, to entertain, and to discover. Like Odysseus and his oar, we all wield symbols of our "driving force." Such symbols might include a textbook, a gavel, a stethoscope, a hammer, a pie pan, a model car, or an airplane. The key is to meditate, reflect, and discuss how it is that the symbol of your "driving force" can also come to represent "the spirit of discriminating wisdom."

My old friend Norbert was a Trager massage therapist. He used a drawing of a pair of hands to represent his "driving force" as a body worker. The same drawing became symbolic of his evolving wisdom. He would speak of one hand grabbing what truly mattered and the other hand letting go of what was undeserving of his time and energy.

Stage II: A comprehensive "driving force" inventory – This stage calls for courage and honesty. It means being willing to acknowledge and feel the attachment you have experienced to your "driving force." Typically, the relationship you have with your "driving force" will not be a lightweight agenda. It can be fraught with passion, devotion, tenacity, and obsession. The fervency with which you live your "driving force" is reflected in the following mantras: I achieve, therefore I am. I build, therefore I am. I acquire wealth, therefore I am. I teach, therefore I am.

Getting clear about how much "driving force" has been your raison d'être can bring up feelings of regret, sadness, and self-incrimination. It becomes obvious how much of the rest of your life was neglected. We can imagine the anger Odysseus feels as he viciously removes the suitors from his home—an anger aimed ultimately at himself over the time spent away from his wife and son. This stage may also call for self-forgiveness related to what was avoided while living your "driving force." Just remember: an attachment to a "driving force" is the stuff of purpose and there will be no perfect balance between your "driving force" and everything else that makes up your life.

Stage III: Grieving the loss of the spirit of the original "driving force" – This constitutes a sizable death. The "driving force" gave your life meaning and purpose. As your raison d'être, it also infused you with personal worth. You knew you were okay because your "driving force" reminded you daily. I have often heard people declare with pride that they never took a sick day off from work. Upon hearing such an announcement, I often wonder if they simply could not take a day off for fear of losing personal value.

Your "driving force" did not simply provide meaning, purpose, and self-esteem. It was also your conduit to a well-lived life. You likely learned to succeed and fail and come to know the joys and sorrows of love. On some level your "driving force" enabled you to serve others and to make, at least, some small difference. As the spirit of your original "driving force" wanes, so does your identity.

Stage IV: Surrendering to a "driving force" identity crisis – As the spirit of your "driving force" recedes, so does the identity it inspired. Helen Luke again: "He was appalled that the words of Teiresias all those years ago had been so completely blotted out from his conscious mind; and he remembered many other things too, every one of his adventures in turn with their moments of courage, skill, faithfulness, pride, cunning, deceit, and folly. Most vividly of all came the memory of that foolish arrogance which had been the beginning of the evils brought upon him by the great god of the sea."

At this stage, it is important to tell the old stories of your "driving force." Tell them in honor of the life they drove. It can be especially important to speak of the darker themes—arrogance, greed, vanity, false-modesty, and so on—allowing your stories to carry more honesty. This is a time to welcome the depths of your humanity, stripped of its illusions of perfection. Another level of self-forgiveness can take place now due to the honesty and compassion you offer your stories.

An identity crisis at this time in your life can be challenging. It is okay to acknowledge uncertainty about your life mattering. You are in transition. The spirit of the old "driving force" is fading while the new "driving force" has yet to make itself known. It can be helpful to exchange such stories with honest peers. Let yourself feel the loss of who you were, the sadness, regret, and joy. Even if you are continuing to work with your original "driving force," it might very well take on new meaning. Your identity will not shift dramatically over the course of a weekend but rather gradually over time.

We see this gradual evolution of meaning in a passage by the renowned psychotherapist Sheldon Kopp: "And so it is with me as well. I do psychotherapy not to rescue others from their craziness, but to preserve what is left of my own sanity. Not cure others, but to heal myself." Kopp captures the nature of a morphing "driving force." He describes himself as considerably less heroic, refocusing attention on what is in his control. I would only add that attending to his own sanity may be a significant healing ointment for his patients.

It is important throughout any crisis of identity to remind yourself that this is not the end of your life, but rather the end of a particular way you lived your "driving force." You can remember that you are the one awaiting the message from the stranger who reveals the evolving spirit of a "discriminating wisdom."

Stage V: Come to know the stranger – One thing clear for Odysseus was that the journey foretold by Teiresias would bring no glory. An attachment to glory is always double-edged. On the one hand, you get to bask in praise and honor. On the other hand, there is a dependency on sustained performance and being recognized by others. Glory frames power as something given to you from without. It points you away from your inner world and the stranger who awaits your arrival.

This stage distinguishes elders from those who simply grow old. Elders visited the stranger periodically along the way, if only for a brief encounter. It may have been in response to the loss of a high school sweetheart, a failed marriage, or the death of a friend or relative. Rather than hide behind a veil of bravado or denial, you paused. In that momentary rendezvous, the stranger extended an invitation to your inner world. There was at least some stumbling across a landscape carved by sorrow, grief, remorse, and disillusionment.

The elder understands the hero as a knight of the ego. The elder is willing to accept the knight's evolving deference to the stranger. However, many will not relinquish their loyalty to edicts issued by the ego, which are driven by ambition, worldly projects, and campaigns. One who has simply accumulated years, convinced that the ego's mandates were all that there was, will likely not meet the stranger. The elder accepts the stranger's invitation to reclaim the ordinary, open to wonder and awe, bowing to both beauty and being in the presence of the sacred. The elder acknowledges all that has been given, as gratitude eclipses pride, honesty replaces inflation, and acceptance trumps volition.

Stage VI: A time for sacrifice – "Odysseus took the road that led into the woods. He knew now what this sacrifice meant: three offerings of the driving power of his masculinity, which had carried him through so many trials but had also been given over to pride and ambition and greed of achievement" (Luke). It helps to understand this stage if we recall that the phrase "to make holy" is a root meaning of the word *sacred*. During this stage, we make the journey holy.

The stranger instructs Odysseus to offer three sacrifices: a white ram, a red bull, and a breeding black boar, the latter beast possibly signifying the eminent birth of Odysseus's elderhood. He had pridefully taken all the credit for the Greek victory at Troy rather than offer sacrificial thanks to Poseidon. It is never too late in old age to credit our successes to forces larger than ourselves. Such a ritualistic gesture rightsizes the ego. Thus, Odysseus goes home to Ithaca, continuing to make offerings to the Gods while rendering blessings to the journey he was given.

Wisdom is held in our willingness to render our lives sacred or holy. The word *heal* means "to make whole." We can see Odysseus's time with the stranger as a time for healing. You, too, can bring healing to your life, making it whole. The simple act of being mindful of how your arrogance may have brought excessive commendation to some accomplishment, ignoring others who made important contributions, is a way to sacrifice pride in support of healing.

James, a client of mine, explained how he decided to sacrifice arrogance. When he turned 60, he committed to sending notes of appreciation to those who helped or supported him along the way:

"I sent a note of thanks to my primary school basketball coach who devoted time and energy to our team. When I sprained my ankle, he took me to his father's apartment. Gently coming to one knee, the elderly gentleman took my ankle in his hand and prayed for healing. I also sent a note to a cousin who moved next door when I was five. I instantly gained a big brother who was five years older than me and who made sure I was included in the neighborhood activities," explained James, with a sparkle in his eyes resembling that of a child offering an account of the Christmas gifts he received.

James has forwarded over a dozen notes of gratitude. He inspires me to take a gratitude inventory of my own. As I offer my thanks either in writing or verbally, I hear my ego say, "Can't we claim that some wonderful act is only about us?" The elder in me laughs at the notion that something could only be about me. I find that I am also appreciative for that level of mirth.

Stage VII: Attending to your soul's task – By now, the ego has hopefully gained a more manageable composure, less interested in exhibiting its sovereignty. Somewhat emancipated from the ego's rule, elders can be more receptive to identifying and attending the soul's task.

Recently, I had what I call an important elder dream. In this dream my wife invited me to attend a ritual which she described as part of my initiation into elderhood. We traveled by automobile to a remote mountain area until we reached a cottage near the summit. A gentle snow fell as we approached, greeted by swirling chimney smoke. The cottage's many windows made it easy to see a half dozen folks gathered around the fireplace.

Upon entering, we were warmly greeted by people casually dressed. My wife seemed to know several of them. The leader stepped forward and introduced himself and the plant-medicine ritual, which was to begin soon. His demeanor was invitational, receiving each of our questions as if it had a level of considerable appropriateness. His tone was cordial as he explained we would be smoking an extract from a tree grown in Iraq. He went on to assure us that our experience with the plant would not last more than thirty minutes.

I waited until several people partook of the plant from a robust drag on a long medicine pipe. I stepped in for a turn and took a large inhale from the pipe, held the smoke for a couple of seconds, and gently lay back on the mat. I immediately knew what the leader meant when he said, "You'll experience a loss of ego." With my eyes closed, I saw a kaleidoscope of colors accompanied by a constant roar. Once I got through my initial fear, I heard the following voice: "We love you [said over and over again] … We breathe you … You only fear receiving our love … You are our brother … You are he who breathes gently into the light."

As soon as I awoke, I wrote down the messages I heard before filling in the rest of the dream. I had a strong intuition that "breathing gently into the light" was meant to be the task of my elderhood. I felt deeply grateful to have received information so relevant to being an elder.

I immediately began to employ the mantra of "breathe gently into the light" to determine what I would consider right action. Most of the time I knew what action was to be taken or not taken. Sometimes, only in retrospect, would I know that I took the wrong action. But it was never a big deal. All that mattered was my willingness to translate the mantra into real choices.

I believe you have a soul's task that relates to you as an elder. Remain loyal to your curiosity about your task, and more will be revealed to you. Do what you can to interrupt complexity wherever possible. Remain devoted to a simple curiosity. As Kopp reminds us: "To be simple-minded enough to ask, 'Who am I?' is to begin to become wise."

The Unsettlement/Grace Polarity

The aging apprentice is asked to creatively work with the unsettlement/ grace polarity. This polarity allows one to remain intimate with fate and therefore continue to be informed by past and current experiences. Let us first look at the benefits of remaining unsettled.

Unsettlement

"People wish to be settled: only as far as they are unsettled is there any hope for them" (Ralph Waldo Emerson). What is the hope of remaining unsettled? If hope is the capacity to live intimately, then living intimately requires our participation. An old definition of the word *settle* is "come to rest," thereby suggesting that we cannot participate in a state of rest.

Intimacy is dynamic. It exists only in movement. Fate provides endless opportunities for movement, because fate is itself unsettled. We cannot join fate unless we, too, are unsettled. Fate visits us with a vast diversity of folks whose personalities will have us feeling loved, betrayed, forgotten, dismissed, ignored, and revered. Each is a gift. We are asked with each encounter to decide who we are. Do we respond with detachment, resentment, indifference, gratitude, forgiveness, or sorrow? Fate also comes to us through natural events such as birth, death, illness, disaster, and aging.

A man chooses to watch endless ballgames on television while his partner dances, plays, works, studies, and embarks on adventures. He chooses to be settled, disengaging from the partner who is unsettled. Unsettlement means we are touched and moved by and with the disruptive nature of fate. This man is neither touched nor moved by his partner's unsettlement. He is not encouraging intimacy.

Obviously, there are many psychological reasons to remain settled. Aging can offer specific challenges to our unsettlement. It is easier to be emotionally retiring if we are experiencing a disability or chronic illness. When living with some form of infirmity, one may require more support from others to remain unsettled. Isolation can be the death blow of unsettlement.

Isolation has us collapsing into a contracted world where there is little or no movement. It is critical to be in the presence of those who know how to age youthfully, remaining unsettled. Purchasing a sports car or a facelift does not necessarily translate into aging youthfully. Nothing contributes more to aging youthfully than embarking on external or internal adventures.

"A sense of limitation and burden need not stop you from being free to live and express creatively" (Thomas Moore). It may be more challenging to get on a plane or hike mountains, but there is no limit to embarking on internal adventures. When asked about a possible bucket list, I typically respond by saying something like, "I want to live the Seven Sustainables—authenticity, compassion, gratitude, integrity, simplicity, courage, and generosity—more completely" or "I want to continue creating the person I came here to be."

The Wild Edge of Aging

Remaining unsettled means living on the wild edge of aging. A fundamental definition of *wild* is "undomesticated." We can understand "undomesticated" as stepping away from being tamed by societal expectations, freeing ourselves from excessive ties to convention. It is not that we desire to become antisocial; we simply resist tapping into truths that live at our core.

The aging apprentice seizes the opportunity to get right with herself or himself. We can interrupt a tendency to be somewhat hypocritical, untying the laces binding us to self-betrayal. Wildness is the erosion of pretense. With a diminished attachment to pretense, we let go of a desire to impress and are free to declare who we are.

Timothy, an 82-year-old client, wildly declared a refusal to continue paying the price for feigning compliance. At the risk of being perceived as a curmudgeon, he committed himself to dismantling anything resembling a façade.

"I was six when my father went off to World War II, and I was determined to help my mom manage life without my father. I did my chores and my schoolwork. When we moved in with my aunt and uncle, I didn't speak of the abuse I received at the hands of my uncle. Once you lock into being good, it's very difficult to unlock the door of the goodness cage. I've spent most of my life making sure that I said and did nothing that others might perceive as disruptive. I remained a good boy much too long.

"I sacrificed being genuine, which means that in so many situations I wasn't really there. I wasn't there to be rejected and dismissed, and I wasn't there to be loved and accepted. Well, goddamn it, I'm here now! Who knows how much time I have left, and I am determined to be here!" asserted Timothy.

Wildness is the combination of desire and satisfaction from living with desire. Timothy is living on the wild edge of aging. We find another expression of wildness in the allegory of the monk accused of impregnating his neighbor's daughter. The neighbor's daughter announces to her parents that she is carrying the monk's child. The parents march next door, accompanied by their daughter, and confront the monk regarding his carnal activity with their daughter. The monk responds by saying, "So be it."

Nine months later, the parents return with the infant, demanding that the monk raise the child. The monk again responds, "So be it," and proceeds to raise the child, offering caring attention, guidance, and stewardship over the boy's natural gifts.

Twenty-one years later, the daughter confesses to the parents that the actual father of the child was the butcher's son. The parents make a more modest walk to their neighbor. They apologetically reveal to the monk that the butcher's son is the biological father. The monk once again responds, "So be it."

A Buddhist account of the allegory might place emphasis on the monk's ability to detach from his own desire, which is the cause of suffering. We also might say that the monk depicts an unwavering resiliency to allow for being misperceived.

The resiliency to be severely misperceived suggests that one's goodness has attained a sacred level of interiority. A dependency on external approval has appropriately receded. It may be one's most significant attainment at the wild edge of aging. There may be hurt and regret that the best version of you goes missed. But the elders have cultivated an understanding of where their goodness lives and who is responsible for it.

Being unsettled at the wild edge of aging offers us an accordant tonality. We are less prone to being driven off course by sounds and revelry that are incompatible with where our souls live. We have come to know our place. Seductions calling us to somewhere more grandiose have lost considerable potency. The ego has lost its flair for demonstrating how special it is. Being special has been replaced by an ordinary uniqueness, with the unbridled energy of the original "driving force" being replaced by grace.

Grace

Biologists and astrophysicists tell us that all existence is in a state of expansion and contraction. Everything from our lungs and cells to the galaxy itself is expanding and contracting. Our heavily extroverted culture applauds expansion and abhors contraction, honoring only one half of the beating pulse of all life. This is why we often feel shame when moving into the contracted state of depression. It may be challenging for us to appreciate most contracted states. Grace is a contracted state by virtue of being receptive.

An old definition of the word *grace* is "God's unmerited favor, love, or help." Of course, every religion claims its God to be the universal source of grace. For our purposes, fate is the "help and favor" offered by your God and by my God.

The challenge is to remain receptive to what fate offers us. Otherwise, grace cannot happen. At times, the people and events that come to us are fortuitous, making it easy to see favor coming our way. A healthy baby being born, a loved one recovering from illness, a gathering of well-wishers blessing our retirement, an adult child attaining a much-desired professional position: these are all examples of favorable life events.

But fate will also bring the less favorable. Defeat, loss, pain, and sorrow will also be included in fate's delivery. Still, even the most devastating of fate's blows can be a gift. As Kathleen Dowling Singh reminds us: "Terminal illness causes us, many for the first time, to look within. It well might be the only experience powerful enough to force most of us to begin looking at who we think we are and what we think this life is about."

It is only human to protest such happenings. Our hope is to move beyond the protest and bring some measure of grace to what fate presents. In fact, the aging apprentice has had numerous opportunities to protest the unpleasant, and now a measure of acceptance breathes life into grace. Where does such acceptance come from?

Johann Wolfgang von Goethe shed some light on the above question when he wrote: "Happy the man who early learns the wide chasm that lies between his wishes and his powers." The kind of learning to which Goethe refers would be laced with some level of repeated acceptance, neither turning against ourselves nor against fate. Such evolving acceptance finds us coming to terms with our place in the universe. It is a gradual ego adjustment to a fascination with grandiosity, a willingness to acquiesce to the immensity of the unknown.

The Blocks

Let us examine some of the common blocks interfering with our coming to know grace. Franciscan mystic Richard Rohr suggests: "The flow of grace through us is largely blocked when we are living inside a worldview of scarcity, a feeling that there's just not enough: enough of God, enough of me, enough food, enough health care to go around, enough mercy to include and forgive all faults." It can be difficult to outgrow scarcity or an attachment to deprivation. Living with a "worldview of scarcity" might just be the ego's last stronghold.

The aging apprentice is asked to release the ego's claim to surplus by embracing deprivation. Indulging in deprivation is the only way to feel entitled to receive. The problem is that receiving interrupts our attachment to deprivation. It therefore becomes important not to notice some offering being made to us. When my mother turned 99, I called to make a plan to celebrate her birthday. She invariably responded with, "Nobody has called about my birthday," a claim she has restated throughout the years. My untoward reaction was softened as I recalled that she loses any semblance of deservedness if she notices what is being given.

After letting go of an arrogant reaction to my mother's attachment to deprivation, I try paying attention to my own hold on deprivation. I see it manifested in a variety of thoughts: not enough money, not enough appreciation of my contributions, not enough time, and not enough mercy. It is so helpful to remain mindful that consciousness of scarcity is a circuitous way of claiming we deserve more. As we step out of deprivation, our vision begins to broaden, enabling us to see the favor the gods bestow upon us.

A second block to grace is cynicism. Cynicism is the loss of faith that we can actually be recipients of divine help. Cynicism is a protection against disappointment and hurt. It grows out of being disillusioned, which happens as some cherished belief is torn to shreds. We suspend all belief in the possibility of being delightfully surprised and blessed. Of course, we cannot risk noticing some favor attempting to make its way to us, which would ruin our alleged safety and make us vulnerable to disappointment.

In order to inoculate ourselves against inflictions of cynicism, we might need to grieve the loss of certain beliefs and accompanying dreams. Beliefs and dreams offer structure, meaning, and stability to our lives. To be shattered is to suffer a significant loss. In order to sustain a sense of resiliency, we must grieve these losses; otherwise, we cannot let go of them, which leads us to build a case against dreaming and life itself.

On close examination, when we are willing to grieve the loss of some belief that once scaffolded our way of living, we discover we were asking too much of that belief. We may have believed that betrayal is an aberration to a good relationship, that kindness can cause others to become kind, or that accommodating others will inevitably lead to their treating us with compassion. Most beliefs that get fractured reveal a level of naïveté that needed to die in order for us to live life on life's terms. Becoming more realistic does not mean becoming cynical. It means accepting what fate offers by remaining devoted to responding creatively.

The third block against grace is heroism. Here the issue is not so much that favor and help do not exist, but rather that we simply do not need them. Obsessive self-reliance eliminates being touched by grace. This heroic obstruction of grace is vividly depicted in Odysseus' story. It is not until he falls into deep sorrow and helplessness that Athena implores Zeus to allow her to help him. It is as if Athena knows that Odysseus' heroic fortification against grace has been lifted.

Theologian Paul Tillich captures Odysseus' encounter with grace: "Grace strikes us when, year after year, the longed-for perfection of life does not appear, when the old compulsions reign within us as they have for decades, when despair destroys all joy and courage."

Recently I traveled to Spain, where I was scheduled to teach, only to be stricken with a viral bronchitis. During an orientation meeting where teachers were being introduced to participants, I sat struggling to breathe. A woman approached me, gently laid her hand on my shoulders, and said, "Come with me."

Instantly, I had a double reaction to her invitation. On the one hand, I felt so miserable that I would have followed anyone anywhere in hope of some relief. On the other hand, I wondered: Who is this stranger and where is she taking me?

She escorted me to a kitchen area where she boiled water, pouring it into a large bowl with newly cut thyme. As I leaned over the hot vapors emanating from the bowl, she placed a towel over my head to contain and direct the flow of steam directly to my face. After several deep breaths, I could feel the bronchial congestion breaking up.

"Are you doing okay? I'm going to leave now. I'll check with you in the morning," she said.

After fifteen or twenty minutes of breathing the hot mist, I removed the towel and welcomed a cool, easy breath. My entire body seemed more relaxed, less labored. However, I continued to grapple with the meaning of this woman's offering. I was determined to explain her generosity.

I thought, "Maybe she's attracted to me," which I dismissed when I added that she didn't know me and was about thirty years my junior. I tenaciously tried on another interpretation, which was that she was exercising a benevolent paternal projection onto me. That was certainly more plausible than my initial thoughts. I soon became aware that I was struggling to receive the offering without accounting for it with some acceptable rationale. Obviously, it was not easy for me to accept her kindness. My heroic inclinations were attempting to block this occasion of grace.

The next morning, she approached me and asked how I was doing and whether I would be open to receiving therapeutic massage aimed at addressing upper respiratory congestion. I agreed. Rather than ruminate about what was motivating this offering, I surrendered to receiving it with gratitude. Months later, I came to see myself in that moment as a student of grace, gradually accepting the favor bestowed upon me by the gods and delivered by this kind woman.

The heroic ego is so attached to being in control that it leaves us confused and surprised by unsolicited help. I have consistently witnessed grace in action at twelve-step meetings. Someone details the wrongs enacted, the people hurt and disappointed, and the failure to be truly responsible for one's own life, only to be the recipient of genuine acceptance.

The aging apprentice can be more curious about the presence of grace and what it means to prime oneself to receive favor and help. As I write this, sitting on a beach, a woman walks by collecting bits of trash strewn about. Nothing about her suggests she has been hired to do this task. She is simply choosing to bring more beauty to the environment. Before now, I would not have seen her actions as a favor to me. It is a reminder to see grace as relational. Someone is serving as an external resource, which we must notice and be willing to receive.

Giving Grace to Ourselves

We can also offer grace to ourselves. The first way this happens is by pausing, interrupting a sense of urgency, and preventing hasty action. Grace can be the favor we give ourselves to become more settled. Grace manifests as ease. We can continue to be curious about opportunities allowing more ease to touch our lives.

The second way we can invite grace is by working with our emotions. Emotions can be unsettling by nature. Sometimes being emotionally unsettled leads to a variety of useful results. We might say something that needs to be said. We might take an action that has been long in coming. Unsettled emotions can be useful catalysts when we embark on needed change. Yet many of our emotional experiences are not asking for some truth to be spoken or action to be taken. We just feel stuck in our sadness, jealousy, fear, anger, or frustration.

Feeling bogged down with emotion can leave us unsettled, with little or no sense of ease. What keeps us in the grips of an emotion are the stories we attach to it. We almost never allow ourselves to feel sad and nothing more. We create endless stories about the shortcomings of others or ourselves, as well as stories about being unloved by others.

Our aging takes on an aura of grace when we interrupt our narratives and remain focused on feeling the emotion alone, on our own terms. I recently felt overcome by sadness and decided to let go of any story that emerged in conjunction with it. For the first time in years, I gracefully felt my sadness.

We can build a resiliency for remaining focused on an emotion by closing our eyes, sensing where the emotion is in our body, and imagining the energy of the emotion spreading throughout the body. For example, if we feel sadness in our chest, we might redirect the energy of the sadness to our abdominal area, to our pelvis, and down our legs.

A third way we can bestow grace upon ourselves is in those rare moments when we feel and know our essential goodness. Such a moment of welcome allows us to reunite with ourselves. Such a belonging settles the soul in place, at home with itself. This return to our own goodness may be the most significant responsibility of elders. It opens our eyes to beauty, love, possibility, and acts of grace. Without it, we lie in wait for someone to notice we are deprived of our own goodness. We may even find ourselves deluded enough to think someone can love us in lieu of loving ourselves.

We have no time for such deprivation. Death is on its way and is willing to take us before we are able to undo being separated from ourselves. When we pass to the other side in unity with ourselves, our work on the planet is likely complete. Whatever spiritual path we have been on is honored.

Becoming More Relational

Jim, a 58-year-old CEO of a small research firm, became increasingly curious about his capacity to be relational in light of a personal tragedy.

"Steve, a twenty-year colleague of mine, died last week. Steve was a really good guy, a friend. I didn't really know him," Jim reported, seemingly unaware of the incongruity of what he was saying.

"Jim, I hear you describing Steve as a really good guy, a friend of yours whom you didn't know. What do those three descriptions of your relationship with Steve say to you?" I asked, hoping he might have some consideration of the inherent discrepancy.

"Yeah, I get it. How would I know he was a great guy and my friend if I didn't know him?" Jim asked, knowing the question was awakening him to something larger.

"What is Steve's death calling you to?" I asked, confident that he was on to something important.

"Well, I've got to say, I don't wonder enough about my relationships. You know, was I really curious about who Steve was? Or, for that matter, do I wonder enough about anybody who matters to me? I don't think I even understand what I mean to people," Jim disclosed, earnestly displaying his concern as he leaned forward, his words carrying a tone of worry.

Jim had begun to take inventory of ways he may have blocked being more relational. Taking such an inventory is the starting place. Below are some steps to make us more relational.

An honest relational inventory – Describing yourself as relational means you are willing to engage and relate to others. This might entail more conversation, more play, giving and receiving help, going on adventures, having meals together, studying or attending lectures, going to films and plays, praying together, and learning to create more depth and meaning in a relationship.

Deepening a relationship bids us to be curious and intrigued about discovering who we are as we genuinely participate in a relationship. Here are some questions that can help guide the inventory: Who knows me? Who feels known by me? How do I know when someone is a friend? Am I able to identify what is needed to move an acquaintance toward friendship? How do I decide it is appropriate to be more transparent with someone? What frightens me about getting closer to someone?

Making peace with fear – When becoming more relational means playing shuffleboard or bridge, feeling scared may not be an issue. When we are ready to get closer to someone, we can fear fumbling, being rejected, feeling inadequate or uncertain. When being relational means opening the heart, risks will be taken. Wishing the fear away is a waste of time and energy. Better to learn how to regulate the nervous system, walking between fear and safety. It is both humbling and courageous to be one who is scared yet willing to take risks.

Slow enough for attunement – Being attuned to another person means adjusting to the other. We adjust to the unique feelings, thoughts, and needs of the other. We adjust to their energy field, which may be heavily vibrational (agitated, frantic, angry, worried) or contracted (depressed, repressed, fatigued, even-tempered). When we attune to each other, we adjust our thoughts, feelings, and behaviors to create resonance between us. We can understand psychological resonance by way of an analogy to music. Musical notes are in a state of resonance when instruments or voices amplify them. So it is with psychological resonance. One person speaks with a certain tone while both the content and its tonality are amplified by the listener.

For example, I might speak to a friend about my sadness and helplessness in response to a family member being recently diagnosed with a chronic illness. My friend acknowledges both the diagnosis and my emotional reaction to it. The acknowledgement includes a tone that is somber, sympathetic, and tenderhearted.

Remaining an apprentice to love – "The world is violent and mercurial—it will have its way with you. We are saved only by love—love for each other and the love that we pour into the art we feel compelled to share: being a parent; being a writer; being a painter; being a friend. We live in a perpetually burning building, and what we must save from it, all the time, is love" (Tennessee Williams). Williams captures the insecure and unpredictable nature of fate as "violent and mercurial" in his image of the "burning building." Given the nature of fate, he declares that only love is worth saving when faced with such a journey.

Many times have I entered the burning building, desperately attempting to save pride, recognition, a bottle of Canadian whiskey, a reputation, looking good, and some profound insight into the Grand Mystery. What we attempt to save is supposed to bring us love. The irony is that we seldom go in to save love itself. Aging affords numerous opportunities to enter the "burning building," until we discover only love is worth saving, only love can save us.

No spiritual path or psychological modality will likely change the world from being "violent and mercurial." We can, however, make choices that bring some level of calm, clarity, and compassion to our trips into the "burning building." Holding on to love as a learning priority means the apprentice must commit to unity consciousness. The word *advaita* in Sanskrit means "not entirely one, neither two." When becoming more relational, we can retain our uniqueness while refusing to support divisiveness.

Separation from others occurs for a variety of reasons. We might pull away because they look different, have differing beliefs, or worship differently. This suggests you need sameness to feel good about yourself. Such separation is asking for more love of who we are, without seeking external confirmation from those who look like us or believe as we do.

We might also disconnect because we view something in others that is difficult to accept about ourselves: "It's not that I'm self-righteous, but I can sure spot it in him." Projecting on others what we reject about ourselves can be extremely divisive. This disconnect is asking for more mindfulness of who we are and more acceptance of what we discover about ourselves.

Another form of division occurs when we decide that someone or some group is inferior to us. Marking them as inferior makes us feel superior. Divisiveness or a lack of unity consciousness is really a distorted love story. We attempt to secure love by being unloving. As an apprentice to love we are continually asked to find endearment for ourselves without subjugating others.

Initially, a commitment to live with more unity consciousness means living the question: How do I attempt to secure love by thinking and acting in some divisive way? This is the hard work of becoming more relational. It actually means being a student of divisiveness. We were taught to compare and contrast ourselves to others with some hope of coming out on top. I have witnessed those who compare themselves to others and incessantly define themselves as unworthy. They invariably take great joy in seeing someone they admire make a serious mistake. Divisiveness has its toxic tentacles whether we vault ourselves to the top or remain a bottom feeder.

The second step in undoing an attachment to duality consciousness or divisiveness is to identify and feel the emotions that drive us into division. Fear, self-loathing, anger, envy, and vindictiveness are the typical emotional energies pushing us to division. The key is to stay with these emotions and deconstruct the tales of inferiority we spin around others.

The third step is to face how we feel about ourselves when letting go of our divisiveness as a way to massage self-contempt. We may need to feel our self-imposed rejection for a while. It can be very helpful to affiliate with those who have walked the path of undoing duality consciousness. Others may hold compassion for us while we learn to give it to ourselves.

"The man who has never made a fool of himself in love will never be wise in love" (Theodor Reik). Remaining an apprentice to love guarantees we are visited by Parsifal, the fool. There is always plenty of foolishness to go around if we dare to love, stepping into one of the deepest mysteries of the human experience. We will run into the "burning building" again and again, dragging out everything but love. We will pursue those who want nothing to do with us and walk right by love when we could have reached out and touched it. Hopefully, the aging apprentice has learned self-forgiveness for all the fumbling incurred while endeavoring to create loving relationships.

Mercy

I return to imperfection to find myself there. At 72, and on a good day, such a return has less angst, less of a sense of failure, and more acceptance of the man I find there. It may be the gift of disillusionment. So many times I have convinced myself of being much larger than I actually am, only to be severely disillusioned.

In my imperfection, I find the man that I am. In my perfectionism, I find the man I should be, some unattainable version of myself, always striving to be lovable enough. The voice of mercy says, "It's okay to simply be who I am."

The aging apprentice is well aware of what it means to live the paradox of inexhaustible growth. The paradox declares, "I'm absolutely lovable the way I am, and I'm committed to learning and growing." Trapped in endless striving, most of us have stumbled away from the "I'm enough" portion of the counsel. Others withdraw into an extended mediocrity of self-indulgence, sacrificing even a modicum of striving. When we genuinely love ourselves, we also love the journey. The paradox is more easily lived. Self-endearment flows into curiosity and intrigue with regard to how much can be learned and loved.

I recall the words of Yeats: "But one man loved the pilgrim soul in you, / And loved the sorrows of your changing face." The pilgrim is the apprentice willing to journey, meandering through tireless strivings to get life right, finally allowing life to get you right. Only then does a sense of purpose emerge. The pilgrim has learned to triumph over defeat and over victory. Such victories have neither fractured your rapport with fate nor left you yearning to be someone you are not, deeply deserving of mercy. Rather than get a facelift, you could love "the sorrows of your changing face."

You dared to make the pilgrimage. You faced defeat, loss, and rejection. You faced the unknown, sometimes with a fervent honesty and other times overwhelmed into a pretense of certainty. You faced the disappearance of a dream, a dream that brought hope and faith to your spirit. You faced a child-step toward addiction and possibly the end of a young life. You faced love drained of warmth and devotion. You faced losing your place, not knowing where belonging might await you. Yes, by all means, love "the sorrows of your changing face." Those furrows give testimony to your love of life.

Mercy is a kindness that comes unexpectedly, not one that is anticipated. Often, it is a kindness that must wrestle its way through conventional values and precedent that would issue some edict of condemnation. Mercy is found in opening eyes, empowered by an enlargement of the heart.

"He that is without sin among you, let him first cast a stone." These words of Christ cited in the Gospel of John are a good example of mercy pushing its way through a thicket of old law. Christ calls the scribes and Pharisees to a higher vision as they prepare to stone a woman accused of adultery. These words of mercy call to remain self-focused, undistracted by the wrongdoings of others. It may be that the aging apprentice has grown tolerant and accepting of her or his own shortcomings. Striving has become like a worn piece of cloth, no longer able to hold the weight of excessive self-righteousness.

Aretha Franklin, the renowned singer, offered mercy to Angela Davis, who she felt had been unjustly accused. In 1970, Franklin posted bail for her. Franklin's minister-father told her she did not know what she was doing. Franklin's reaction to her father's warning was: "Angela Davis must go free. Black people will be free. I've been locked up [for disturbing the peace in Detroit] and I know you got to disturb the peace when you can't get no peace." Risking some unfavorable paternal response, Franklin pushed past her father's admonition. She found the path to mercy, the one she would walk.

The aging apprentice has learned to remove the yoke of convention, especially when it denigrates the heart. It may be that conscious aging abates the need to prove something. When your energy subsides and you are more aware of your life ending, mercy may be more available. Mercy is a deep relational offering. With less of a need to demonstrate some unique prowess, you are less divisive, now able to see how much we all deserve kindness.

Getting Ready to Leave

I do not want to leave. It all feels like some old fraternity trick where I was blindfolded and driven to some unfamiliar location. The task was to successfully find my way back to campus. I wonder: Do we die and find ourselves in some unknown place and then need to find our way back to Earth? Or, do we die to find ourselves in no unfamiliar place?

Part of my reluctance to leave is that it has taken years to acquire some vague understanding of myself and those I love. I have also gained cursory insight into the human experience in general. How can I leave when I feel so deeply unfinished? How much comfort have I acquired through my alleged knowing?

It is not so much that thinking proves my existence. Rather, my mental musing offers an endless assortment of stories, furnishing me with an opportunity to archive a life. These narratives allow me a moment of escape from the immensity of my helplessness. I take great comfort in fooling myself about how much I can control. I have no need to prove I exist; rather, I am dedicated to believing I hold some jurisdiction over my experience.

Life can easily be reduced to a boundless set of vignettes where I see myself performing at least what I believe to be some small measure of power. In such illusory moments, I am convinced that I matter. Of course, to matter as a result of performing is ephemeral, removed of substance and soul. It is extremely unlikely that as a performer I can step from doing to being.

The eyes of the aging apprentice have begun to see doing for what it is. On some basic level, it is a way to have a body. Bodies seem to take well to action. However, an aging body feels its encroaching limits. My physical strength and suppleness begin to elude me. My immediate recall of names seems to have taken up some repose, requesting my patience.

From the Greek, the word *perform* means "to work out." Up and through midlife, we are working out a great deal. All of these varied performances are a way to create a life. We get educations, create relationships, work jobs, and establish homes, all of which offer us life experience. The ego hopes to gain satisfaction through all of these actions. Yet performing takes on a new level of meaning when we hope for our performances to be witnessed by others, applauded, and rewarded. This level of alleged control is challenging to relinquish. We do not want to give up the seductive belief that we can lure others into appreciating and loving us.

"We cannot take control, and this is our dying, as we have to gradually let go of our need for control, our small self-serving world-views, and our comforting certitudes about which we are really not certain at all. It is dying that we must both allow from our side and allow to be done to us—in other words, both an active and receptive surrender" (Richard Rohr). Rohr's quote reminds us again that a vital life direction is not trying to get life right but rather allowing life to get us right. Dying is life striving to get us right by bridging the gap between doing and being. In our aging fragility, doing and performing find their rightful size as we humbly accept how much has actually been out of our control throughout the entire journey. An obsession with doing and performing ultimately atrophies, not leading to feelings of worthlessness but rather to a welcoming of being.

This receptivity to being does not need to happen in heavily abstract ways but rather in simple, concrete expressions. Recently, I was watching a scene from the 2018 film *A Star is Born*, in which a man is championing the gifts of a singer he believes in. He gently coaxes her onto his stage, helping her push through her fear and reluctance to claim her gift and bring it to the world. Tears streamed down my face in response to his offering of faith and guidance and the woman's receptivity to birthing her gift. I later realized that I had stepped into being as I opened my own heart to the blessing of a mentor. Being is allowing ourselves to be touched by the sacred, by that which truly matters.

With a heartening reception to being, we are readier to stay and readier to leave. This may be the last polarity we are asked to outgrow. Each breath becomes more authentic as illusions of control recede. We understand being as living more truthfully with regard to our control and our performances. Thus, fate is enlivened to move us, touch us, teach us, and heal us. We have attained a new acceptance of fate's immensity and mystery. It is in such an acceptance that we come to know the embrace of being.

My prayer is that in my final hours I might utter the last lines from the poem "At Peace" by Amado Nervo:

> I loved, I was loved, the sun caressed my face.
> Life, you owe me nothing, Life, we are at peace!

A Blessing for the Aging Apprentice

Your "driving force" now asks for transformation. It was the energy
thrusting you into the depth and breadth of life. Your talent, your
ambition to build, create, lead, and explore. All the while, convinced it
was your way to really be someone.

Fate allowed you to dance with her in Victory and in Defeat. She
was the one creating you, attempting to get you right, when you
were convinced you were up to the business of getting life right. Your
triumphs allowed Fate to point you toward Humility, Simplicity, and
Gratitude.

Defeat was her chance to bring you closer to asking for help,
acceptance, and letting go. The story of your apprenticeship has
deepened. You now live in a larger narrative, laced with the gifts of
what both Victory and Defeat have brought to you.

You know now where your essential goodness lives, and who is
responsible for it. Such knowing beats with the pulse of Wisdom. Your
divine spark was never meant to be proven. Now, welcome the fool who
believed that enough success would make you enough.

With ambition finding a comfortable repose, Grace gently finds its
way to you. Grace happens to you as you relinquish your hold upon
determination. Grace is the softness of a will that has been worn by the
crashing waves of Fate.

Mercy and Love now find the place in your soul where they always
belonged. Mercy issues a kindness, ending illusions of separation. Your
loving always held a vision of your purpose. It was the reason you
chose to live, and now it frees you to leave.

Being a devoted apprentice was living wisely. Wisdom was never
meant to be a measure of how much you know. It was always an act

of devotion allowing people, places, and experiences to penetrate and inseminate you. Birthing you into larger stories of Grace, Mercy, and Love.

Notes

Chapter 1

Epigraph

Blake, William. "Proverbs of Hell." *The Marriage of Heaven and Hell* (1793). LibQuotes. Accessed April 21, 2017. https://libquotes.com/william-blake/quote/lbt2i5a.

25-26

Meade, Michael. *Why the World Doesn't End: Tales of Renewal in Times of Loss.* Seattle: Greenfire Press, 2012.

28

Kopp, Sheldon. *The Hanged Man: Psychology and the Forces of Darkness.* Palo Alto: Science & Behavior Books, 1974.

29

Jung, Carl. "Two Essays on Analytical Psychology." *The Collected* Works, Vol. 7. (1953). Edited by Gerhard Adler & translated by F.C. Hall, Ed. 2. Princeton: Princeton University Press/Bollingen, 1966.

Chapter 2

40

Gray, James P. "It's A Gray Area: Einstein's Brilliant Thoughts Pertinent to Today's Woes." *Los Angeles Times,* May 31, 2013. https://www.latimes.com/socal/daily-pilot/opinion/tn-dpt-me-0602-gray-20130531-story.html.

40

Richard Rohr. "Seeing Truly." *cac.org,* Center for Action and Contemplation, July 15, 2016. https://cac.org/seeing-truly-2016-07-15/.

41

Augustus Masters, Robert, PhD. "Spiritual Bypassing: Avoidance in Holy Drag." April 29, 2013. https://www.robertmasters.com/spiritual-bypassing.

42

Campbell, Joseph. *The Hero with a Thousand Faces,* Ed. 2. Princeton: Princeton University Press/Bollingen, 1968.

42

Teilhard de Chardin, Pierre. "Patient Trust." Accessed February 1, 2017. https://alifesworkmovie.com/2015/05/patient-trust-a-poem-by-pierre-teilhard-de-chardin/.

47

Kurtz, Ron. *Body-Centered Psychotherapy: The Hakomi Method: The Integrated Use of Mindfulness, Nonviolence, and the Body.* Mendocino: LifeRhythm, 1990.

53

Hesiod, David W. Tandy, and Walter C. Neale. *Hesiod's Works and Days.* Berkeley: University of California Press, 1996.

56

West, Thomas G. and Plato. *Plato's Apology of Socrates: An Interpretation, with a New Translation.* Ithaca: Cornell University Press, 1979.

62

Einstein, Albert. A well-known quote by the scientist with an unidentified exact origin.

Chapter 3

Epigraph

Eliot, T.S. *After Strange Gods: A Primer of Modern Heresy.* Page-Barbour Lectures at the University of Virginia, 1933 (Classic Reprint, 2018). London: Faber and Faber, 1934.

72

Niebuhr, Reinhold. "The Serenity Prayer." Tag line to a sermon (1943).

72

Pope John XXIII. "Personal Quotes/Biography." Internet Movie Database. Accessed October 10, 2018. https://www.imdb.com/name/nm1537862/bio#quotes.

73

Merton, Thomas, and Thomas P. McDonnell. *A Thomas Merton Reader.* Garden City: Image Books, 1996.

73

Kornfield, Jack. *The Wise Heart: A Guide to the Universal Teachings of Buddhist Psychology.* New York: Bantam Books/Random House USA, 2009.

77

Chodron, Pema. "Spiritual Quotation." Quoted by John Welwood. *Towards a Psychology of Awakening: Buddhism, Psychotherapy, and the Path of Personal and Spiritual Transformation* (2000). Spirituality & Practice: Resources for Spiritual Journeys. Accessed February 8, 2017. https://www.spiritualityandpractice. com/quotes/quotations/view/35422/spiritual-quotation.

81

Weller, Francis. "The Wild Edge of Sorrow: The Sacred Work of Grief" (2019). Francis Weller. Accessed October 7, 2019. https://www.francisweller. net/the-wild-edge-of-sorrow-the-sacred-work-of-grief.html.

81

Gawande, Atul. *Being Mortal: Medicine and What Matters in the End.* New York: Picador, 2014.

82

Rohr, Richard. "Seeing Truly." Center for Action and Contemplation. June 23, 2016. https://cac.org/seeing-truly-2016-07-15/.

Chapter 4

Epigraph

Hemingway, Ernest. "Ernest Hemingway." *New York Journal-American,* July 11, 1961. LibQuotes. https://libquotes.com/ernest-hemingway/quote/ lbw4j8s.

91

Mares, Théun. "Cry of the Eagle: The Toltec Teachings, Vol. 2." *Lessons of Life: Internal dialogue whispers all day long* (blog). December 24, 2018. https://livefabulouslife.com/2018/12/24/internal-dialogue-whispers-all-day-long/.

92-93

Barrett, William. *The Illusion of Technqiue: A Search for Meaning in a Technological Civilization*. Garden City: Anchor Press/Doubleday, 1979.

95

Oriah Mountain Dreamer. "Today's Poem: The Invitation." Quoted by Dr. Karin Lawson. *Dr Karin Lawson* (blog). April 20, 2017. https://drkarinlawson. com/todays-poem-the-invitation/.

97

West, Thomas G. and Plato. *Plato's Apology of Socrates: An Interpretation, with a New Translation*. Ithaca: Cornell University Press, 1979.

104

Nouwen, Henri J. *Intimacy: Pastoral Psychological Essays*. San Francisco: Harper & Row Publishers, 1969.

Chapter 5

Epigraph

Emerson, Ralph Waldo. "The Wisdom of Ralph Waldo Emerson." Academy of Ideas: Free Minds for a Free Society, March 22, 2014. https:// academyofideas.com/2014/01/the-wisdom-of-ralph-waldo-emerson/.

112

Winnicott, Donald. "Donald Winnicott: Psychotherapy." The School of Life Articles. Accessed June 28, 2018. https://www.theschooloflife.com/ thebookoflife/the-great-psychoanalysts-donald-winnicott/.

112

Fromm, Eric. *The Heart of Man: Its Genius for Good and Evil*. New York: Harper & Row, 1980.

123

Mandela, Nelson. Quoted by Eamon Gilmore. "If you want to make peace with your enemy, you have to work with your enemy. Then he becomes your partner" Article. Organization for Security and Co-operation in Europe, April 27, 2012. www.Osce.org/cio/90075.

Chapter 6

131

Mr. Purrington (Lewis Lafontaine). "Carl Jung 'The Secret of the Golden Flower' – Quotations." *Carl Jung Depth Psychology Site* (blog). April 21, 2020. https://carljungdepthpsychologysite.blog/2020/04/21/carl-jung-the-secret-of-the-golden-flower-quotations/#.YFYIXIWRKjoC.

134

Jung, Emma, and Marie-Luise von Franz. *The Grail Legend.* Princeton: Princeton University Press, 1998.

144

Jung, Emma, and Marie-Luise von Franz. *The Grail Legend.* Princeton: Princeton University Press, 1998.

144

Saint Augustine of Hippo. "Content Library." One Journey. Accessed February 25, 2018. https://onejourney.net/saint-augustine-of-hippo-quote-men-go-abroad-to-wonder-at-the-heights-of-mountains-at-the-huge-waves-of-the-sea/.

146

Frey, Angelica. "'The Odyssey' Quotes Explained." ThoughtCo. Updated December 18, 2018. https://www.thoughtco.com/the-odyssey-quotes-4179126.

150

Homer. *The Odyssey.* Translated by Robert Fitzgerald (1998). "Odysseus as A Heroic Hero in Homer's 'The Odyssey.'" Cram. Accessed May 1, 2017. https://www.cram.com/essay/Odysseus-As-A-Heroic-Hero-In-Homers/F3C4MFE2AC.

Chapter 7

Epigraph

Plotinus. "Plotinus Quote." Quoted by Arthur Hilary Armstrong. *Plotinus: Selections from His Major Writings* (1962). AZQuotes. Accessed February 9, 2017. https://www.azquotes.com/quote/870229.

158

Emerson, Ralph Waldo. "Quote from Ralph Waldo Emerson." The Quotations Page. Accessed March 6, 2018. http://www.quotationspage.com/quote/9184.html.

160-161

Gen. 32:22-31 *Holy Bible, New International Version*®, NIV®. Copyright ©1973, 1978, 1984, 2011 by Biblica, Inc.™ Used by permission of Zondervan. All rights reserved worldwide.

161

1 John 4:5 *Holy Bible, New International Version*®, NIV®. Copyright ©1973, 1978, 1984, 2011 by Biblica, Inc.™ Used by permission of Zondervan. All rights reserved worldwide.

Chapter 8

179

Rilke, Ranier Maria. "Letters to a Young Poet." Accessed May 15, 2017. http://www.columbia.edu/~ey2172/rilke.html.

180

Lane, David. "The Missing Nuance: The Integral Myth - Ken Wilber as Religious Preacher," A Four-Part Critique, Part Four. IntegralWorld. Accessed March 16, 2017. http://www.integralworld.net/lane118.html.

180

Twain, Mark. "A Pilot's Needs." *Life on the Mississippi* (1883). Accessed January 10, 2017. https://www.mtwain.com/Life_On_The_Mississippi/13.html.

182

West, Thomas G. and Plato. *"Plato's Apology of Socrates": An Interpretation, with a New Translation*. Ithaca: Cornell University Press, 1979.

183

Barrett, William. *The Illusion of Technqiue: A Search for Meaning in a Technological Civilization*. Garden City: Anchor Press/Doubleday, 1979.

189

Kashdan, Todd. *Curious? Discover the Missing Ingredient to a Fulfilling Life*. New York: Harper, 2010.

195
Nietzsche, Friedrich. A well-known quote by the philosopher with an unidentified exact origin.

Chapter 9

Epigraph
Yeats, William Butler. "When You Are Old." *The Rose* (1893). LibQuotes. Accessed December 29, 2017. https://libquotes.com/william-butler-yeats/quotes/When-You-Are-Old.

203
Kopp, Sheldon. *The Hanged Man: Psychology and the Forces of Darkness.* Palo Alto: Science & Behavior Books, 1974.

206
Kopp, Sheldon. *The Hanged Man: Psychology and the Forces of Darkness.* Palo Alto: Science & Behavior Books, 1974.

207
Emerson, Ralph Waldo. "The Wisdom of Ralph Waldo Emerson." Academy of Ideas: Free Minds for a Free Society, March 22, 2014. https://academyofideas.com/2014/01/the-wisdom-of-ralph-waldo-emerson/.

207
Moore, Thomas. *Ageless Soul: The Lifelong Journey Toward Meaning and Joy.* New York: St. Martin's Press, 2017.

210
Singh, Kathleen Dowling. Quoted by John M. Gerber. *The Grace in Dying: A Message of Hope, Comfort, and Spiritual Transformation.* "Caregiver Suffering and Spiritual Healing." Changing the Story. July 19, 2018. https://changingthestory.net/2019/04/12/caregiver-suffering/.

210
Von Goethe, Johann Wolfgang. *Goethe's Works,* Vol.1 (1885). "Johann Wolfgang Von Goethe Quote." AZQuotes. Accessed May 10, 2017. https://www.azquotes.com/quote/852849.

210

Rohr, Richard. "Worldview of Abundance." Center for Action and Contemplation, May 15, 2017. https://cac.org/worldview-of-abundance-2017-05-24/.

212

Tillich, Paul. "Quotes from the Works of Paul Tillich." Trinity in You, August 26, 2020. https://trinityinyou.com/quotes/paul-tillich/.

216

Williams, Tennessee. Cited from a conversation with Jim Grissom, New Orleans, 1982.

217

Reik, Theodor. *Love and Lust: On the Psychoanalysis of Romantic and Sexual Emotions* (ed. 1970). LibQuotes. Accessed November 10, 2017. https://libquotes.com/theodor-reik/quote/lbn0g1a.

218

Yeats, William Butler. "When You Are Old." *The Rose* (1893). LibQuotes. Accessed March 18, 2017. https://libquotes.com/william-butler-yeats/quotes/When-You-Are-Old.

219

John 8:7, *Holy Bible, New International Version*®, NIV®. Copyright ©1973, 1978, 1984, 2011 by Biblica, Inc.™ Used by permission of Zondervan. All rights reserved worldwide.

219

Franklin, Aretha. "Aretha Says She'll Go Angela's Bond If Permitted." *Jet,* December 3, 1970.

220

Rohr, Richard. "Dying by Brightness." Center for Action and Contemplation, October 3, 2018. https://cac.org/dying-by-brightness-2018-10-07/.

221

Nervo, Amado. "En Paz [At Peace]." *Obras Completes de Amaro Nervo.* Translated by Fr. Juan Romas. Madrid: Biblioteca Nueva, 1920.

Permissions

Chapter 2

Epigraph

Wilson, David Sloan. Interviewed by Krista Tippett. Excerpt from BECOMING WISE: AN INQUIRY INTO THE MYSTERY AND ART OF LIVING by Krista Tippett, copyright © 2016 by Krista Tippett. Used by permission of Penguin Press, an imprint of Penguin Publishing Group, a division of Penguin Random House LLC. All rights reserved.

55

Bly, Robert and Kabir. "The Guest Inside You." *Kabir: Ecstatic Poems* by Robert Bly. Copyright © 2004 by Robert Bly. Reprinted by permission of Beacon Press, Boston.

Chapter 3

77

Moore, Thomas. *Original Self: Living with Paradox and Originality*. New York: Perennial, 2001. Used with permission.

80

O'Donohue, John. *Eternal Echoes: Celtic Reflections on Our Yearning to Belong*. New York: Perennial, 2002. Used with permission.

Chapter 5

123

Frankl, Viktor E. *Man's Search for Meaning: An Introduction to Logotherapy*. Boston, MA. 2006. Reprinted by permission of Beacon Press, Boston.

Chapter 6

Epigraph

Steinbeck, John. Excerpt from THE ACTS OF KING ARTHUR AND HIS NOBLE KNIGHTS by John Steinbeck, edited by Chase Horton, copyright © 1976 by Elaine Steinbeck. Used by permission of Viking Books, an imprint of Penguin Publishing Group, a division of Penguin Random House LLC. All rights reserved.

140

Johnson, Robert. *He: Understanding Masculine Psychology*. New York: Harper Perennial-Revised Edition, 1989. Used by permission of HarperCollins Publishers and Jerry M. Ruhl, PhD.

141

Johnson, Robert. *He: Understanding Masculine Psychology*. New York: Harper Perennial-Revised Edition, 1989. Used by permission of HarperCollins Publishers and Jerry M. Ruhl, PhD.

143

Johnson, Robert. *He: Understanding Masculine Psychology*. New York: Harper Perennial-Revised Edition, 1989. Used by permission of HarperCollins Publishers and Jerry M. Ruhl, PhD.

153

Tippett, Krista. Excerpt from BECOMING WISE: AN INQUIRY INTO THE MYSTERY AND ART OF LIVING by Krista Tippett, copyright © 2016 by Krista Tippett. Used by permission of Penguin Press, an imprint of Penguin Publishing Group, a division of Penguin Random House LLC. All rights reserved.

Chapter 7

172

Moore, Thomas. Excerpt from DARK NIGHTS OF THE SOUL: A GUIDE TO FINDING YOUR WAY THROUGH LIFE'S ORDEALS by Thomas Moore, copyright © 2004 by Thomas Moore. Used by permission of Gotham Books, an imprint of Penguin Publishing Group, a division of Penguin Random House LLC. All rights reserved.

Chapter 8

Epigraph

Ladinsky, Daniel and Hafiz. Excerpt from "The Great Work" from the Penguin publication *The Gift: Poems by Hafiz* by Daniel Ladinsky, copyright 1999 and used with permission.

181-182

Firestein, Stuart. *Ignorance: How It Drives Science.* Copyright © 2012 by Stuart Firestein. Reproduced with permission of the Licensor through PLSclear.

188

Firestein, Stuart. *Ignorance: How It Drives Science.* Copyright © 2012 by Stuart Firestein. Reproduced with permission of the Licensor through PLSclear.

Chapter 9

200

Luke, Helen M. *Old Age: Journey Into Simplicity.* New York: Bell Tower, 1987. Reprinted by permission of Apple Farm, Three Rivers, MI, 2021.

204

Luke, Helen M. *Old Age: Journey Into Simplicity.* New York: Bell Tower, 1987. Reprinted by permission of Apple Farm, Three Rivers, MI, 2021.

Thorough efforts have been made to secure all permissions. Any omissions or corrections will be made in future editions.

About the Author

Paul Dunion, EdD, is a wholistic psychological healer, teacher, and author, also calling himself an eclectic mystic committed to remaining mindful of life as a mysterious and unpredictable journey. Paul teaches how to make peace with the unknown, evoking within each of us a proclivity for wisdom.

Employing an existential modality as well as a somatic approach to treating trauma, he is trained in EMDR and is a graduate of the Somatic Experiencing Institute. He earned his Doctoral degree in Counseling and Consulting Psychology from the University of Massachusetts at Amherst and his M.A. in Philosophy from the University of Connecticut.

As a professor of Philosophy and one who guides healing and growth, Paul has spent forty years examining the kinds of life choices that can yield the wisdom path. He focuses on what it means to see life as offering an Initiation, guiding and challenging us to find our way to our own depths. Committed to a Socratic method of teaching, Paul's intention is to serve as a muse, awakening the truths that live in his students.

A steadfast believer in the power of community, Paul founded Boys to Men, a Connecticut mentoring program for teenage boys, and COMEGA, the semi-annual Connecticut Men's Gathering, now in its 30th year of service. Paul also created The Croton Mystery School as well as offered many workshops to assist others in crafting a devotion to living in unity with life. Paul is a Senior Faculty Member/Expert with Mobius Executive Leadership, where he teaches at Mobius' Next Practice Institute, offers supervision for their therapists, and delivers customized Leadership Immersions globally.

Storytelling, speaking and writing are some of Paul's strongest gifts. He is a regular contributor to Medium and SelfGrowth and has published dozens of articles and blogs pertaining to human potential in various journals and platforms including HuffPost. His works include 5 books. *Seekers: Finding Our Way Home*, received high praise from Writers Digest Self-Published Book Awards who called it "a thought-provoking work that will benefit readers at any point in life….This is the type of book that people should read and return to again and again. A wonderful book." His title *Dare to Grow Up: Learn to Become Who You are Meant to Be* has been adopted as a classroom text by the Hamline University School of Business.

Regarding *Wisdom: Apprenticing to the Unknown and Befriending Fate*, Paul says: "I wrote this book because I've believed in the possibility of wisdom since I began studying philosophy at age 19. I was deeply moved by Socrates' response to his friend Chaerephon, who is told by the Delphinic Oracle that Socrates is the wisest man in Athens. Initially puzzled, Socrates recalls a recent conversation with another who believed himself to be indisputably knowledgeable. Socrates says, 'Maybe she's right. The fellow I was just speaking to actually believes he knows something.' Thus, began my introduction to curiosity having a primary place on the path to wisdom. What I have been naive about is just how much of an ego adjustment it would take to point me in the right direction. I also wrote this book because it hurt my ears everytime I heard the word *wisdom* referred to in some demeaning way, when information through technology has appeared to become sacrosanct."

He advances the vision that "as we release our strivings to control and dominate life, we engender an attitude of unity consciousness, such mindfulness yielding the depth and meaning of living life relationally. We come to know genuine belonging both with ourselves and to our lived experience."

Please learn more about Paul and his offerings at
www.pauldunion.com.